lonely planet

SRI LANKA

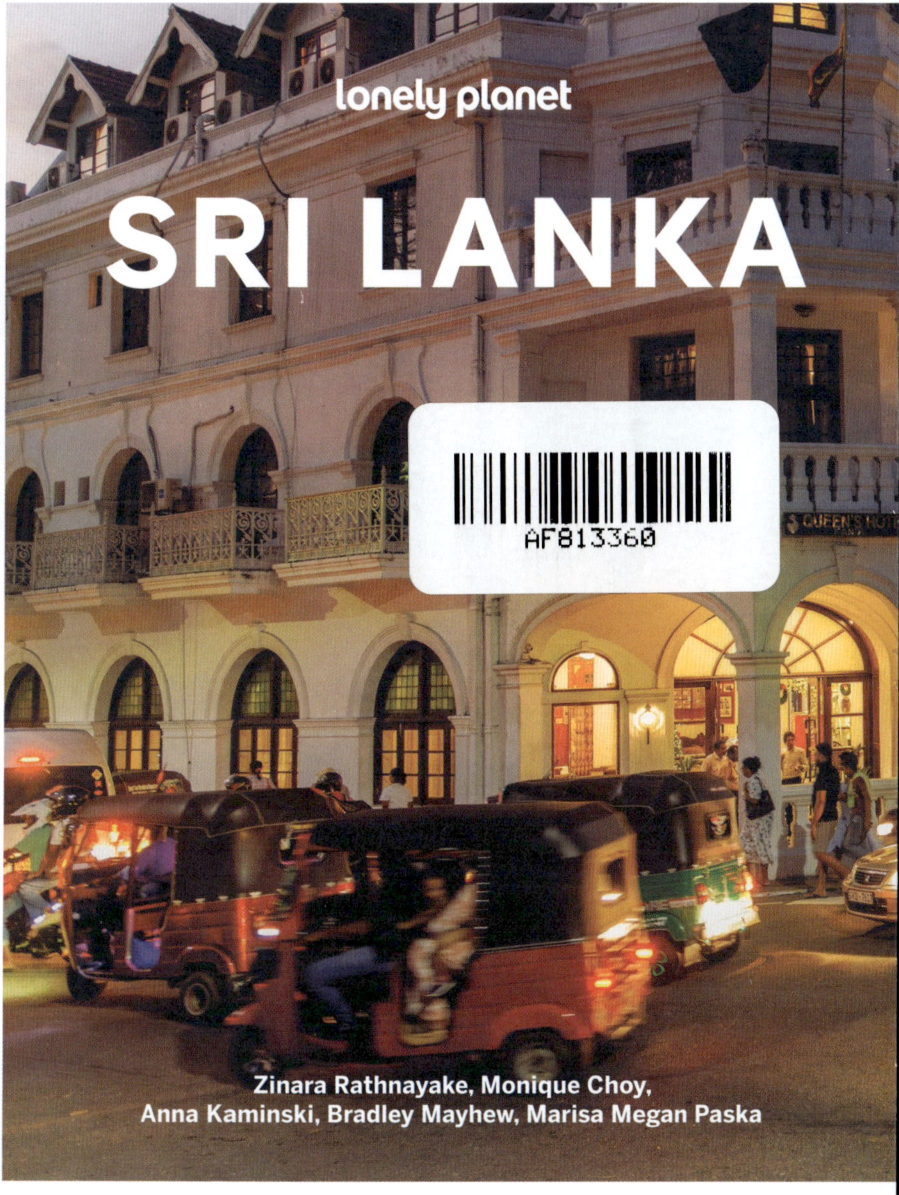

Zinara Rathnayake, Monique Choy,
Anna Kaminski, Bradley Mayhew, Marisa Megan Paska

JAVA

Laze on secret, powder-soft beaches. Catch rolling waves. Circle ancient stupas and marvel at museum-like cities of former royals. Spot elusive wildlife and spy on marine animals. Ride the rails curving through terraced tea estates. Discover the present through a 2000-year-old past. Hike cloud-wrapped sacred mountains. Immerse yourself in artistic heritage. Tuck into plates of rice and curry, sip arrack and drift into the slow rhythm of the island.

This is Sri Lanka.

TURN THE PAGE AND START PLANNING YOUR NEXT BEST TRIP →

0 50 km
0 25 miles
Palk Strait
Kankesanturai
Point Pedro
Karaitivu
Jaffna
Punkudutivu
Velanai
Chavakachcheri
Nainativu
Neduntivu 2 hrs
Neduntivu (Delft)
Jaffna Lagoon
Bay of Bengal
Palaitivu
Palk Bay
Kilinochchi
Putukkudiyirippu
The North 224
Iranaitivu
Mullaittivu
Nanthi Kadal Lagoon
Mannar Island
Tunukkai
Pesalai
Mankulam
Mannar Town
Kokkilai Lagoon
Pulmoddai
Vankala
Vavuniya
Gulf of Mannar
Trincomalee
Medawachchiya
Horowupotana
Portugal Bay
Koddiyar Bay
Kinniya
Wilpattu National Park
Mutur
Anuradhapura
Mihintale
Yan Oya
Kantale
Dutch Bay
Kalpitiya
Maragahawewa
Kala Oya
Ancient Cities 166
Somawathiya National Park
Thambuttegama
Puttalam Lagoon
Uppar Lagoon
Talawila
Ritigala
Kekirawa
Habarana
Hingurakgoda
Flood Plains National Park
Puttalam
Galgamuwa
Minneriya National Park
Sigiriya
Polonnaruwa
Maduru O
Valachchenai

Above Jaffna Fort (p233)

Marisa Megan Paska

@_marisamegan

For such a tiny country, Sri Lanka is jam-packed with things to do. In Kandy, you can dive deep into one of the most culturally significant parts of the country – the ancient arts from the Kandyan dynasty are still very much alive here. Watching Kandyan dancing and drumming – either at a dance show or on the street during Esala Perahera – is absolutely hypnotising, and should not be missed.

Contents

Sri Lanka's shoreline stretches for 1340km. Five out of the world's seven sea-turtle species come ashore here to lay eggs. Monsoon rains affect one coast at a time, making Sri Lanka a year-round beach destination.

STUNNING **SANDS**

Blessed with palm-fringed seaside coves, shallow, clear waters and low-key stretches of golden sand, Sri Lanka has beaches for every traveller's taste. With changing monsoons on opposite coasts, there are beaches year-round at which to swim, sunbathe, party and lounge, or take in sunsets with grilled barramundi and chilled beer. Divers, too, can take advantage of the island's excellent wrecks, caves and shallow reefs.

EPIC_SAM/SHUTTERSTOCK

Above Thuparama Dagoba (p191), Anuradhapura

Left Sea turtle hatchling
Right Dalawella Beach (p30), Unawatuna
Below Beach in Tangalle (p102)

→ DEEP SOUTH SWELLS

Stroll the palm-hugging sea cliffs and bouldered shores, but be cautious while swimming in the beaches between Tangalle (p102) and Tissa, as strong currents are frequent.

MAMA_MIA/SHUTTERSTOCK

FRESHLY GRILLED

Nothing quite screams Sri Lankan like retreating to a beach shack for grilled seafood or battered cuttlefish, washed down with a glass of Lion beer.

FROM LEFT: KE.BE/SHUTTERSTOCK, MARIUS DOBILAS/SHUTTERSTOCK

↑ FOLLOW THE SUN

Avoid monsoons, and go where the beaches are at their best: the east coast from May until September; the south coast from November to April.

Best Beach Experiences

- **Find your favourite sun-soaked beach along the south coast.** (p92)
- **Stroll along Tangalle's wild, wave-swept coastline.** (p102)
- **Explore the depths of the marine world in Kirinda.** (p98)
- **Chase the wind in Kalpitiya's flatwater lagoons.** (p70)
- **Go snorkelling in Pigeon Island Marine National Park off the coast in Nilaveli.** (p208)

CAPTIVATING CULTURE

A series of historical migrations from India, the Arab world and the Malay Archipelago, coupled with centuries of trade, colonisation and war, have resulted in a society of diverse cuisines, traditions and faith. While nearly 75% of the population are ethnically Sinhalese, there are also Tamils, Moors, Malays, Memons, Dutch Burghers and small settlements of indigenous Veddah, the island's earliest remaining inhabitants.

Temple of the Tooth

Buddhist faith

The holiest place of worship for Sri Lankan Buddhists, this temple houses the enshrined canine tooth of the Buddha. Tour the magnificent Royal Palace Complex, home to Sri Lanka's last kings before Kandy fell into the hands of the British.

8min east of Kandy

▸ p158

St Anthony's Shrine

Roman Catholic church

This 18th-century shrine traces its origins to a Catholic priest from India who built a mudbrick chapel here. While the original building was targeted during the Easter bombings in 2019, the rebuilt church continues to be an important place of worship.

15min north of Colombo

▸ p49

Jami Ul-Alfar Masjid

Indo-Islamic architecture

Smack dab in bustling Pettah Market, Jami Ul-Alfar Masjid has intricate red-and-white brickwork and pomegranate-shaped domes. It is one of Colombo's oldest mosques.

8min northwest of Colombo

▸ p49

FROM LEFT: SEAN HSU/SHUTTERSTOCK, ANNA KAMINSKI, XANDRA R/SHUTTERSTOCK

Nallur Kandaswamy Temple

Iconic Hindu temple

Jaffna houses the ornate entrance towers of the island's most important Hindu shrine. During the annual 25-day temple festival, devotees engage in penance, drums beat and chariot processions parade statues of Hindu deities.

8min northeast of Jaffna

▶ p233

Gal Oya

Last indigenous community

Traditionally hunter-gatherers living in the dense forests, Sri Lanka's indigenous Veddah people were displaced by large-scale irrigation projects. Join a jungle walk led by a community member at Gal Oya Lodge to learn about their way of life.

34min northeast of Bibile

▶ p215

Galle Fort

Sri Lanka in miniature

This 300-year-old fortified town was a key trading hub that fell first into the hands of the Portuguese, then the Dutch and the British. It is home to residences, schools, mosques, Buddhist temples and Catholic churches.

4min south of Galle

▶ p116

South coast surf season from November to April; East coast from May to October.

Communities like SeaSisters are making the ocean accessible for women in a male-dominated local surf culture.

Peak kitesurfing season from May to September; beginner season from December to March.

CATCH A WAVE

With year-round warm waters and consistent swells, Sri Lanka is one of Asia's best surfing destinations. Advanced surfers – and those looking to step up their game – are drawn to reef and point breaks along the south and east coasts. Beginners can ease in on the South's gentle, rolling waves and sandy, sheltered breaks tucked into picturesque coves. With steady, fast wind conditions, there's something for kitesurfers, too, both learners and experts.

Left Surfer, Weligama (p97)
Right Hiriketiya (p97)
Below Kitesurfers, Kalpitiya (p70)

→ SOMETHING FOR EVERYONE

The South is home to a mix of mellow beach breaks and demanding reef breaks. Base yourself in Weligama, Ahangama or Hiriketiya (p97).

MARIUS DOBILAS/SHUTTERSTOCK

GO EAST

Experienced surfers will like catching waves in surf spots in and around Arugam Bay (p216), 343km east of Colombo. Look for Peanut Farm, Okanda and Pottuvil Point.

FROM LEFT: NILANKA SAMPATH/SHUTTERSTOCK, SEANKELLYPIX/SHUTTERSTOCK

↑ CHASING THE WIND

Kalpitiya (p70) is the capital of kitesurfing in Sri Lanka, with shallow flatwater lagoons and two wind seasons. Quiet Kappalady village nearby makes a great base.

Best Surfing Experiences

- **Ride the rolling waves in some of Asia's best surf spots in Arugam Bay.** (p216)
- **Chase the wind and find your favourite kitesurfing spot in and around Kalpitiya.** (p70)
- **Launch your surfer life at a surf camp in Ahangama or Weligama.** (p97)
- **Learn to tackle soft, gentle waves in a perfect horseshoe bay in Hiriketiya.** (p97)

KNOW THE WILD

Over 7000 wild Asian elephants live in Sri Lanka.

The Sri Lankan elephant is the largest and darkest of Asian elephants.

Estimated number of leopards in Sri Lanka: 700 to 1000.

WONDROUS WILDLIFE

Home to sweeping dry grasslands, shadowy central highlands forests and marshy wetlands along the coast, Sri Lanka is a biodiversity hotspot, and has worked to conserve wildlife with its network of national parks and nature reserves. From the elusive leopard to pods of spinner dolphins, and from sea turtles to parades of wild elephants that feed, bathe, play and nap in isolated waterholes, there's plenty to see.

Left Leopard, Yala National Park (p106)
Right Elephants, Minneriya National Park (p180)
Below Spinner dolphin, Kalpitiya (p71)

→ THE GATHERING

The July-to-October dry season sees large herds of Asian elephants – about 300 to 400 – gather at reservoirs in Kaudulla and Minneriya (p180).

MILES ASTRAY/SHUTTERSTOCK

SRI LANKAN LEOPARD

This elusive big cat is Sri Lanka's pride. Head to quieter national parks like Kumana and Wilpattu, or visit low-key parts of the popular Yala National Park (p106).

FROM LEFT: MARTIN MECNAROWSKI/SHUTTERSTOCK, MICHAEL NOLAN/ROBERTHARDING/GETTY IMAGES

↑ MARINE LIFE

Mirissa (p100) is a hub for whale-watching. From November to April, Kalpitiya (p71) is ideal for spotting hundreds of playful spinner dolphins and the occasional killer whale.

Best Wildlife Experiences

- **Spot leopards on a jeep safari to Yala National Park.** (p106)
- **Watch wild elephants gather in their hundreds in Kaudulla or Minneriya.** (p180)
- **Marvel at migrant flamingos turning Mannar's marshes a stunning pink.** (p238)
- **Jump on a jeep safari to Sri Lanka's largest national park Wilpattu.** (p72)
- **Walk the jungles at night in Sigiriya to spot a nocturnal primate.** (p176)

RIDING THE RAILS

For a small island, Sri Lanka has some epic train journeys. In the Hill Country, diesel locos snake past rolling tea gardens, tumbling waterfalls and colonial-era railway stations. Along the southwest coast, trains glide by the sea, passing coconut-lined beach towns. Make sure to munch on the lentil fritters peddled by vendors squeezing through the busy carriages. It's quintessentially Sri Lankan.

FROM TOP: BADA1/SHUTTERSTOCK, MAKSIM GULYACHIK/SHUTTERSTOCK

→ TOURIST TRAINS

Special trains like Ella Odyssey and Calypso run from Colombo to Badulla, and briefly halt at key stops, like the St Clair Falls and Nine Arches Bridge.

Best Railway Experiences

- **The Kandy–Badulla route is often regarded as one of the world's most beautiful train journeys.** (p128)
- **Sit by the window for unparalleled sea views on a train from Colombo to Galle.** (p80)
- **Watch trains roll across the Nine Arches Bridge in Ella.** (p128)
- **Get mesmerised by the views at Idalgashinna Railway Station.** (p129)

★ BOOK YOUR SEAT

Some trains on popular tourist routes have reserved and non-reserved cars. Consider booking your seat through the official website (seatreservation.railway.gov.lk).

Top Train journey through the Hill Country tea estates (p128)
Left Calypso tourist train

Rice and coconut form the base of Sri Lankan cooking.

Days revolve around short eats (an umbrella term used for sweet and savoury bakery delights).

Tea, often made with powdered milk and sugar, is a local favourite.

HUEY MIN/SHUTTERSTOCK

FEASTS FOR DAYS

Sri Lankans love to feast. This is evident in everything from lunchtime rice and curry (pictured) to teatime snacks and after-work parties. From Sunday gatherings centred on seafood stews in the North to coconut milk and jaggery custards prepared for Eid, or cricket matches on TV – even when Sri Lanka is losing – anything, anywhere is reason enough to celebrate over food, drinks and music.

Best Food & Drink Experiences

- **Sip cocktails under the coconut canopy in Hiriketiya.** (p108)
- **Learn to cook crab curry with a Jaffna local.** (p229)
- **Chow down on plates of rice and curry in Colombo.** (p50)
- **Set out for an arrack tasting at Ropewalk inside Galle Fort Hotel.** (p119)
- **Feast on freshly caught seafood at Club. Ceylon.** (p84)

ANCIENT KINGDOMS

For over 2000 years, ancient dynasties in Sri Lanka rose to power, and fell. The erstwhile royals built temples, palaces and castles – where art and architecture were given prominence. These ancient sites and ruins are scattered across the island, particularly within the cultural triangle of Anuradhapura, Polonnaruwa and Kandy.

FROM TOP: ALONANOLA/SHUTTERSTOCK, DESIGNFACTS/SHUTTERSTOCK

→ DESIGN DETAILS

At the entrance to most temples is a *sandakada pahana*, also known as a moonstone. These ornate semicircular stone slabs show the ongoing cycle of birth, existence and death in Buddhism.

Best Ancient Kingdom Experiences

- **Be enchanted by the views, frescoes and water gardens of Sigiriya.** (p172)
- **Traverse the monasteries and ruins of a former kingdom in Polonnaruwa.** (p182)
- **Walk around massive stupas and a 2300-year-old sacred tree in Anuradhapura.** (p188)
- **Climb the ornamental stairway of a medieval citadel in Yapahuwa.** (p196)

← CAVE PAINTINGS

Cave temples, like the UNESCO-listed Dambulla (p178), contain impressive religious art. History enthusiasts will appreciate the paintings at the 2nd-century Ridi Vihara, and Aukana for its Buddha image carved out of a single rock face.

Top Dambulla cave temple (p178)
Left Moonstone (p195)

CREATIVE HEART

Across Sri Lanka, settlements evolved and flourished through artistic traditions like pottery, batik, handloom and maskmaking, where artisan families passed their skills on to the next generation. The island has also produced prominent architects like the late Geoffrey Bawa and the iconic late Minnette de Silva, who continue to inspire artists today.

FROM TOP: MARIA STUDIO/SHUTTERSTOCK, GUZEL GASHIGULLINA/SHUTTERSTOCK

→ BATIK ART

A fabric dyeing method that uses wax resist to create beautiful designs, batik is now being championed by young and contemporary artists (p83).

Best Creative Experiences

- ▸ **Get to know Colombo through the works of Geoffrey Bawa.** (p78)
- ▸ **Meet the artists and craftspeople in and around Hikkaduwa.** (p82)
- ▸ **Spend a night at Geoffrey Bawa's country estate Lunuganga.** (p77)
- ▸ **Shop for fair-trade artisanal products at the Saturday Good Market in Colombo.** (p60)
- ▸ **Tour Colombo's best contemporary galleries.** (p56)

← GEOFFREY BAWA

Known as the pioneer of tropical modernism, the late architect (p55) created work that responds to light, air and climate, incorporating local building practices and materials.

Top Geoffrey Bawa's Lunuganga country estate (p77)
Left Batik handicraft

ISLAND **TRAILS**

Few people associate Sri Lanka with rugged peaks, mountain trails weaving through mist-shrouded hamlets and natural pools hiding in deep jungle. Yet with its rainforests, tea gardens, tropical grasslands and coral-made offshore islands, this small country is an excellent and diverse place to walk, hike and cycle. These are some of Sri Lanka's most extraordinary outdoor adventures.

Sri Pada (Adam's Peak)

Holy mountain

Climb 5500 steps to Sri Pada – a sacred mountain for pilgrims of diverse faiths – for sunrise views. Atop the hill is a footprint believed to be of Adam, Buddha and the Hindu god Shiva.

1¼hr southwest of Hatton

▶ p146

Sinharaja

A tropical rainforest

Crisscrossed by waterways, this dense forest shelters 95% of the birds and 50% of the mammals and butterflies found only in Sri Lanka. The rainforest is largely free from human activity, with trees that are relics of supercontinent Gondwanaland formed 600 million years ago.

2½hr northeast of Galle

▶ p150

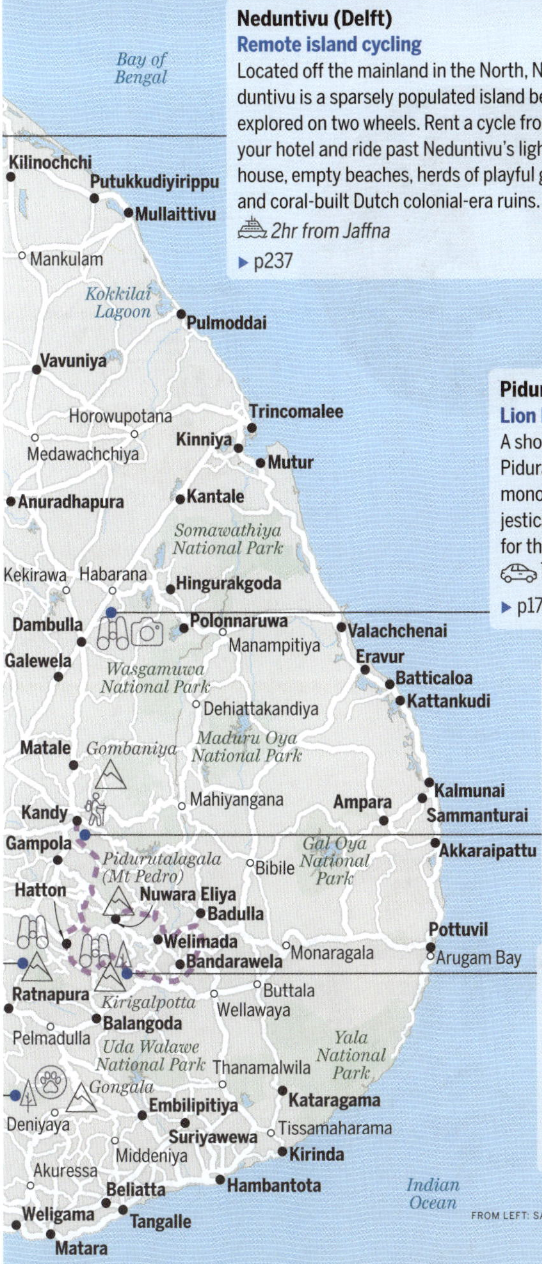

Neduntivu (Delft)

Remote island cycling

Located off the mainland in the North, Neduntivu is a sparsely populated island best explored on two wheels. Rent a cycle from your hotel and ride past Neduntivu's lighthouse, empty beaches, herds of playful goats and coral-built Dutch colonial-era ruins.

2hr from Jaffna

▶ p237

Pidurangala

Lion Rock views

A short but demanding hike takes you to the top of Pidurangala rock. Your reward: fabulous views of the monolithic rock fortress of Sigiriya, which juts majestically over the green jungle. Allow about an hour for the journey up, and go for sunrise or sunset.

10min from Sigiriya

▶ p174

The Pekoe Trail

Tea country walk

This 300km route through the Central Highlands passes tea estates, small settlements, Hindu temples and rolling mountains. Walk the entire trail, or pick one of its 22 stages. Stage 1 begins at Ceylon Tea Museum.

20min south of Kandy

▶ p130

Horton Plains National Park

Mist-swathed plains

This is a wild grassland plateau 2000m above the sea with rocky pools and waterfalls. Walk the 10km loop past World's End, which offers views all the way to the coast.

1hr from Nuwara Eliya

▶ p144

FROM LEFT: SAIKO3P/SHUTTERSTOCK, DEVAKA SENEVIRATNE/SHUTTERSTOCK

Sri Lanka in SUMMER

JUNE

Peak season in the North and East; fabulous for beach days in Nilaveli, Uppuveli and Passekudah, and cultural trips to Jaffna.

Short but heavy monsoon downpours affect the southwest coast and Hill Country, particularly in the evening; low accommodation prices and thinner crowds.

↙ Community Meals

Full moon in June (Poson Poya) marks Buddhism's introduction to Sri Lanka, celebrated with *dansel* (free food and drink stands on the streets).

↗ Surf's Up

Strong swells make this the best time for intermediate and pro surfers in Arugam Bay; a few beginner surf spots, too.

Average daytime max: 31°C
Days of rainfall: 15

JULY

CLOCKWISE FROM MAIN: IACOMINO FRIMAGES/SHUTTERSTOCK, PIXELSTUDIO SL/SHUTTERSTOCK, SHARA S. KODIKARA/GETTY IMAGES, EPIC_SAM/SHUTTERSTOCK, PHOTO WICKY/SHUTTERSTOCK, THE ROAD PROVIDES/SHUTTERSTOCK

↘ Esala Perahera

Annual 10-day festival (August/July) brings throngs of dancers, drummers and stilt walkers in a nighttime cultural procession.

Kandy, p160

▸ kandyesalaperahera.com

Also a 10-day vibrant festival in Kataragama with acts of self-mortification.

▸ rmkd.lk

Kitesurfing

Strong, consistent winds and flatwater lagoons in Kalpitiya make summer prime time for expert kitesurfers. Not ideal for beginners.

Kalpitiya, p70

↑ Nallur Festival

This 25-day celebration heats up the city with vibrant processions, music and acts of self-mortification. High demand for accommodation.

Jaffna, p233

▸ nalluran.com

Average daytime max: 30°C
Days of rainfall: 9

AUGUST

Average daytime max: 30°C
Days of rainfall: 9

Elephant Assembly

Wild elephants scout for water and food during the dry months of July and August (through to October), gathering in their hundreds around massive lakes near Sigiriya.

Minneriya and Kaudulla national parks, p181

Packing Notes

Umbrella and raincoat for afternoon showers. Dry bag for water activities and bug repellent to stay safe from mosquitos.

Shoulder season around the country; generally a good time to visit with fewer crowds and low prices.

Arugam Bay surfing continues until October, but evening showers start to loom in the North, East and Colombo. Rainfall is heavier in November.

Arugam Bay, p216

↙ Highland Trekking

Sunny, dry weather in Central Highlands makes it the best time to walk the Pekoe Trail (pictured left) or trek in the Knuckles Conservation Forest (pictured below).

Pekoe Trail and the Knuckles, p130 & p162

▸ thepekoetrail.org

← Whale-Watching

Blue whales and dolphins begin to migrate to the calmer seas in Mirissa (pictured far left); large pods of spinner dolphins in Kalpitiya from November through to April.

Mirissa and Kalpitiya, p100 & p71

SEPTEMBER

Average daytime max: 30°C
Days of rainfall: 15

OCTOBER

Sri Lanka in AUTUMN

CLOCKWISE FROM MAIN: MARTIJN VAN DEN ENK/SHUTTERSTOCK, SHALOM RUFEISEN/SHUTTERSTOCK, ANNA KAMINSKI, NURPHOTO/GETTY IMAGES, MALIKA JAYATHILAKE/SHUTTERSTOCK

↘ Deepavali

Also called Diwali, the Hindu festival of lights sees temple celebrations, the lighting of oil lamps and vibrant floor art.

Book Fair

Colombo's biggest annual book fair typically falls in September or October. Crowds arrive in the thousands at Bandaranaike Memorial International Conference Hall (BMICH).

▶ cibf.lk

↑ Migratory Birds

Birds arrive at coastal wetlands in Bundala, Mannar and Jaffna. Birdwatching season runs November to April, peaking around February. Greater flamingos (pictured above) in the North.

Mannar, p238

NOVEMBER

Average daytime max: 30°C
Days of rainfall: 17

Average daytime max: 31°C
Days of rainfall: 15

Packing Notes

Cottons and linens for humidity and sunscreen to stay safe from the sun. A raincoat comes in handy.

Peak season for travelling, except for the east coast, which experiences rains. Accommodation prices soar; book ahead.

Demand for accommodation peaks during December and January. View tours and overnight adventures in advance at lonelyplanet.com.

↘ New Year's Day

Most locals celebrate by preparing *kiri bath* (rice cooked in coconut milk) to invite good fortune for the new year.

↖ Tropical Christmas

Christmas celebrations, from carols to galas, during the month of December. Colombo (pictured left) lights up. Good time to sample Sri Lankan Burgher treats.

DECEMBER

Average daytime max: 31°C
Days of rainfall: 10

JANUARY

Sri Lanka in WINTER

CLOCKWISE FROM MAIN: MARIUS DOBILAS/SHUTTERSTOCK, MIHIDUM JAYASINGHE/SHUTTERSTOCK, SAMANWEERATUNGA/SHUTTERSTOCK, J_K/SHUTTERSTOCK, BATSAC/SHUTTERSTOCK

The Galle Literary Festival

Kicks off towards the end of January every year along with art trails and culinary pop-ups with renowned chefs.

▶ galleliteraryfestival.com

↖ Rolling Waves

The south-coast surf season is in full swing. Head to Weligama (pictured above), Ahangama and Hiriketiya.

Weligama, Ahangama and Hiriketiya, p97

↑ Holy Pilgrimage

December marks the beginning of Sri Pada (Adam's Peak) climbing season (continues until May) with dry, clear and cool weather. Crowds peak on full moon.

Sri Pada, p146

Average daytime max: 31°C
Days of rainfall: 4

FEBRUARY

Average daytime max: 32°C
Days of rainfall: 4

Pongal

In January Hindus gather at temples to celebrate the three- or four-day harvest festival with traditional feasts and sweets.

Packing Notes

Dressy outfits for beach resorts and a sweater for central mountains. Sunscreen, SPF 50 or higher, is essential.

Peak tourist season comes to an end. Sunnier, drier and hotter days, but lower prices as crowds leave. Generally a good time to travel.

In May, monsoons loom along the southwest coast. Beach and surf activities shift to the east coast towns like Trincomalee, Nilaveli and Arugam Bay.

↘ Sinhala & Tamil New Year

Usually on 13 or 14 April, with rituals, games and traditional sweetmeats at auspicious times. Businesses close; buses and trains are packed before and after as locals travel home.

↘ Spring Time

Synonymous with the flowering of red coral trees and the birdcalls of Asian koel. The second half of April is school holidays and peak domestic tourist season.

MARCH

Average daytime max: 32°C
Days of rainfall: 7

APRIL

Sri Lanka in SPRING

CLOCKWISE FROM MAIN: MRK-FRAMES/SHUTTERSTOCK, NILANKA SAMPATH/SHUTTERSTOCK, KUSHAN KALPA/SHUTTERSTOCK, SHUTTERLK/SHUTTERSTOCK, INTREEGUE PHOTOGRAPHY/SHUTTERSTOCK

Turtle Nesting

Turtles nest year-round, but reach a peak from April to July in Rekawa. Also a great time to see hatchlings. But pick an ethical tour.

Rekawa, p103

↗ Vesak

Buddhists celebrate the birth, enlightenment and nirvana of Buddha, with meditation, *dansel,* lanterns and illuminated structures depicting Buddha's past lives.

↑ Adventure Time

Ideal time to raft the river rapids as monsoons arrive in May (through to December). Check for weather updates and seasonal floods.

Average daytime max: 32°C
Days of rainfall: 12

MAY

Average daytime max: 31°C
Days of rainfall: 16

Packing Notes

Sunscreen and hat for scorching heat, electrolytes for high humidity, umbrella for scattered showers.

THE WEST COAST
Trip Builder

TAKE YOUR PICK OF MUST-SEES AND HIDDEN GEMS

For a vibrant mix of beach, city, art and architecture, take a trip along the island's west coast. The lively Sri Lankan capital is a destination in itself, and you aren't too far away from sprawling beaches, water sports, wildlife and the country home of Sri Lanka's most celebrated architect.

Trip Notes

Hub towns Colombo, Bentota, Kalpitiya

How long Allow 7 days

Getting around Major towns are connected by regular buses, with several trains running south from Colombo. Ride-shares (cars, tuk tuks and motorbikes) are popular in Colombo and Negombo. Otherwise, hire a tuk tuk through your accommodation or get your own wheels.

Tips For faster travel times, use expressways where you can. Trains to Hikkaduwa and Bentota offer stunning sea views.

Kalpitiya
Lounge on powder-sand beaches. When – and if – you're bored, kite-surf on flatwater lagoons and hop on a boat to see playful spinner dolphins and the occasional killer whale.
3½hr from Colombo

Negombo
Get lost in the bustle of morning fish markets in this airport town. Explore sandy resort beaches, Catholic shrines and Hindu temples, and savour boat-to-table dining.
20min from Bandaranaike International Airport

Bentota
Discover the world of Geoffrey Bawa at his country estate Lunuganga, stroll his brother's landscaped garden at Brief, go jet skiing, and paint folk masks with artisans.
1½hr from Colombo

Wilpattu

Scout for the elusive leopard and wild elephants in the dry evergreen forest and grasslands of Sri Lanka's largest national park. You'll need a 4WD with a driver.

2hr from Kalpitiya

Colombo

Marvel at the iconic Jami Ul-Alfar Masjid, tour Geoffrey Bawa's urban residence, browse art galleries and munch *vadai* (lentil fritters) at Galle Face Green (pictured) – especially on a weekend evening.

40min from Bandaranaike International Airport

Hikkaduwa

Spot turtles, go on a river safari and watch sunsets on sunkissed beaches with fresh-off-the-boat seafood feasts. Pick only an ethical turtle hatchery.

2hr from Colombo

GALLE & THE SOUTH

Trip Builder

TAKE YOUR PICK OF MUST-SEES AND HIDDEN GEMS

Find your favourite Sri Lankan beach town on this epic south-coast road trip. You'll be rewarded with stretches of sun-filled bays, surf villages, arrack taverns, and rice and curry spreads in family-run settings. Spot marine mammals, stroll centuries-old forts, cycle through paddy fields and escape to rain-fed jungles.

Trip Notes

Hub towns Galle, Weligama, Hiriketiya, Deniyaya

How long Allow 7 to 10 days

Getting around Rent a car or motorbike, hire a tuk tuk, or hop on one of the many buses that run along the beach road or interiors.

Tips Be on the alert for road traffic, as public buses can be quite aggressive. Hire an experienced local driver if you aren't comfortable driving yourself.

Galle
Stroll the 300-year-old Galle Fort, where you can dine alfresco, shop for handlooms and watch sunsets from the ramparts. Follow the locals outside the fort to after-work taverns.
2hr from Colombo

Unawatuna
Go partying or head to quieter Dalawella Beach to see turtles swimming in clear blue waters. Cycle along paddy-lined roads to visit a rock temple.
14min from Galle

CLOCKWISE FROM TOP LEFT: SOFT_LIGHT/SHUTTERSTOCK, KAREL BARTIK/SHUTTERSTOCK, MARIUS DOBILAS/SHUTTERSTOCK

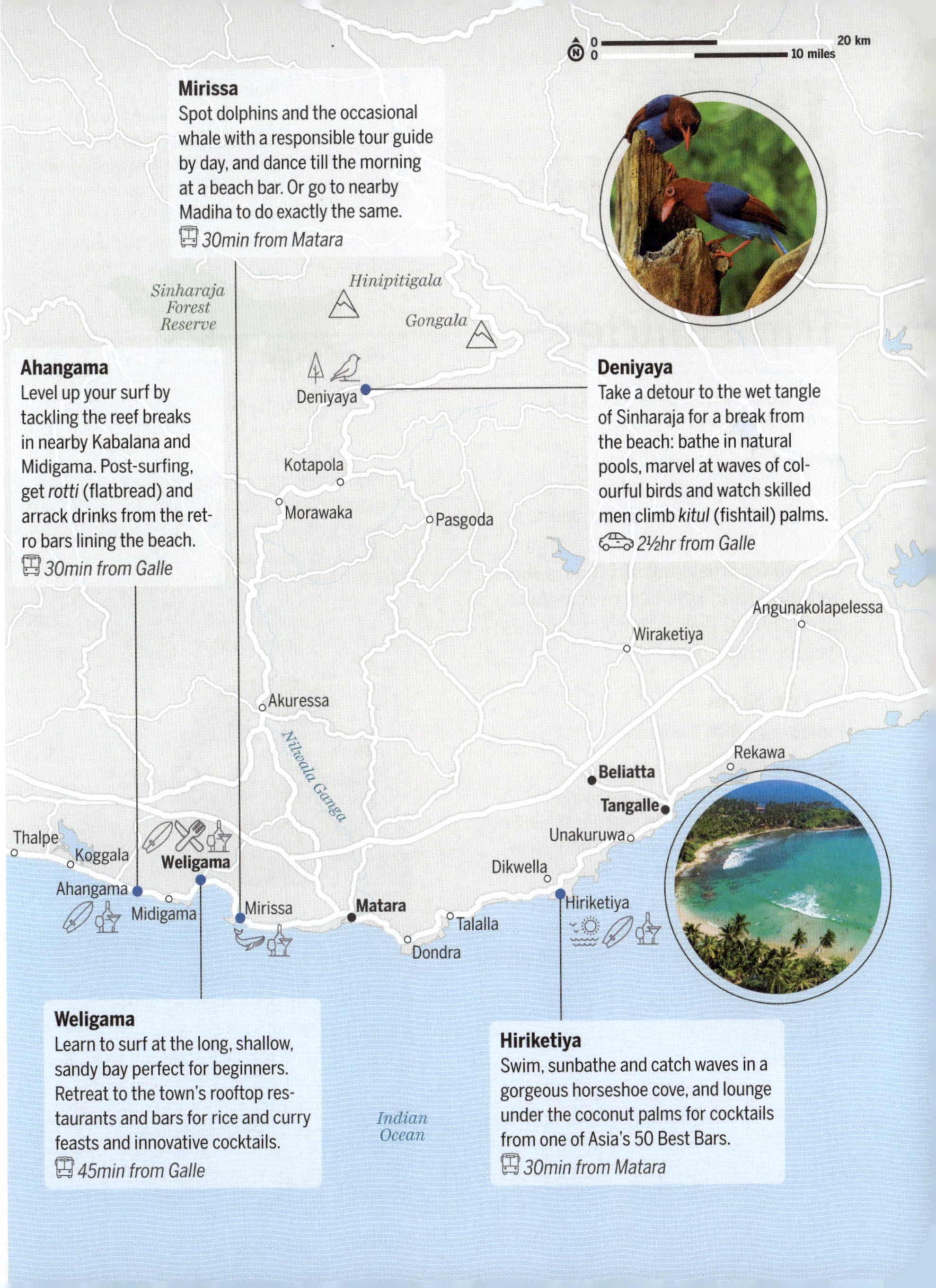

Mirissa
Spot dolphins and the occasional whale with a responsible tour guide by day, and dance till the morning at a beach bar. Or go to nearby Madiha to do exactly the same.
30min from Matara

Ahangama
Level up your surf by tackling the reef breaks in nearby Kabalana and Midigama. Post-surfing, get *rotti* (flatbread) and arrack drinks from the retro bars lining the beach.
30min from Galle

Deniyaya
Take a detour to the wet tangle of Sinharaja for a break from the beach: bathe in natural pools, marvel at waves of colourful birds and watch skilled men climb *kitul* (fishtail) palms.
2½hr from Galle

Weligama
Learn to surf at the long, shallow, sandy bay perfect for beginners. Retreat to the town's rooftop restaurants and bars for rice and curry feasts and innovative cocktails.
45min from Galle

Hiriketiya
Swim, sunbathe and catch waves in a gorgeous horseshoe cove, and lounge under the coconut palms for cocktails from one of Asia's 50 Best Bars.
30min from Matara

THE NORTH-EAST
Trip Builder

TAKE YOUR PICK OF MUST-SEES AND HIDDEN GEMS

This Northeast road trip dives deep into Sri Lanka's Tamil heartland, with its offshore islands and wild marshes, which are home to birdlife. Treat yourself to lazy days on white-sand beaches, or make the most of local feasts, temple trails and cycling adventures.

Trip Notes

Hub towns Jaffna, Trincomalee

How long Allow 10 days

Getting around Main towns are connected by regular buses during the day; ferries run to smaller islands. Cycle, bike or hop on a tuk tuk to get around small towns and villages.

Tips With little road traffic, the countryside is excellent for cycling. Birdwatching season – particularly for migratory flamingos – runs from November until April.

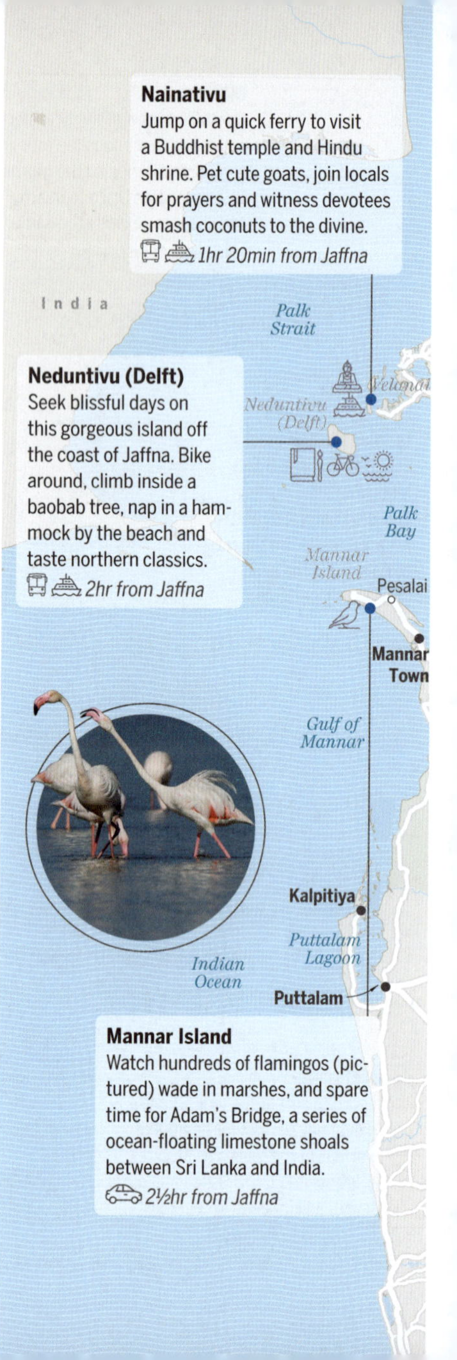

Nainativu
Jump on a quick ferry to visit a Buddhist temple and Hindu shrine. Pet cute goats, join locals for prayers and witness devotees smash coconuts to the divine.
1hr 20min from Jaffna

Neduntivu (Delft)
Seek blissful days on this gorgeous island off the coast of Jaffna. Bike around, climb inside a baobab tree, nap in a hammock by the beach and taste northern classics.
2hr from Jaffna

Mannar Island
Watch hundreds of flamingos (pictured) wade in marshes, and spare time for Adam's Bridge, a series of ocean-floating limestone shoals between Sri Lanka and India.
2½hr from Jaffna

FROM LEFT: PRAMIL THARANGA/SHUTTERSTOCK, DENIS COSTILLE/SHUTTERSTOCK, TUUL & BRUNO MORANDI/GETTY IMAGES

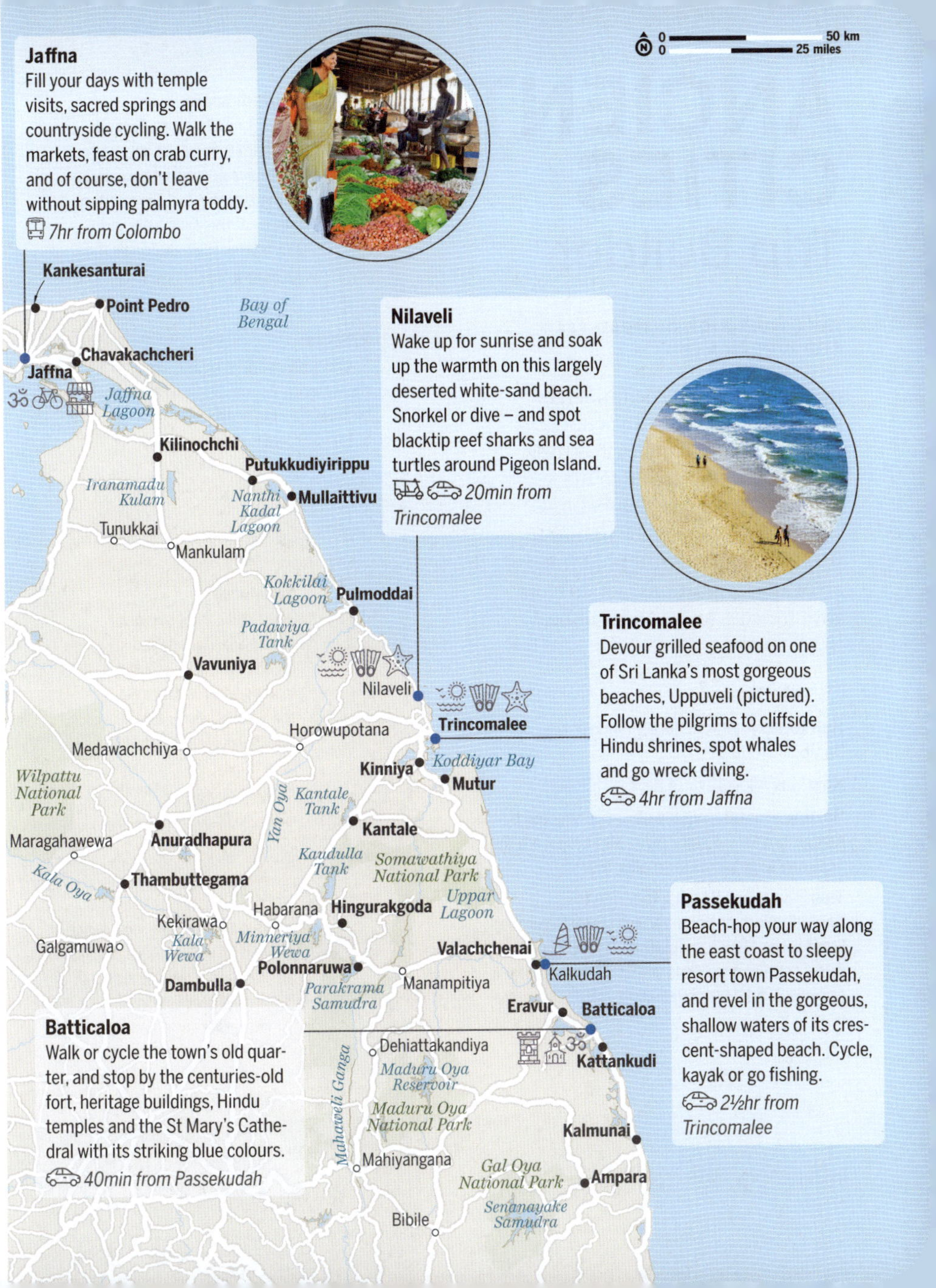

Jaffna

Fill your days with temple visits, sacred springs and countryside cycling. Walk the markets, feast on crab curry, and of course, don't leave without sipping palmyra toddy.

7hr from Colombo

Nilaveli

Wake up for sunrise and soak up the warmth on this largely deserted white-sand beach. Snorkel or dive – and spot blacktip reef sharks and sea turtles around Pigeon Island.

20min from Trincomalee

Trincomalee

Devour grilled seafood on one of Sri Lanka's most gorgeous beaches, Uppuveli (pictured). Follow the pilgrims to cliffside Hindu shrines, spot whales and go wreck diving.

4hr from Jaffna

Passekudah

Beach-hop your way along the east coast to sleepy resort town Passekudah, and revel in the gorgeous, shallow waters of its crescent-shaped beach. Cycle, kayak or go fishing.

2½hr from Trincomalee

Batticaloa

Walk or cycle the town's old quarter, and stop by the centuries-old fort, heritage buildings, Hindu temples and the St Mary's Cathedral with its striking blue colours.

40min from Passekudah

ANCIENT CITIES
Trip Builder

TAKE YOUR PICK OF MUST-SEES AND HIDDEN GEMS

This culture-rich itinerary connects Sri Lanka's ancient kingdoms, cave temples and rock castles with the chance to throw in a wildlife safari. History buffs will have endless opportunities to stroll through centuries-old ruins of erstwhile civilisations, get up close with frescoes and wander offbeat small towns.

Trip Notes

Hub towns Anuradhapura, Polonnaruwa, Dambulla, Kandy

How long Allow 12 to 14 days

Getting around Main towns are connected by regular buses. Tuk tuks, bikes and cycles are the best way to get around smaller towns.

Tips Save time by taking the train to Anuradhapura or Polonnaruwa (from Colombo). From there, stick to public buses; there are no direct train connections within the region. Get a taxi or tuk tuk for convenience.

CLOCKWISE FROM TOP: RADCHUK O.S/SHUTTERSTOCK, M.L.NUWAN/SHUTTERSTOCK, GORAN_SAFAREK/SHUTTERSTOCK

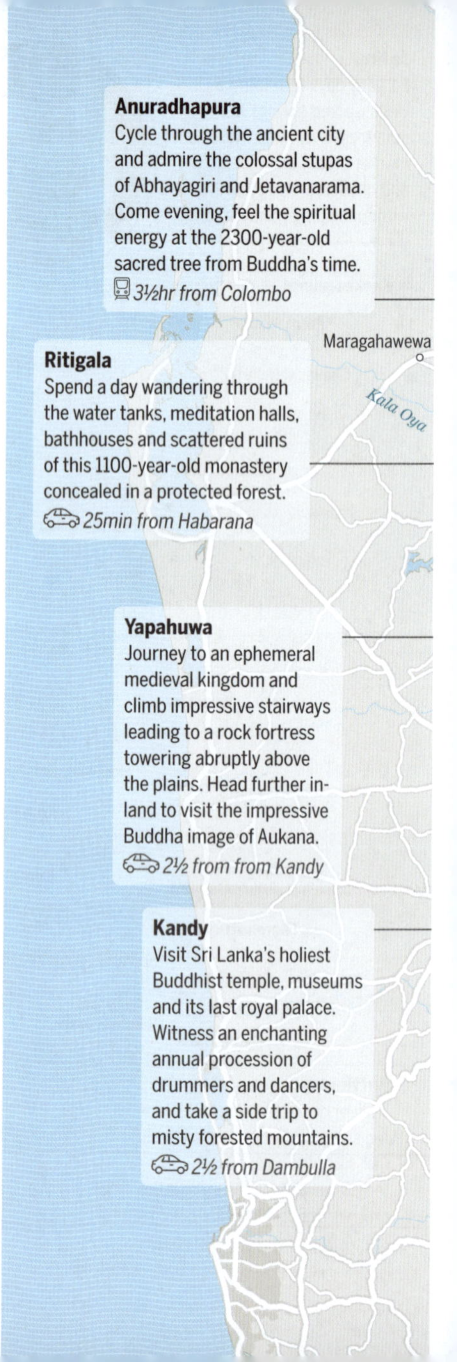

Anuradhapura
Cycle through the ancient city and admire the colossal stupas of Abhayagiri and Jetavanarama. Come evening, feel the spiritual energy at the 2300-year-old sacred tree from Buddha's time.
3½hr from Colombo

Ritigala
Spend a day wandering through the water tanks, meditation halls, bathhouses and scattered ruins of this 1100-year-old monastery concealed in a protected forest.
25min from Habarana

Yapahuwa
Journey to an ephemeral medieval kingdom and climb impressive stairways leading to a rock fortress towering abruptly above the plains. Head further inland to visit the impressive Buddha image of Aukana.
2½ from from Kandy

Kandy
Visit Sri Lanka's holiest Buddhist temple, museums and its last royal palace. Witness an enchanting annual procession of drummers and dancers, and take a side trip to misty forested mountains.
2½ from Dambulla

Habarana

Take a break from history lessons and temples, and go on a safari to Kaudulla or Minneriya national parks, where you can spot elephants, birds and deer.

30min from Dambulla

Sigiriya

Reach the summit of a short-lived, fortified capital (pictured) built atop a single rock rising dramatically above the jungle. Hike the neighbouring Pidurangala for epic sunrise views.

1½hr from Anuradhapura

Polonnaruwa

Gaze at the magnificent ruins, monk baths, ornate moonstones and images of Buddha cut out of a single slab of granite in and around the ancient Royal Palace.

2hr from Anuradhapura

Dambulla

Wander rock cave temples (pictured) to marvel at Buddha images and walls covered in centuries-old art. Detour to Aukana for the magnificent Buddha carved out of a single rock face.

80min from Anuradhapura

THE HIGH-LANDS
Trip Builder

TAKE YOUR PICK OF MUST-SEES AND HIDDEN GEMS

Journey to Sri Lanka's spectacular Central Highlands by train. Then trek through tea gardens, climb sacred mountains, hike rugged peaks and plunge into secret waterfalls. This itinerary will give you plenty of opportunity to discover wilderness and sleepy mountain villages.

Trip Notes

Hub towns Nuwara Eliya, Ella, Kitulgala, Haputale, Hatton

How long Allow 10 to 12 days

Getting around Trains can be slow, but they pass through stunning landscapes. Driving is risky on twisty roads, so stick to tuk tuks or buses to get around small towns.

Tips Tourist trains connect Hill Country towns with Kandy and Colombo; book ahead. Pack sweaters; carry a raincoat and umbrella.

Kitulgala
Trek through the the island's last primary rain-forest, teeming with birdlife, and bathe in ice-cold cascades. Ride river rapids, too – Kitulgala is the hub of white-water rafting.
2½hr from Kandy

Hatton
Take advantage of the signposted Pekoe Trail (pictured) for treks through the tea country. Summit Sri Lanka's holiest mountain for sunrise views, chase waterfalls and kayak in a picture-perfect lake.
2hr from Kandy

CLOCKWISE FROM TOP LEFT: HILDAWEGES/GETTY IMAGES, ANNA KAMINSKI, ANNA KAMINSKI

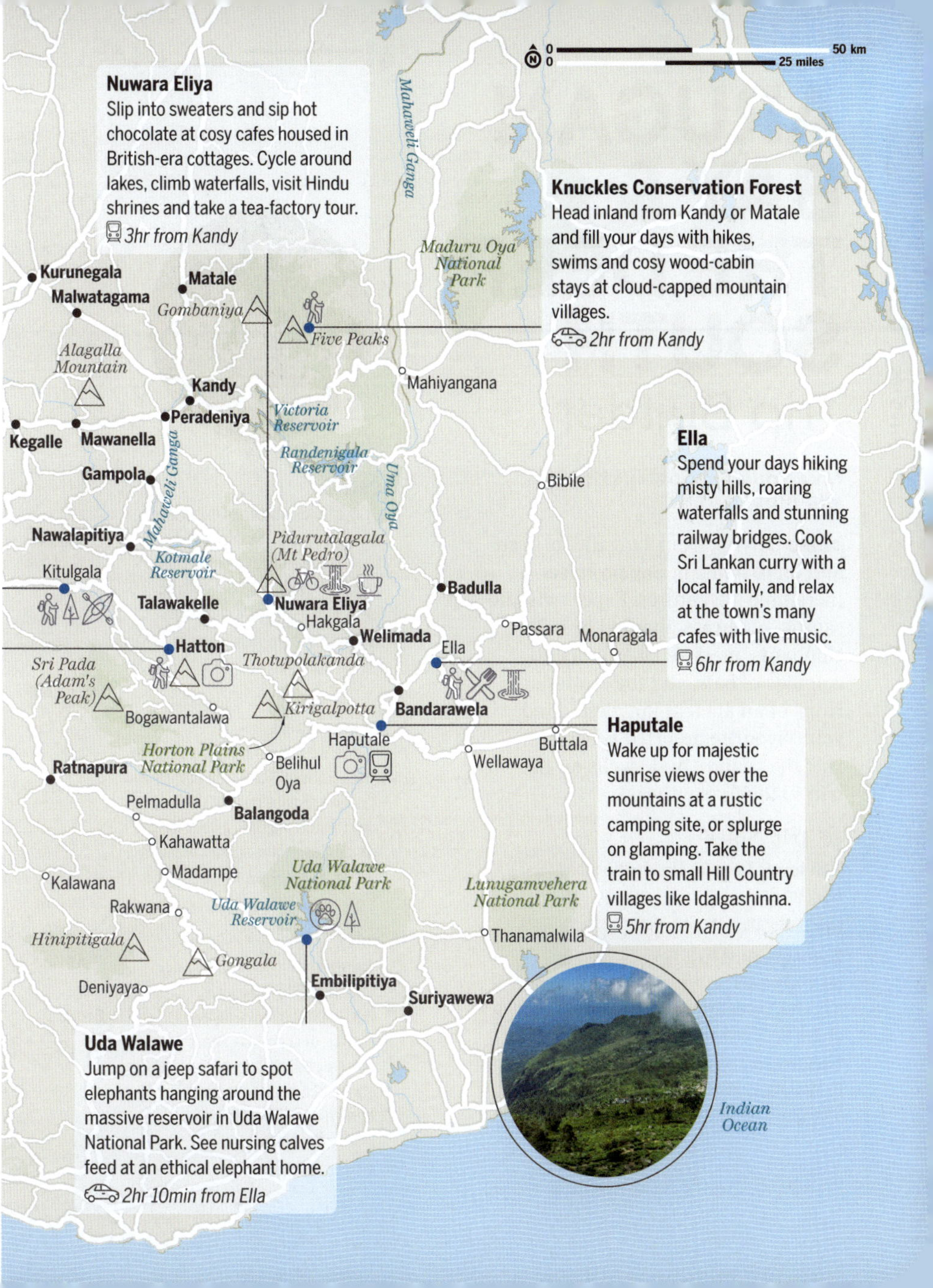

Nuwara Eliya

Slip into sweaters and sip hot chocolate at cosy cafes housed in British-era cottages. Cycle around lakes, climb waterfalls, visit Hindu shrines and take a tea-factory tour.

3hr from Kandy

Knuckles Conservation Forest

Head inland from Kandy or Matale and fill your days with hikes, swims and cosy wood-cabin stays at cloud-capped mountain villages.

2hr from Kandy

Ella

Spend your days hiking misty hills, roaring waterfalls and stunning railway bridges. Cook Sri Lankan curry with a local family, and relax at the town's many cafes with live music.

6hr from Kandy

Haputale

Wake up for majestic sunrise views over the mountains at a rustic camping site, or splurge on glamping. Take the train to small Hill Country villages like Idalgashinna.

5hr from Kandy

Uda Walawe

Jump on a jeep safari to spot elephants hanging around the massive reservoir in Uda Walawe National Park. See nursing calves feed at an ethical elephant home.

2hr 10min from Ella

ARUGAM BAY & THE DEEP SOUTH
Trip Builder

TAKE YOUR PICK OF MUST-SEES AND HIDDEN GEMS

Driving from Tangalle to Tissa and on to Arugam Bay promises incredible adventures. Expect wildlife safaris, highways guarded by wild elephants, massive lakes home to colonies of bats, and the scattered ruins of an ancient kingdom. Find your favourite deserted beach and surf the island's best swells on this trip to the far southeast.

Trip Notes

Hub towns Tangalle, Tissamaharama (Tissa), Arugam Bay

How long Allow 7 to 10 days

Getting around Past Tangalle, roads are relatively quiet, so experienced drivers can rent a tuk tuk or car to drive around. Otherwise, hop on tuk tuks; PickMe is popular.

Tips The Southern Expressway, which extends to Mattala, is faster and safer for driving. Don't feed or try to touch wild animals.

CLOCKWISE FROM LEFT: OLIVER STREWE/GETTY IMAGES, THEPHOTOGRAPHERSL/SHUTTERSTOCK, WILD SRILANAKA/SHUTTERSTOCK

Buttala
Stay at a lake cabin to experience rural village life. Devour local food, trace ancient temple ruins, and drift away in a boat to spot birds and lonely bull elephants.
1½hr from Tissa

Kataragama
Set base in a safari lodge close to Yala National Park's quieter Block 5, have picnics by the Gin River and watch pilgrims give offerings to deities at this sacred precinct.
30min from Tissa

Tangalle
Beach-hop to Rekawa to find your secret wild-wavy stretch of shoreline. Feast on seafood, sip cocktails and watch nesting turtles at night – but give them plenty of space.
3hr from Colombo

Gal Oya

Take a detour enroute to Arugam Bay for jungle walks and boat safaris run by the Veddah, the island's last remaining indigenous people. Spy on elephants swimming in the lake.

3½hr from Tissa

Arugam Bay

Surf some of Asia's best swells and wander through hermits' caves in Kudumbigala. Worth noting that most of Arugam Bay's surf breaks are only for the intermediate and expert surfers.

3hr from Tangalle

Kumana National Park

Leave the crowds behind and spot leopards, sloth bears, elephants and massive crocs with their mouths wide open at this wild riverine grassland. Over 250 bird species nest and breed here.

1hr from Arugam Bay

Tissamaharama

Safari to Yala National Park – to spot leopards, sloth bears (pictured) and elephants in the wild. Watch sunsets over the town's lake, birdwatch in Bundala National Park and scout for ancient ruins.

1½hr from Tangalle

7 Things to Know About SRI LANKA

INSIDER TIPS TO HIT THE GROUND RUNNING

1 Tea Country

Sri Lanka is one of the world's largest tea exporters. The industry is built on the backs of Malaiyaha Tamils, Sri Lanka's most socioeconomically marginalised community with little to no opportunity to step outside the estates they are born into. When you visit tea estates, be mindful of their history, avoid photography without consent and don't support exploitative tea-plucking experiences that profit from their struggles.

▶ See more about Ceylon tea on p136

2 Cooling Off

Sri Lanka experiences scorching hot, humid weather throughout, except in Hill Country towns like Nuwara Eliya. Make sure to follow these tips to stay comfortable:

Clothing Stick to easy, flowing, summery clothing, and natural fabrics like cotton and linen.

King coconuts Packed with electrolytes, orange-hued king coconuts are what locals sip to stay hydrated.

Cooling wipes It's difficult to find unscented wipes here, so carry plenty of them to get rid of the sweat.

3 Short Eats

Tied to island life are a range of sweet and savoury snacks like fish rolls (deep-fried breaded rolls loaded with spicy canned tuna) and sugar-sprinkled tea buns. These are sold everywhere from fancy bakeries to street carts.

▶ See more about short eats on p52

4 Poya Days

Every full moon *(poya)* is a public holiday in Sri Lanka, reflecting Buddhist religious significance. Sale of alcohol and fresh meat is prohibited on these days.

▶ See more about *poya* on p149 and p193

5 Everyone's Family

You'll notice locals pop into a grocery store and address the shopkeeper as uncle or aunty, or *ayya/anna* (elder brother) and *akka* (elder sister). The two people – more often than not – aren't related. It's a customary way to show respect to everyone, including strangers. If someone looks younger, they'll be called *malli/thambi* (younger brother) or *nangi/thangachi* (younger sister).

6 Local Lingo

Island mannerisms and words that may help you to make friends along the way:

Machan – a common way to address friends; similar to 'dude' or 'bro'

Aiyo! – for expressing disappointment, surprise or pity

Gihin ennam (Sinhala); poittu varen (Tamil) – meaning 'I'll go and come back.' Use this when you depart; Sri Lankans never say goodbye

Plain tea – use this to order a cup of black tea; tea is often served with milk

Keeya da? – to ask the price of an item or service; avoid *kopamana da,* which is too formal

Worth noting: Sinhala phrases like *stutiyi* (thank you), *ayubown* (a way of greeting), and *karunakarala* (excuse me) are almost never used in daily life, although hotels and guides may use them. Stick to English words.

The ubiquitous nod: The side-to-side head waggle can mean anything from a strong yes to complete no, or maybe.

▶ See more about language on p256

7 Sweet Cinnamon

For generations, Sri Lanka has been known to produce the world's best cinnamon, with commercial cultivation beginning from the Dutch colonial times in the 17th and 18th centuries. Cinnamon here has an inviting scent. It's soft, sweet and light brown, compared to widely used cassia cinnamon, which is hardier, stronger, spicier and dark brown.

▶ See more about cinnamon on p95

Read, Listen, Watch & Follow

READ

The Seven Moons of Maali Almeida (Shehan Karunatilaka; 2022) Darkly funny murder mystery amid the civil war.

Gamperaliya (Uprooted; Martin Wickramasinghe; 1944) Traditional village life coming undone under modernisation.

Funny Boy (Shyam Selvadurai; 1994) Sexual identity politics and ethnic tensions.

Running in the Family (Michael Ondaatje; 1982) A memoir of sorts by the Sri Lankan–born poet and writer.

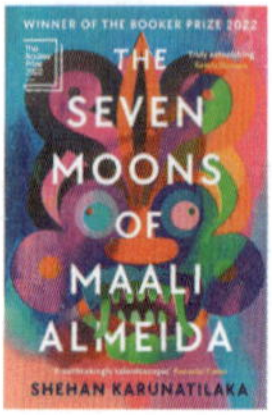

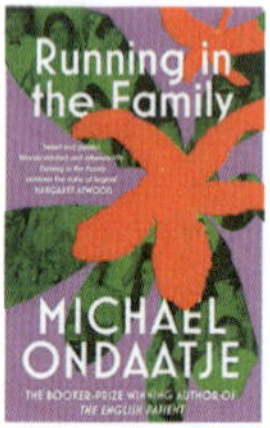

LISTEN

Made in Jaffna (Shan Vincent de Paul; 2021) Album by Jaffna-born Canadian artist on Tamil identity and resilience.

MCC Cowdrey Lecture (Kumar Sangakkara; pictured; 2011) Lecture by then cricket player on how cricket unites all, blurring ethnic lines.

Surangani (Dinesh Kanagaratnam; 2008) A Tamil-Sinhala remix of the Sri Lankan Baila (music genre with Afro-Portuguese roots) hit.

Nim Him Sewwa (Pandit WD Amaradeva; 1978) Island's immortal wedding romance song by an eminent vocalist.

PA IMAGES/ALAMY

Enjoy Enjaami
(Dhee ft Arivu; 2021) Singer Dhee and rapper Arivu explore landless struggles through Arivu's grandmother, a Sri Lankan tea-estate worker.

WATCH

Demons in Paradise (pictured; Jude Ratnam; 2017) Trilingual documentary explores the aftermath of war.

Butterfly Symphony (Jayantha Chandrasiri; 2013) Musical romance film about a student's journey to adulthood.

The Complex Human Geography of Sri Lanka (Alex Rothman; 2022) Kiwi videomaker dives into the island's different ethnic communities.

Gharasarapa (Jayantha Chandrasiri; 2018) Supernatural romantic horror film on folklore rituals.

Death on a Full Moon Day (Prasanna Vithanage; 1997) Film about a father who refuses to believe his soldier son died during a civil war.

COLLECTION CHRISTOPHEL /ALAMY

FOLLOW

@PoornaThenaturegirl Country life farm and cooking youtuber.

Newswire (newswire.lk) News aggregator with weather alerts.

@lostinlanka Inspiring Instagram for island stories.

@destination_srilanka Sri Lanka Tourism's official account.

Sri Lanka Cricket (srilankacricket.lk) Updates on tournaments and ticket sales.

COLOMBO

FINE DINING | ART & DESIGN | COLONIAL HISTORY

RESEARCHED BY MONIQUE CHOY

Wander chaotic Pettah Market and snap a selfie at the candy-striped **Jami Ul-Alfar Masjid** (p49)
10min from Fort

Sample sensational local curries on a banana leaf at **Upali's** (p50)
10min from Fort

Indulge in a massage from blind and vision-impaired practitioners at **Thusare Talking Hands** (p59)
8min from Fort

Sticky-beak inside a stylish architect's home at **Geoffrey Bawa House** (p55)
10min from Fort

Take in contemporary art and design at iconic **Barefoot** (p120)
12min from Fort

Watch the sun sink into the ocean from a beanbag on the beach in **Dehiwala** (p61)
25min from Fort

COLOMBO
Trip Builder

Colombo thrums with energy, from its busy markets to its cafe culture and contemporary-art scene. It's a city obsessed with design, especially design that fuses traditional artisan techniques with modernism – you'll see it in everything from architecture to home furnishings, visual art to fashion.

FROM TOP: LEEYAKORN06/SHUTTERSTOCK, GEOGPHOTOS/ALAMY
PREVIOUS SPREAD: ELEN MARLEN/SHUTTERSTOCK

Practicalities

ARRIVING

The Colombo–Katunayake Expressway brings you from the airport to the city within an hour. With luggage, rideshare or taxi are your best options; for rideshares you'll need mobile (cell) coverage.

CONNECT

Wi-fi is readily available in hotels, cafes and restaurants, though speed and reliability can be iffy.

MONEY

Larger hotels and restaurants accept electronic payment, though you'll still need cash for smaller places. ATMs are plentiful.

WHERE TO STAY

Area	Pros/Con
Colombo Fort & Pettah	Downtown has international hotels, close to Galle Face Green. Busy and businesslike.
Kollupitiya, Cinnamon Gardens & Borella	Cafes, shops, galleries and restaurants; good base for sights north and south. Pricey.
Bambalapitiya, Wellawatta & Mt Lavinia	Bambalapitiya offers cafes; Wellawatta and Mt Lavinia are southern beach suburbs. Further from sights.

GETTING AROUND

Tuk tuk Agree a price before embarking; bring correct fare, as most drivers don't carry change.

Uber and PickMe Rideshares by tuk tuk, car or motorbike eliminate hassle of haggling, directions and correct change.

Walking Colombo is walkable, despite the heat.

TOP: NGOC TRAN/SHUTTERSTOCK
BOTTOM: FANFO/SHUTTERSTOCK

EATING

Street food is special in this city, from *kotthu rotti* (stir-fried flatbread with veggies, meat and egg; pictured top left) to lunch packets (rice-and-curry meals in takeaway parcels). Vendors at Galle Face Green are famed for *isso vadai* (deep-fried prawn and lentil snacks) and Colombo is the best place to try Burgher specialty *lamprais* (riced cooked with curry in a banana leaf; pictured bottom left).

Best leafy courtyard cafe
Life's Good Kitchen (p61)

Must-try local curry
Curry Pot (p50)

DEC–MAR
Dry, warm weather and fewer showers. High season.

APR–MAY
Increasing thunderstorms and humidity. Sinhala and Tamil New Year in April.

JUN–SEP
Regular afternoon showers and strong winds. Low season.

OCT–NOV
The wettest time of the year, with high humidity.

01 Meander Through PETTAH MARKET

MAD MARKET | COLONIAL HISTORY | DIVERSE FAITHS

Packed into a tangle of streets, Pettah has been a vibrant trading area since the early 1800s under British colonial rule. The mad market energy here contrasts with moments of devout contemplation in the many houses of worship of different spiritual traditions.

GEORGE PACHANTOURIS/GETTY IMAGES

Trip Notes

Getting here Located between the Fort and the main train station in downtown Colombo, Pettah is easily reached by tuk tuk.

When to go Avoid the hottest part of the day (1pm to 4pm) when the crowds and chaos can be overwhelming. Come in July/August to catch Vel celebrations.

Top tip Cool down with a king coconut from street vendors, or slip into the respite of the covered market areas.

Vel Celebrations

In July or August, Colombo's Hindus celebrate Vel, when the god of War, Murrugan (also known as Skanda), vanquished evil. A joyous procession departs from Pettah's two Kathiresan temples, featuring a colourfully decorated chariot conveying Murrugan's sacred spear *(vel)* amid festive drumming, chanting and incense.

01 Snap a selfie with the candy-striped **Jami Ul-Alfar Masjid** (pictured pp44-5); you can also take a look at the interior outside prayer times. The building may look compact, but this Tardis can hold up to 10,000 worshippers.

02 Housed in the former home of Dutch governor Thomas van Rhee, and reopened in 2025 after refurbishment, the **Dutch Museum** preserves household goods, weapons and model ships from the Dutch colonial era.

03 Pettah Market is packed with household goods, pungent spices and tech gear. One of the most atmospheric parts is the **Vegetable Market**, a covered walkway housing a riot of colour, smells and sounds.

04 Dedicated to Skanda, the Hindu God of War, the **New Kathiresan Kovil** (pictured above) was built by devotees from the neighbouring Old Kathiresan Kovil. It's located on Sea St, the gold-trading area.

05 One of Sri Lanka's most important Catholic churches, **St Anthony's Shrine** was targeted in the 2019 Easter Sunday suicide bombings. A memorial inside is dedicated to the 93 people who lost their lives.

FROM TOP: PICTURE ALLIANCE/GETTY IMAGES, ELEN MARLEN/SHUTTERSTOCK

02 Dining & NIGHTLIFE

ROMANTIC DINING | LANEWAY COCKTAILS | ROOFTOPS

Sri Lanka is one of the world's great food destinations. From amazing street food to Burgher *lamprais*, Jaffna crab curry to British high tea, you can taste your way through Sri Lankan history. The nightlife is equally satisfying, whether you're watching the sunset from a rooftop, sipping cocktails at a cool laneway bar or downing a cold beer from a beanbag on the beach.

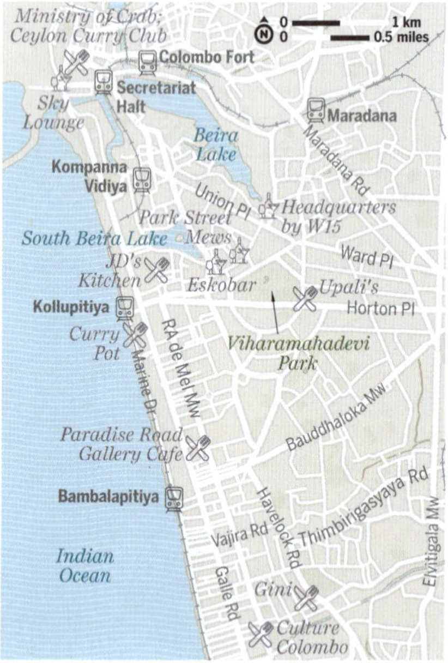

How to

When to go Happy-hour deals reward you for spending sunset on a rooftop, but the vibe doesn't really start simmering till later in the night.

Getting around Be cautious walking the streets late at night, as you would in any big city.

Drink like a local Lion Lager and Heineken Lanka are the most popular local beers, or try coconut-based arrack. Don't bother with wine – it's typically expensive, inferior and imported.

Memorable meals As its name suggests, **Dutch Hospital** was a 17th-century hospital serving employees of the Dutch East India Company. Today, it's home to excellent restaurants, including **Ministry of Crab** and **Ceylon Curry Club**.

Alternatively, eat without blowing your budget at local stops such as **Curry Pot**, **Culture Colombo** and **JD's Kitchen**. **Upali's** is a local fave with outstanding Sri Lankan dishes like 2000-year-old *hathmaluwa* (seven-in-one curry).

For a romantic meal head to **Paradise Road Gallery Cafe**, housed in Geoffrey Bawa's former office; or lovely **Gini**, specialising in live-fire cooking. Travel south to the **Mt Lavinia Hotel** to learn about its tragic love story.

Night Shift A cobbled alley of old warehouses, **Park Street Mews** has been converted into a cool nightlife destination with fairy lights, street art and boutique bars and restaurants. Expect live

AMIT_THAKARE/SHUTTERSTOCK

music, outdoor seating, DJs, open kitchens and a lively buzz.

Good weather, great views and a booming cocktail culture finds locals enjoying sundowners on rooftops across the city. Catch views of the shore from the **Sky Lounge** at the Kingsbury. Head to **Headquarters by W15** for perfect views of the Lotus Tower, or to **Eskobar** for a cool South American theme with velvet curtains, mezcal and cachaça cocktails.

Wellawatta, **Dehiwala** and **Mt Lavinia** are the closest swimming beaches to the city, and the golden sand is lined with simple restaurants and beach clubs like **Soul Beach**.

Colombo's LGBTIQ+ Scene

June is when we celebrate Pride. A bunch of different organisations do events, but the main one is Equal Ground (equal-ground.org). It has arts and performances and poetry, and a rainbow double-decker-bus parade ending with a Pride party and a kite festival; it generally happens in Mt Lavinia Beach.

But beyond that, nothing happens. There are no gay bars or clubs or restaurants. I'm probably the only one who has a Pride flag. But honestly, any of the clubs and bars, like in Park St, are very open-minded; there are no dramas.

Tash de Silva, *owner of 'Stache cafe. @the.stache_brunch*

Top Ministry of Crab

COLOMBO
Short Eats

01

02

03

04

05

01 Vadai
Deep-fried snacks made from flour and a variety of lentils and other legumes – the perfect combo of crunchy outside and chewy inside.

02 Isso vadai
A *vadai* topped with prawns *(isso)* and served with tangy sauce and a squeeze of lime. Specialty of the stalls on Galle Face Green.

03 Ulundu vadai
More doughy than ordinary *vadais*, these doughnut-shaped fritters are made from skinned black lentil flour to create a crispy exterior and fluffy interior.

04 Chinese rolls
Riffing on spring rolls, Sri Lankan–style Chinese rolls are battered before frying, and filled with veg (usually potato) and meat, fish or egg.

05 Mas rotti
Flatbread filled with spicy meat, onions and potatoes (sometimes egg) and pan-fried to flaky perfection – *kulkul mas rotti* are chicken, *harak mas rotti* are beef.

06 Elawalu roti
The veg version of *mas rotti* – charred flatbread wrapped into a parcel filled with chunky potato-based veg curry.

07 Maalu paan
A triangle-shaped, golden brioche-style bun filled with spicy potato and fish, usually mackerel (*maalu* means fish in Sinhala; *paan* means bread).

08 Maalu patti
Another *maalu* option, these small deep-fried crescents resemble empanadas. Inside is an aromatic mix of fish, potatoes and spices.

09 Maalu cutlet
Crispy breadcrumbed fish balls deep-fried until a deep golden brown. Typically made from canned mackerel, potatoes and spices.

10 Sareta talla
'Hot butter cuttlefish' is made by tossing scored cuttlefish in a rich sauce of butter, chilli and garlic to make a crunchy, chewy snack.

11 Kimbula banis
Sugar-dusted treat of fluffy sweet bread wrapped into a croissant-like roll resembling a crocodile (*kimbula* means crocodile in Sinhala).

01 SZEFEI/SHUTTERSTOCK. **02** SHUTTERVISTAS/SHUTTERSTOCK. **03** ZUEAHMAD/SHUTTERSTOCK. **04** LAZHKO SVETLANA/SHUTTERSTOCK. **05** MARIA STUDIO/SHUTTERSTOCK. **06** LAZHKO SVETLANA/SHUTTERSTOCK. **07** KOKOFOUNDIT/SHUTTERSTOCK. **08** CHARITH BANDARA/SHUTTERSTOCK. **09** LAZHKO SVETLANA/SHUTTERSTOCK. **10** RUWAN WALPOLA/SHUTTERSTOCK. **11** FATHIMA FAROOK/SHUTTERSTOCK

03 Art & DESIGN

TROPICAL MODERNISM | GALLERIES | TRADITION

Colombo punches above its weight in contemporary art. The city is obsessed with design, especially design that fuses traditional artisan techniques with modernism – you'll see it in everything from architecture to home furnishings, visual art to fashion.

GEORGE PACHANTOURIS/GETTY IMAGES

How to

Getting here/around You can walk between many art spaces in the area around Viharamahadevi Park; otherwise grab a tuk tuk.

When to go Museums and galleries are the perfect choice to avoid the heat of the day, or whenever a monsoonal downpour rolls in.

Top tip Book a day or two ahead to visit Geoffrey Bawa's home; no need to reserve ahead anywhere else.

GEOGPHOTOS/ALAMY

SLSK PHOTOGRAPHY/SHUTTERSTOCK

Bawa Bonanza

The father of tropical modernism, architect Geoffrey Bawa (1919–2003) fused ancient and contemporary influences, using courtyards, pathways and light wells to link indoor and outdoor spaces. With interiors open to sun and rain, he brought the outside in and created contemplative spaces between functional rooms, and portals offering glimpses of spaces yet to be entered.

At the end of a quiet cul-de-sac is the **house** where the master architect lived from 1960 to 1970, meticulously preserved just as he left it. The space amalgamates four small terraced homes acquired at different times, and offers a fascinating look at how Bawa managed small and unusual spaces to dramatic effect.

You can visit plenty of other Bawa-designed buildings around town, from **Seema Malakaya**,

Tradition Meets Modernity

A strong movement in Sri Lankan design, spearheaded by creatives like Barefoot founder Barbara Sansoni and batik artist Ena de Silva, is the fusion of traditional skills with modern design. **Barefoot** brings incredible colour combinations to handloom technique, while **Urban Island** works with palmyra artisans to craft stunning modern baskets.

Top left Seema Malakaya
Left Sri Lankan Parliament (p56)
Above Barefoot

the lovely meditation hall in Beira Lake; to the home he designed for lawyer Aelian Kannangara, now the **Geoffrey Bawa Space** housing temporary exhibitions; to his former office, now the **Paradise Road Gallery Cafe**; and the impressive **Sri Lankan Parliament**.

Brush Up on Your Art History

While the **National Art Gallery** undergoes renovations, you can take a captivating walk through Sri Lanka's historical kingdoms at the **National Museum of Colombo**. Look for the throne of Sri Vikrama Rajasinha, the last king of Kandy, which was looted by British soldiers in 1815 and returned to Sri Lanka by King George V in 1934. Upstairs galleries are devoted to Sri Lankan arts, crafts and culture. Just outside is an open-air gallery on the pavement of the **Green Path**. For several decades, artists from around Sri Lanka have gathered here to sell their work.

Colombo's Best Contemporary Galleries

Founded by Barbara Sansoni, the most recognisable designer in Sri Lanka, **Barefoot Gallery** encourages artist experimentation. **Paradise Road** was started by Shanth Fernando in 1987. In 2009 his daughter opened her own gallery, **Saskia Fernando Gallery**, and a second **branch** in 2025. These two galleries are known for their rigorous selection processes and for actively developing artists' careers.

There's also the new **Curado Art Space**, and here at **Radicle**, we focus on emerging artists.

Mandira Runatunga *is an assistant lecturer and curator at the University of Visual and Performing Arts and curator of Radicle Gallery. @radiclegallery*

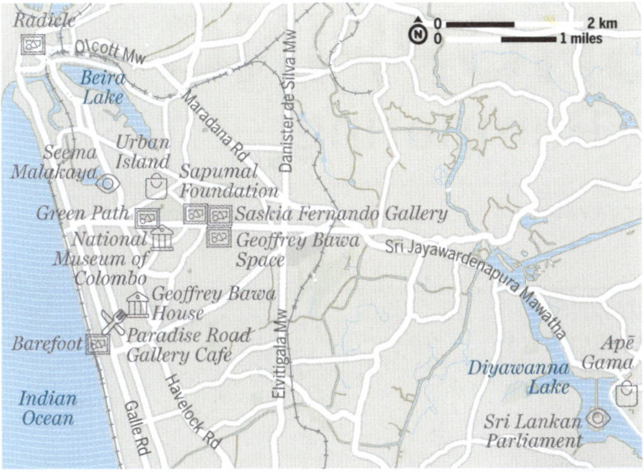

Left National Museum of Colombo
Below Mask, Laksala

Nestled in suburban streets not far away is the **Sapumal Foundation**, in a typical Colombo bungalow. It was originally the home of artist **Harry Pieris**, a founding member of the famed Group of '43 art movement, which marked the emergence of Sri Lankan modernism. It's now a gallery housing a permanent collection filled with the work of his circle.

Meet Artisans at Work

A model of a traditional Sri Lankan village, **Apē Gama** has palm-thatched mudbrick buildings scattered under shady trees. It sounds a bit cheesy, but this is actually a cultural centre in active use by community groups for education, festivals, school celebrations and performances by local dance and music groups.

Dotted around the grounds are artisan workshops where skilled makers are busy working lathes, weaving baskets and tightening drumskins; they're all happy to chat with visitors. You can purchase work directly from the artists, or there's a branch of the government craft store **Laksala** on the grounds. The **Ceylon Crafts Museum** is also here, displaying award-winning examples of traditional crafts such as lace-making, lacquerwork, mask-making and metalwork.

04 SHOPPING & Pampering

FASHION | HOMEWARES | AYURVEDA

A little retail therapy goes so well with a spot of self-care, don't you think? Seek out home-grown fashion, homewares and stylish souvenirs then relax with Sri Lanka's age-old Ayurvedic natural therapies, aromatic massage, and beauty treatments from across Asia.

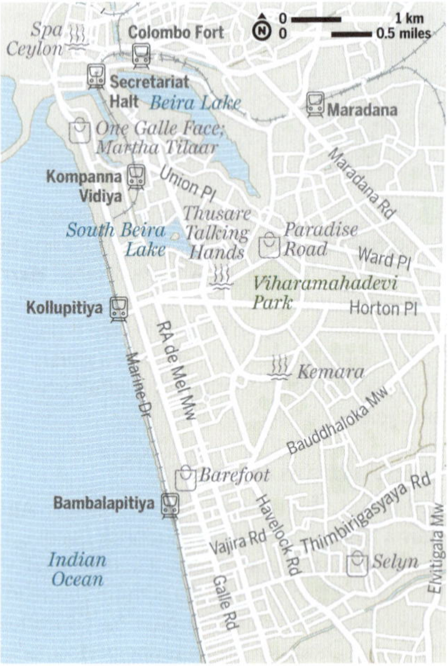

How to

Getting here A walkable cluster of Sri Lankan brands can be found in the Viharamahadevi Park area, including Paradise Road, Odel's flagship department store, Cotton Collection and Urban Island.

When to go As with galleries and museums, air-conditioned stores and spas provide great refuges from heat and rain.

Bargaining While you might be able to bargain at the Pettah Market, it's not done at more upmarket retail outlets.

Shop Beyond the Malls

In Colombo, you could spend a week hanging out in malls like **One Galle Face** among international brands like Birkenstock, Mango, Tommy Hilfilger and Swarovski. But look a little further afield and you'll discover local brands you won't find elsewhere.

The unmissable brands are **Barefoot** (fashion, toys and homewares) and **Paradise Road**; while handloom fabric producer **Selyn** is a fair-trade-certified handicrafts company with stunning clothing, sarongs and homewares.

Colombo-Style Pampering

A local sensation, **Spa Ceylon** offers Ayurveda wellness and products perfumed with the likes of night jasmine, neem and tea tree at around 40 colourful locations throughout the city, many with a spa and massage centre.

SLSK PHOTOGRAPHY/SHUTTERSTOCK

Top Spa Ceylon

All-natural, holistic massages, facials and other treatments are offered at gorgeous **Kemara**, which also has a cafe with a menu free of gluten, grain, dairy and sugar. Indonesia's herbal therapy empress **Martha Tilaar** has a branch in luxe One Galle Face mall. Go here for *rupasampat wahyabi-antara*, the Javanese art of inner and outer beauty.

For highly skilled and more budget-friendly massage, there's no better option than **Thusare Talking Hands**. This social enterprise trains blind and vision-impaired practitioners in oil-free shiatsu acupressure massage. It also offers manicure and pedicure treatments by deaf nail artists.

What Is Ayurveda?

This 3000- to 5000-year-old tradition of natural therapy emphasises the balance of body, mind and spirit through calibrating the three bio-energies known as *doshas*. The word Ayurveda comes from the Sanskrit words *ayur* (life) and *veda* (knowledge).

Typical massage treatments include *abhyanga* (oil massage), *udvartana* (exfoliating powder massage), *pindasweda* (massage with warm herbal bundles) and *padabhyanga* (foot massage). Other Ayurvedic treatments include *panchakarma* (purification and detoxification), *shidohara* (pouring warm oil onto the forehead), *swedana* (steam therapy), as well as dietary and wellness advice.

Listings

BEST OF THE REST

Sights in the City

Lotus Tower

Opened in 2022, the lovely Lotus Tower, with its rainbow of changing petal colours, is a landmark throughout the city. At 356m it's the tallest building in South Asia, and the 19th tallest in the world, with an elevator that zips you to the top in 48 seconds.

Gangaramaya Temple

The revered Buddhist temple complex is a treasure vault, packed floor to ceiling with offerings left by Buddhist devotees. Across the road, Seema Malakaya is a small but atmospheric spiritual centre designed by Geoffrey Bawa in 1985.

Chill Out with the Locals

Galle Face Green

Gathering at Galle Face Green every evening to watch the sunset, play music and eat street food is an unwritten tradition in Colombo. For a few months during the economic crisis in 2022, it became the scene of the Aragalaya ('the Struggle' in Sinhala), a huge, organised and peaceful protest camp.

Saturday Good Market

On Saturdays (9am to 5pm, rain or shine) head to Colombo Racecourse for this super-chill outdoor market with a curated list of stalls and traders, including many charity and fair-trade organisations.

Viharamahadevi Park

Considered the lungs of Colombo, Viharamahadevi Park is green and peaceful, benefiting from a canopy of tall and shady trees.

Yoga, Meditation & Astrology

Soul Theory

A full schedule of daily classes for all levels, as well as meditation, reiki and Vedic astrology readings in a lovely space opening on a Zen garden. Check Instagram for the schedule.

Ishtara

Holistic wellness centre offering daily yoga, as well as meditation, sound healings and tarot, in a lovely studio next to the Geoffrey Bawa Space. Find the schedule on Instagram.

Nanda Sri Hatha Yoga Institute

Respected yoga teacher Guru Nanda Siriwardana runs this Nugegoda-based school. The centre has been established for over 30 years, and focuses on correct technique.

Hit the Beach

Wellawatta Beach

Clusters of simple open-air eateries with tables in the sand, known as *wadiyas* in Sinhala, serve inexpensive and delicious seafood here. The celebrated Jaffna ice cream shop Rio is

TRABANTOS/SHUTTERSTOCK

Viharamahadevi Park

on the main road, offering old-school sundaes served in a parfait glass.

Dehiwala Beach

Further south is a string of beach-club restaurants. Upmarket Soul Beach has a pool and live music on weekends, while at CanLanka there's a food court with budget beer, burger and takeaway options and the Plan B club upstairs with DJs.

Mt Lavinia Beach

The public beach here is more chill, with boogieboard rental on the sand, while the exclusive Mt Lavinia private beach is for guests of the Mt Lavinia Hotel only.

Cafe Culture

Life's Good Kitchen $$

Gorgeous courtyard cafe dripping with shady foliage; you'll feel like you're in a treehouse. International menu with good veg and vegan options.

Department of Coffee $$

With macchiatos, honey oat-milk lattes, Vietnamese *phins,* French presses and single-origin pour overs, this spot take its coffee very seriously.

'Stache $$

Laid-back LGBTIQ+-owned cafe, tucked away in a quiet street serving Sri Lankan food with a brunch twist.

Radicle $$

Sharing space with a contemporary-art gallery in the historic De Mel building in Fort, Radicle roasts its own beans and crafts its own matcha from five different cultivars.

Black Cat Cafe $$

A hip cafe in a lovely heritage house east of Viharamahadevi Park with books, board games and a program of author talks and live music.

SLCRAZYARTIST/SHUTTERSTOCK

Dehiwala Beach

High Tea

Crave $$$

The Hilton does an epic high-tea buffet on Saturday in a buzzy atmosphere with international sweets and savouries. There are two sittings – 12.30pm to 2.30pm and 3pm to 5pm. Wear loose pants.

Galle Face Hotel $$$

Sip in style at the venerable Galle Face Hotel with a platter (Monday to Thursday) or buffet (Friday to Sunday) high tea. The gracious veranda overlooks the ocean.

Paradise Road Tintagel $$$

This gorgeous old mansion was the former home of Prime Minister SWRD Bandaranaike (and also where he was assassinated). Choose the alfresco courtyard or the lavish lobby to sample fresh scones and baked treats in sumptuous surrounds.

Dilmah t-lounge $$

More affordable than the grand hotels, this is a great place to sample Sri Lanka's famed silver tip tea. Your order comes with a timer to ensure the perfect steep. Book ahead for high tea.

WEST COAST

BEACHES | DESIGN | WATER SPORTS

RESEARCHED BY BRADLEY MAYHEW

WEST COAST
Trip Builder

Scuba divers, kitesurfers and lovers of interior design will adore the west coast, as will anyone pressed for time; almost everything is less than a two-hour drive from the main international airport.

Watch the sun set over the Indian Ocean in **Negombo** (p68)
15min from Colombo Airport

Overnight in one of Geoffrey Bawa's iconic hotels in **Bentota** (p79)
2hr from Colombo

Remember 2004's devastating tsunami at Peraliya's **Community Tsunami Education Centre** (p81)
10min from Hikkaduwa

CLOCKWISE FROM TOP LEFT: INIGOLAI-PHOTOGRAPHY/SHUTTERSTOCK, AURORE KERVOERN/GETTY IMAGES, SHASHH/SHUTTERSTOCK, ISHITA BHOWMIK/SHUTTERSTOCK
PREVIOUS: SOFT_LIGHT/SHUTTERSTOCK

N
0 — 50 km
0 — 25 miles

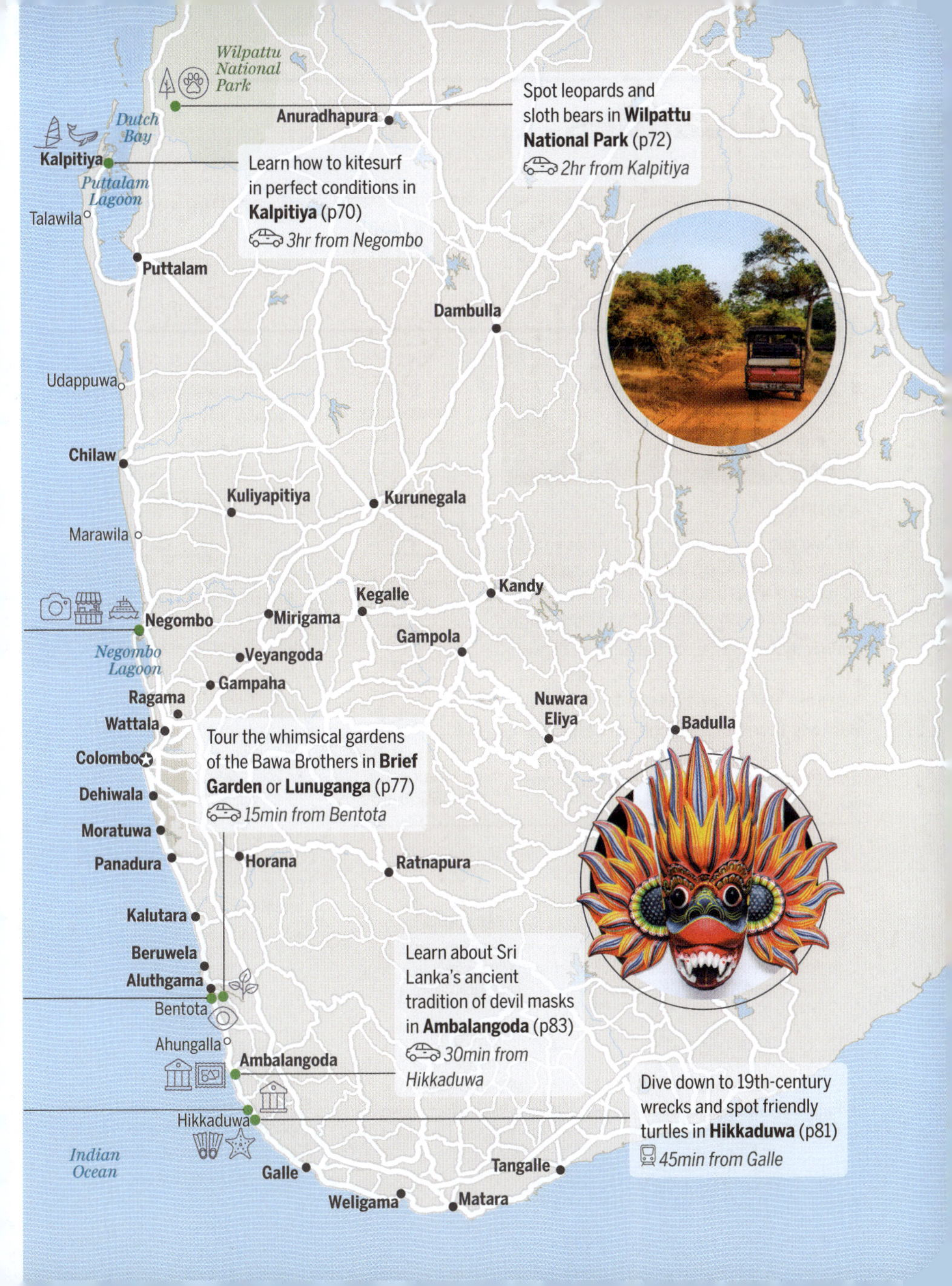
Wilpattu National Park
Dutch Bay
Kalpitiya
Puttalam Lagoon
Talawila
Puttalam
Anuradhapura
Spot leopards and sloth bears in Wilpattu National Park (p72)
2hr from Kalpitiya
Learn how to kitesurf in perfect conditions in Kalpitiya (p70)
3hr from Negombo
Dambulla
Udappuwa
Chilaw
Kuliyapitiya
Kurunegala
Marawila
Kandy
Kegalle
Negombo
Mirigama
Gampola
Negombo Lagoon
Veyangoda
Gampaha
Ragama
Wattala
Nuwara Eliya
Badulla
Colombo
Tour the whimsical gardens of the Bawa Brothers in Brief Garden or Lunuganga (p77)
15min from Bentota
Dehiwala
Moratuwa
Panadura
Horana
Ratnapura
Kalutara
Beruwela
Aluthgama
Bentota
Ahungalla
Ambalangoda
Learn about Sri Lanka's ancient tradition of devil masks in Ambalangoda (p83)
30min from Hikkaduwa
Hikkaduwa
Dive down to 19th-century wrecks and spot friendly turtles in Hikkaduwa (p81)
45min from Galle
Indian Ocean
Galle
Tangalle
Weligama
Matara

Practicalities

BADAI/SHUTTERSTOCK

ARRIVING

Air Colombo Bandaranaike Airport is closer to Negombo (10km, pictured) than Colombo, making Negombo an obvious first or last night. Hikkaduwa is only two hours away on the Southern Expressway.

Train Frequent coastal commuter trains between Colombo and Galle stop in southern west-coast towns like Bentota and Hikkaduwa.

Bus Local buses connect southern west-coast towns every 15 minutes. Express direct buses to/from Colombo take the faster Southern Expressway (with tolls).

HOW MUCH FOR A

Prawn curry
Rs 2000

Lunuganga tour
US$20

Wilpattu National Park safari
US$60–100

WHEN TO GO

NOV–APR
Dry weather and calm seas for peak season beach fun, surfing and diving.

FEB–OCT
Spot animals in Wilpattu National Park, especially June to September.

MAY–OCT
Rain and low-season prices in the south. Perfect kitesurfing in Kalpitiya.

MID-DEC–MAR
Second kitesurfing season in Kalpitiya, plus dolphin and whale spotting.

GETTING AROUND

Train The scenic coastal line between Colombo and Galle is a popular way to get around the southwest coast.

Bus Local buses stop a lot but run frequently and almost always have a seat. Connections thin considerably in the northwest, but there are still hourly buses.

Scooter Places like Hikkaduwa rent scooters if you have a license, and they can be a fun way to get around.

Tuk Tuk Apps like PickMe work in most towns and are a cost-effective option within and between towns. Negombo is a popular place to rent your own tuk tuk.

EATING & DRINKING

The best food options on the west coast are, of course, seafood, with most restaurants offering some kind of fried fish (pictured top right) or fish or prawn curry (pictured bottom right). Negombo and Hikkaduwa are the best places for international options, and Negombo fish market is a fabulous place to get a sense of the breadth of local produce, even though much of it is earmarked for export. Hikkaduwa is the place to get poke bowls, cold-pressed juices and good coffee.

Best waterside location
Windy Waves (p84) & Malli's Seafood Restaurant (p84)

Must-try seafood
Club. Ceylon (p84)

CONNECT & FIND YOUR WAY

Wi-fi Every hotel and restaurant offers reliable internet. Mobile phone and data connections are good along the west coast.

Navigation A single road connects all the towns of the west coast and rarely strays more than 200m from the ocean. Only the Kalpitiya peninsula offers some minor navigational challenges.

WHERE TO STAY

The west coast has some of the country's most stylish accommodation. For quieter options look for coastal places between the main towns, or head inland, even just a few hundred metres, for the best value.

Town	Pros/Cons
Negombo	Lots of choice, from family guesthouses to beachside resorts, but heavily touristed.
Bentota	Excellent for top-end accommodation, with some of Sri Lanka's most stylish boutique and designer options.
Hikkaduwa	All budgets covered, with the quietest options away from the road. Potentially noisy at weekends.

PADI CERTIFICATION

Bring your PADI scuba card if you want to dive in Kalpitiya or Hikkaduwa. Both places offer refresher dives if you are a bit rusty.

MONEY

ATMs are everywhere along the west coast. The exception is the Kalpitiya peninsula, so be sure to bring cash for Kalpitiya stays (though the kitesurfing resorts take cards).

05 Negombo PIT-STOP

SUNSETS | SEAFOOD | LAGOON TOURS

Given that it's just 10km from Sri Lanka's main airport, Negombo has long been a favourite first- or last-night stopover, but there's more to the town than that. Its morning fish market is possibly the most interesting in the country, sunsets from the strip's main beach are legendary and boat trips around the Negombo lagoon are sublime. Stay an extra day; Negombo is worth it.

How to

Getting here Taxis and tuk tuks make the 9km trip from Colombo Bandaranaike International Airport, and buses and trains run frequently to Colombo.

When to go December to April is peak season, with clear skies and calm seas, but July to September also brings good weather. At other months expect some rain, rougher seas and hotel discounts.

Offbeat cultural experience Visit one of Negombo's many churches on a Sunday.

Negombo's Fish Market

Make your jet lag work in your favour by rising at dawn to catch the action at Negombo's **Lellama Fish Market**. The north side houses the main fish auction, where brokers advise fishers on the daily prices and the big boats dock to sell huge yellowfin tuna to buyers from Colombo and beyond. You'll see emperor fish, mahi mahi, cobia, needle fish, *paral* (trevally), octopus, cuttlefish, bottle squid and both lagoon and sea prawns here.

By 9am the market is mostly over, and you should head instead for the smaller *(podi)* **fish market** by the Dutch Fort, where you'll see fish cutters chopping up the day's catch, as thousands of smaller fish dry in lines on coconut mesh. Both markets are closed on Sundays and Catholic holidays.

To get a taste of the day's freshest catch, reserve a table at **Club. Ceylon**, Negombo's finest and most sustainable fish restaurant.

TRABANTOS/SHUTTERSTOCK

Market Culture

I visit Lellama Fish Market most mornings in season, and I just love its unique energy and fantastic atmosphere.

The buyers at the auctions here are real pros and can tell by sight just how fresh a catch is to within an hour or two, and even whether it was line- or net-caught. The sellers are proud showmen and you'll also see older aunties, many of them widows of fishermen, who buy fish here and then resell it at other markets. Many of the families at Lellama have been fishing for seven or more generations.

Liz Norris, *owner-chef at Club. Ceylon restaurant. @clubceylon*

Lagoon by Boat

Negombo's other great experience is a sunset boat trip around the **Negombo Lagoon**. In two hours you'll visit fishing communities, detour up the Dutch-built **Hamilton Canal**, and watch sunset colours blush over the lagoon as men fish from outrigger canoes. If you're a keen birder, get up early and head to the far south of the lagoon into the **Muthurajawela Wetlands**, which is home to over 75 species of birds.

Top Fishing boats, Negombo Lagoon

06 Kitesurfing in KALPITIYA

KITESURFING | WILDLIFE-WATCHING | DIVING

Way out at the far end of the remote Kalpitiya peninsula lies one of the world's best kitesurfing locations. A combination of consistent seasonal wind, shallow warm-water lagoons and picture-perfect ocean sandbars attracts kitesurfers from around the world, making it the perfect place to spend a few days learning an exciting new sport.

MALCOLM P CHAPMAN/GETTY IMAGES

How to

When to go The main kiting season is April to October, with a shorter second season from mid-December to March. January is peak time.

Getting here Several daily buses run direct to Kalpitiya from Negombo and Colombo. Alternatively, change in Palawi junction or Puttalam for an hourly bus to Kalpitiya. A van pickup from the airport costs US$95; this is arranged through the kite resorts.

Top tip Shops in Kalpitiya town close on Friday afternoons and Sundays.

TRABANTOS/SHUTTERSTOCK

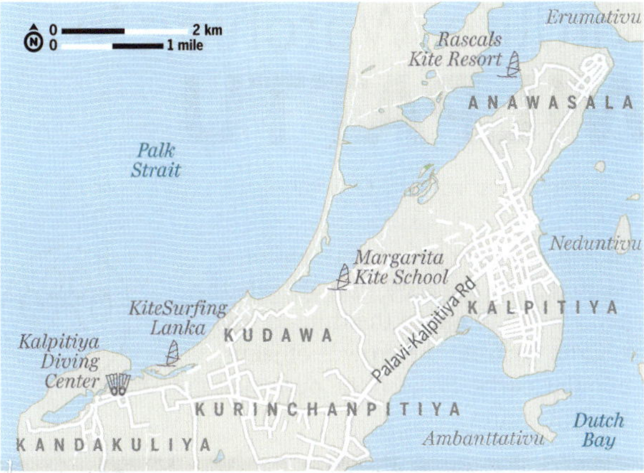

Perfect wind Kalpitiya's big draw is its eight months a year of stable, consistent wind, which blows over flat, warm and shallow lagoons to create perfect kitesurfing conditions. Over a dozen kitesurfing schools and resorts dot the peninsula, notably **Rascals Kite Resort** (rascalskiteresort.com), **KiteSurfing Lanka** (kitesurfinglanka.com) and **Margarita Kite School** (margaritakiteschool.com). Beginners stick to the 2.5km-long Kalpitiya Lagoon, but experienced surfers can head out on boat trips to a host of idyllic ocean islands and sandbars for epic downwinding adventures.

Beginners normally sign up for eight hours of tuition spread over three days, costing around US$480/600 for one/two people sharing an instructor. Weeklong accommodation packages are common, and equipment rental is available if you want to hone your skills.

Dolphins, whales and reefs There's more to Kalpitiya than kites. Between November and April, operators offer early-morning boat trips to see superpods of hundreds of spinner dolphins frolicking in the sparkling ocean waves. Further out to sea are sperm, minke and even majestic blue whales, notably in November and in March/April.

Kalpitiya is also home to Bar Reef, Sri Lanka's largest, and while the coral has suffered from bleaching in recent years, the marine life is excellent during the clearer visibility of November to April. Contact the family-run **Kalpitiya Diving Center** (kalpitiyadivingcenter.com) for a full range of sites.

Top left Kitesurfers, Kalpitiya
Bottom left Dolphins near Kalpitiya

Kitesurfing Tips

I often suggest avoiding the beginning or end of the kiting season to guarantee the best conditions, or at least add on a spare day at this time in case of sub-optimal wind. Remember that kitesurfing is an extreme sport, so ensure that your instructor is IKO-certified. A rescue boat is useful for beginners, even in the lagoon.

You'll want to bring good quality sunglasses and water-resistant sun protection. Water shoes are useful against shells on the lagoon bed; bring your own if you have big feet.

Susantha Fernando, *instructor and owner of Sun Wind Beach Kite Resort. @sun_wind_beach_kalpitiya*

07 Wildlife-Watching in WILPATTU

WILDLIFE | SAFARI | HISTORY

Wilpattu is the largest and oldest of Sri Lanka's national parks, and one of the least visited. This is a park that attracts the more serious wildlife-watcher, willing to put in the time to spot leopards, sloth bears or elephants far from the crowds of jeeps found in Sri Lanka's more popular parks. It's also the perfect stop-off between Kalpitiya and Anuradhapura.

WILD SNAP CREATIONS/SHUTTERSTOCK

How to

Getting here Puttalam to Anuradhapura buses pass 8km south of the main Hunuwilagama gate, but you need your own transport to access the remoter western Eluwankulama gate.

When to go The dry season months of June to September are most popular, followed by October, February and March.

Organise a safari Any accommodation can arrange a six-seater 4WD Hilux or LandCruiser, or try **Leopard Den** (leoparddenwilpattu.com) at Wilpattu Junction.

OMINDU SHEHAN/SHUTTERSTOCK

ROSHANA1986/SHUTTERSTOCK

Far left Leopard in Wilpattu
Bottom left Sloth bear in Wilpattu
Left Kudiramalai Point

On Safari

Thanks to its closure during the majority of Sri Lanka's 26-year civil war, **Wilpattu National Park** has some of the best-preserved natural settings in the nation. It also has some of the most varied landscapes, located at the junction of dry evergreen forests, wetlands and coastal habitats. It even contains several archaeological sites; **Kudiramalai Point**, on the park's western coast, is allegedly where the Sinhala people's ancestors first arrived on the island in 543 BCE.

The dry season is the most popular time to visit, when wildlife tends to concentrate around the 60 or so shrinking sand-rimmed lakes, or *villu,* that give the park its name. This central lakes area is where leopards are most commonly spotted and is about an hour's drive from the main gate.

Most people enter via the main **Hunuwilagama** entrance, but a second less-visited entrance lies further west at **Eluwankulama**. Either way, try to enter the park when it opens at 6am. Apart from the elusive leopards and sloth bears, you'll likely spot crocodiles, cobras and some of the park's 100 bird species, from hornbills to painted storks. To maximise your chances of sightings, prioritise your efforts around dawn and dusk, bring good binoculars and book a good wildlife guide well in advance.

Full-day jeep safaris without a guide cost around US$60 to US$100 per person, which includes around US$37 per person in park fees.

Safari Savvy

When choosing which part of the park to visit, bear in mind that the Western (Eluwankulama) gate has less traffic and accommodation and feels more exclusive, but access can be impossible in the wet season. Elephants are more frequently spotted at the Pomparippu grasslands near this western gate, while sloth bears are more commonly seen nearer the main (Hunuwilagama) gate.

I recommend a two-night minimum stay, with a full-day safari inside the park. Visit the park's central section early in the morning, head to the Kudiramalai ruins at midday, then return south for late-afternoon spotting.

Arran Sivarajah, *safari guide and co-owner of Ceylon Wild Safaris. ceylonwildsafaris.com*

Sri Lankan

WILDLIFE

04

02

03

05

01

06

01 Asian Elephant
Sri Lanka has the highest density of elephants in Asia. See them in Minneriya, Yala or Uda Walawe national parks.

02 Leopard
Just 800 of these big cats are left in Sri Lanka. They're notoriously hard to spot, with Yala and Wilpattu national parks your best bet.

03 Sloth Bear
A nocturnal black bear with a dishevelled look, shaggy mane, long claws and poor sight; sometimes spotted in Yala and Wilpattu national parks.

04 Blue Whale
Drawn by the upswell of deep ocean nutrients, blue whales can be spotted December to April off the coasts of Mirissa or Kalpitiya.

05 Slender Loris
Adorable, disc-eyed primate with pencil-thin limbs. Grey slender loris are easily spotted in Sigiriya; red loris are rarer.

06 Rusty-Spotted Cat
Cuteness overload with the world's smallest feline, which could fit into the palm of your hand.

07

08

10

09

12

11

07 Toque Macaque
Endemic to Sri Lanka, living in troops and with a monk-like 'toque' hairstyle.

08 Olive Ridley Turtle
One of the five types of turtle (also leatherback, hawksbill, loggerhead and green) that lay their eggs on Sri Lanka's west and south coasts.

09 Sri Lankan Junglefowl
The males of Sri Lanka's chicken-like national bird boast vivid colours and a golden mane.

10 Purple-Faced Langur
Endemic to Sri Lanka, seen in lowland rainforest and the highlands around Nuwara Eliya.

11 Asian Water Monitor
Dog-sized semi-aquatic lizard, the world's second largest, often seen at the archaeological sites of Anuradhapura or Polonnaruwa.

12 Sambar
Large maned deer, up to 1.5m tall at the shoulder, with large herds common in Horton Plains National Park.

01 AL CARRERA/SHUTTERSTOCK, **02** HAMID300/SHUTTERSTOCK, **03** MARTIN MECNAROWSKI/SHUTTERSTOCK, **04** B113/SHUTTERSTOCK, **05** ERIC ISSELEE/SHUTTERSTOCK, **06** JIRIK V/SHUTTERSTOCK, **07** PIOTR POZNAN/SHUTTERSTOCK, **08** NILANKA SAMPATH/GETTY IMAGES, **09** PIOTR POZNAN/SHUTTERSTOCK, **10** MARTIN PELANEK/SHUTTERSTOCK, **11** TON PONCHAI/SHUTTERSTOCK, **12** ANAN KAEWKHAMMUL/SHUTTERSTOCK

08 Gardens of the BAWA BROTHERS

ART | SCULPTURE | GARDENS

The lush countryside around Bentota is home to two of Sri Lanka's most beautiful country estates, the former homes of the Bawa brothers, Geoffrey and Bevis, who rank among Sri Lanka's most colourful and intriguing characters. Anyone with an eye for interior decor, garden design or the artistic life will love a day spent exploring these sublime, historic and whimsical retreats.

HEINRICH VAN TONDER/SHUTTERSTOCK

How to

Getting here Lunuganga is 5km southeast of Bentota, and Brief Garden is 8km northeast; a tuk tuk or taxi is the best way to get to either.

When to go Any time is possible, though October to May brings the driest weather.

Tours Visits to Lunuganga are by guided tour only, at 11am, 2pm and 3pm; see geoffreybawa.com/lunuganga for details.

SARAFALLSTROM/SHUTTERSTOCK

RANJANA PERERA/SHUTTERSTOCK

Lunuganga

The father of tropical modernism, renowned Sri Lankan architect Geoffrey Bawa (1919–2003) owed his career change from lawyer to architect to this country estate, known as **Lunuganga** (Salt River; adult US$20), whose construction spanned an epic four decades. Arrive for one of the three daily tours and you'll be led past Bawa's weekend office, the lower lakeshore gardens, past half-hidden works of art and across the hillside that was razed to improve views from the main house (and where Bawa's ashes are buried), all the while learning about Bawa's development of the property into what it is today.

The house itself and the outlying buildings are off limits but are bookable as part of the the impeccable five-star hotel **Teardrop Lunuganga** (teardrop-hotels.com/lunuganga).

Brief Garden

Built on the family's former rubber plantation, **Brief Garden** was the home of Geoffrey's older brother, the Sri Lankan landscape architect Bevis Bawa. Built on a more intimate scale than Lunuganga, the delightful garden is full of hidden nooks and peppered with colourful murals, leering sculptures and homoerotic art.

There are some fascinating details to look out for, both in the garden and the house, notably the mural of Sri Lanka by Australian artist Donald Friend (who came to visit for a week and stayed for six years!) and the Christmas card to Bevis from actress Viven Leigh and her husband Lawrence Olivier.

Far left Lakeshore gardens, Lunuganga
Bottom left and left Brief Garden

Brief Memories

Bevis inherited the house and estate from his parents at age 20. He started the garden in 1929, and it took 20 years to create, although a garden is never really finished. I joined in 1969 as Bevis' secretary.

Bevis was a sociable man and the estate soon became a social hub. Geoffrey would often visit in the evening, and they would drink and laugh like mad; the brothers had a rivalry, but they also loved each other.

I used to walk the garden twice a day, but these days my favourite spot is under the pergola. When I sit here, I feel that I'm part of the garden.

Dooland De Silva, *former head gardener and current owner of Brief Garden.*

09 Geoffrey Bawa's ARCHITECTURE

DESIGN | ARCHITECTURE | STYLE

Sri Lanka's most renowned architect Geoffrey Bawa (1919–2003) created some of the country's most iconic buildings, in a style often dubbed tropical modernism. Visit some of his most stylish creations – destinations in their own right – on this luxurious west-coast itinerary.

JAMES TALALAY/ALAMY

Jetwing Lighthouse Hotel

Trip Notes

Getting here All the hotels are accessible via a combination of bus and tuk tuk.

Visit Most Bawa-designed hotels offer a Bawa-focused tour of their properties, free to guests or around US$10 to non-guests, who should reserve a spot. Be sure to also visit Lunuganga (p77).

Stay All the properties listed here make for fabulous stays; Jetwing Lagoon's garden villa lets you overnight in what was Bawa's office during construction in 1965.

Classic Bawa

Several themes run through Bawa's designs: the use of natural light and ventilation, a love of blending interior and exterior spaces, and the adoption of natural rock features into building design. Look out also for Bawa's love of Portuguese-style roof tiles and of central water pools framed by *araliya* (frangipani) trees.

01 Bawa's first hotel, originally called the Blue Lagoon, **Jetwing Lagoon Wellness** has been remodelled by one of his protégés into a serene wellness hotel featuring Sri Lanka's longest pool.

02 Built in 1969 on the site of the British-era Rest House, **Cinnamon Bentota Beach** has architecture recalling an earlier Dutch fort. Don't miss the colourful batik and fabric ceilings, designed by Ena de Silva and Barbara Sansoni.

03 **Boutique 87** consists of two intimate Bawa-designed villas filled with art and surrounded by lush gardens, a cobalt-blue swimming pool and several faux ruins. Book a tour (US$10).

04 Built in 1981 as the Hotel Triton, **Heritance Ahungalla** has a line of pools that connect sea and sky, alongside several interior tree-filled courtyards. Spot the original lobby elevator.

05 From sculptor Laki Senanayake's epic battle-scene balustrade, to the use of natural rock and the batik ceiling of the Coat of Arms bar, this **Jetwing Lighthouse Hotel** is classic Bawa.

CLOCKWISE FROM TOP LEFT: BRADLEY MAYHEW, MARKO REIMANN/ALAMY, PETER COOK/ALAMY

10 Beach Life in HIKKADUWA

SURFING | SCUBA | NIGHTLIFE

Famed since the 1970s for its surf scene and beachside reef snorkelling, Hikkaduwa has lost its shine in recent years, with the surf scene shifting along the south coast. But there are still good reasons to come to Hikka; families will love spotting turtles from the lovely beaches, divers can explore great wrecks and night owls will find the island's biggest beach parties.

BLAZENKA BABIC/GETTY IMAGES

How to

Getting here Hikka is easily accessible along the coastal highway, 100km south of Colombo and 18km north of Galle. If arriving by train, secure a sea-facing seat in the carriage to take in the superb views.

When to go November to April are the months for both surfing and scuba diving; during other months, the sea is too rough and diving companies relocate to the east coast.

Top tip Hikka's northern beaches are smaller and more crowded; head further south, around the Roman Beach Hotel, for some elbow room.

MARIUS DOBILAS/SHUTTERSTOCK

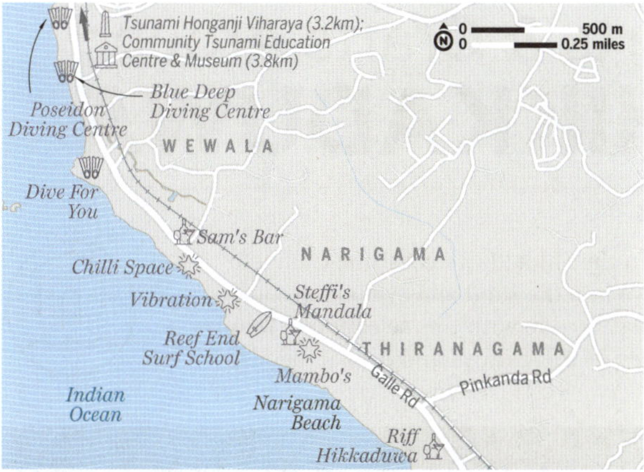

Top left Community Tsunami Education Centre and Museum **Bottom left** Sea turtle

Surf's up Hikkaduwa (pictured pp62–3) is the beach that put Sri Lanka on the global surfing map. The town's mix of shore and reef breaks are good for both beginner and advanced surfers, and schools like **Reef End Surf School** (reefendsurf-school.com) offer tuition and rent boards. Beginners generally stick to the the sandy beach breaks of Narigama beach and further south.

Underwater wonders Hikkaduwa's northern coastline is lined by a shallow fringing reef that has been designated the Hikkaduwa National Park. Tsunami damage and bleaching has degraded the coral in recent years, but the reef is still home to sea turtles, luminescent fish and blacktip reef sharks, and it's incredibly accessible. You can even spot sea turtles from the beach outside the Hikka Tranz Hotel.

Divers will be more excited by two nearby shipwreck sites – the 85m-long *Earl of Shaftesbury*, built in 1847, or the slightly deeper *'SS Conch',* a former oil tanker. Dive centres like **Dive for You** (diveforyou.com), **Poseidon Diving Centre** (diving srilanka.com) and **Blue Deep Diving Centre** (bluedeepdiving.com) operate daily boat dives.

Remembering the tsunami It's worth heading 4km north of Hikkaduwa to Pereliya, where the **Community Tsunami Education Centre and Museum** and the **Tsunami Honganji Viharaya** commemorate the 33,000 Sri Lankans who lost their lives in the 2004 Boxing Day tsunami. It's a sobering, moving visit, and the serene standing Buddha is beautifully framed at sunset.

A Big Night Out

After a hard day's surfing, diving or snorkelling, Hikkaduwa shifts gear to offer some of the biggest beach parties on the coast.

Things kick off sedately enough at the surprisingly affordable rooftop bar of the **Riff Hikkaduwa**. After taking in the town's finest sunset views, move onto hip beachside drinks spots such as **Steffi's Mandala**, sometimes with live music or DJ sets.

For a big night, try **Sam's Bar** for televised football, or one of several late-night, techno-heavy party spots: notably **Mambo's** and **Chilli Space** on Wednesdays and Saturdays, or **Vibration** on Fridays.

11 Arts & Crafts Around HIKKADUWA

BATIKS | MASKS | PAINTING

There's a lot more to the Hikkaduwa coastline than left breaks and beach parties. When the sand and seafood become tiresome, unleash your creative side with this selection of family-friendly artistic experiences in Hikkaduwa and Ambalangoda, 15km to the north.

BADA1/SHUTTERSTOCK

Madu Ganga Boat Trip

One family-friendly excursion north of Ambalangoda is the half-day boat safari (pictured) around **Madu Ganga Lake**, where you'll get to see an island temple, a mangrove tunnel, traditional methods of cinnamon production and a colony of vampire bats, before stopping for a *thambili* (king coconut) from a floating juice bar.

Trip Notes

Getting here/around Tuk tuks can take you to the sites on the fringes of Hikkaduwa. For Ambalangoda frequent northbound coastal buses can drop you at the doors of the two museums.

When to go The crafts workshops are open year-round, though you'll find more courses available in the high-season months of November to April.

Puppets To get a visual sense of Sri Lankan puppetry, visit puppeteersoflanka.com and click on its YouTube channel.

04 The best place to learn about Sri Lanka's devil masks and their symbolism is **Ariyapala & Sons Mask Museum** in Ambalangoda, the island's centre of mask production.

05 Ambalangoda is also famed for its puppetry; learn about this venerable tradition and catch a family-friendly performance in the town's **Puppet Art Museum**.

03 Learn how to paint geometric mandalas at Hikkaduwa's **Lake Hostel**, courtesy of artist Maheesha Sewwandi, a descendent of royal astrologers. She also offers cooking classes.

02 For the best batiks around, head inland from Hikkaduwa to **Genuine Batik Studio**, where J Hirantha Wimalarathne reveals the stunning batik skills inherited from his father and grandfather.

01 **Bokka Almeida Hotel** runs frequent workshops on everything from sculpture and watercolour painting to mask making, batik dyeing and more.

FROM TOP: BRADLEY MAYHEW, BRADLEY MAYHEW

Listings

BEST OF THE REST

Churches

St Mary's Church

The largest Catholic church in Negombo, with a pastel-coloured, neoclassical design and colourful ceiling murals.

St Sebastian's Church

Pay your respects to the 100 people who died at this Katuwapitiya church during the Easter Sunday terrorist bombings of 2019. Look for the memorial and section of wall left unrestored to show the blast marks.

St Anne's Church

This 17th-century Kalpitiya shrine is among the oldest and most popular Christian shrines in the country, featuring a weeklong festival in August that draws thousands of pilgrims.

Buddhist Temples

Kande Vihara Temple

One of the largest Buddha statues in the country, at almost 50m (164ft) tall, with an attached temple complex dating back to 1734; in Aluthgama.

Kothduwa Rajamaha Viharaya

Small island temple, often visited on a boat tour of Madu Ganga Lake. Dating from 1884, the site claims to have once housed the famous Buddha's tooth relic.

Seenigama Muhudu Viharaya

Join locals on a short boat trip out to this island temple just north of Hikkaduwa. It's frequented by victims of theft looking for retribution.

Sunandarama Maha Viharaya

Peaceful temple in Ambalangoda decorated with murals depicting Buddha's past lives and fronted by a spectacularly elaborate entry gate.

Seafood Splash-Outs

Club. Ceylon $$$

This classy restaurant in a Negombo colonial mansion requires reservations to sample Liz Norris' fabulous contemporary seafood, sustainably sourced from the nearby fish market.

Windy Waves $$

Find delicious curry and seafood at this cool, beachfront eatery in Kudawa on the Kalpitiya peninsula; reserve a table on the beach and add a sunset cocktail for the perfect evening.

Vintage Restaurant $$

Crab soup, *paraw* fish and delicious prawn curries make this popular Bentota seafood spot a worthwhile dinner destination.

Malli's Seafood Restaurant $$$

A family-owned restaurant serving Western and Sri Lankan favourites beside the scenic riverfront east of Bentota; book a dockside table for a sunset date.

HIGH FLIERS/SHUTTERSTOCK

Seenigama Muhudu Viharaya

Historical Highlights

Kudiramalai

These 3000-year-old ruins deep in Wilpattu National Park are thought to be of Tambapanni (Copper Sands), where Indian Prince Vijaya landed in 543 BCE to found Sri Lanka's first kingdom.

Dutch Fort

Sign in with the Sri Lankan Navy to tour this 17th-century Kalpitiya fort, with its bat-filled corner tunnels, which once led to the nearby Dutch Reformed Church.

Hamilton Canal

This canal system, aka the Dutch Canal, was built in the 17th century to transport spices to Negombo port. Add a boat tour of the lagoon.

Rent Your Own Wheels

Tuktuk Rental

The most popular tuk tuk rental company on the island, based in Negombo but offering vehicle drop-offs across the country.

Shane Tours 176

Helpful Negombo place for tuk tuk, motorbike and scooter rental. Can help with license paperwork and offers add-ons like luggage racks and Bluetooth speakers.

Department of Motor Traffic

This new counter at the airport arrivals hall arranges temporary driving permits for scooters and cars (but not tuk tuks).

Learn Something

Roman Beach Hotel

This Hikkaduwa hotel offers hour-long cooking demonstrations and tastings, focused on creative ways to use cinnamon in Sri Lankan fusion cooking, from curries to ice cream. The cinnamon is harvested from its own estate.

JIANG_LIU/SHUTTERSTOCK

Hamilton Canal

Elephant Foot

It's hard to think of something more fun than learning to lay down hypnotically danceable rhythms during an hour-long drumming class with Lal Priyanka at Hikkaduwa's Elephant Foot.

Tea Library

If you wish you knew your green from your white tea, or what a monsoon flush is, visit this shop, restaurant and tea room in Hikkaduwa, run by Handunugoda Tea Estate (p95).

Best Local Bars

Sam's Bar

Find your tribe over a selection of draught beers during popular televised football nights at this Hikkaduwa sports bar.

Rodeo Pub

Welcoming bar in Negombo with a great vibe that serves comfort food and sometimes has DJ sets on the weekends.

THE SOUTH

BEACHES | SURFING | WILDLIFE

RESEARCHED BY BRADLEY MAYHEW

THE SOUTH
Trip Builder

The South is an alluring combination of dazzling white-sand beaches, Sri Lanka's hippest surf scene, Buddhist ruins and the chance to spot elephants, leopards and blue whales on one extraordinary coastline. It's a true microcosm of Sri Lanka.

Find out what goes into a perfect cup of Sri Lankan tea at **Handunugoda Tea Estate** (p95)
45min from Galle

Find your perfect stretch of beach, at Goyambokka or **Talalla** (p93)
1-2hr from Galle

Scuba dive on historic wrecks or an underwater chess set at **Unawatuna** (p99)
15min from Galle

Catch your first wave at surf schools in **Weligama** (p97)
1hr from Galle

Spot leopards on a jeep safari through **Yala National Park** (p106)
45min from Tissamaharama
Explore the ancient stupas and water tanks of Buddhist **Tissamaharama** (p105)
4hr from Galle
Kuda Oya
Uda Walawe Reservoir
Uda Walawe National Park
Thanamalwila
Lunugamvehera National Park
Kataragama
Yala National Park
Embilipitiya
Udamattala
Walawe Ganga
Suriyawewa
Tissa Wewa
Yoda Kandiya Wewa
Yoda Wewa
Debarawewa
Tissamaharama
Benda Wewa
Embilikala Kalapuwa
Pallerata Wewa
Kirinda
Angunakolapelessa
Ambalantota
Hambantota
Rekawa
Indian Ocean
0 20 km
0 10 miles

Practicalities

VIRTUALEXPLORING/SHUTTERSTOCK

ARRIVING

Galle Most people start or end their south coast travels in Galle (p110). Trains from Colombo run via Galle and Weligama to Matara and Beliatta, near Tangalle. The inland Southern Expressway extends to Hambantota, with express air-con buses to Colombo running from Tangalle and other destinations. A taxi to the airport takes around three hours.

Hill Country Bus connections to the Hill Country include a Matara-to-Bandarawela service, via Tangalle and Haputale, passing near Ella.

HOW MUCH FOR A

One-hour surfing lesson Rs 5000

Two-tank scuba dive US$90

Whale-watching excursion US$60

WHEN TO GO

MID-DEC–APR
High season with low rainfall, good diving, surfing, whale-watching, leopard-spotting.

JUL–AUG
The spectacular and little-known Kataragama Festival (p105).

MAY–OCT
The southwest Yala monsoon brings rain and rough seas.

NOV–MID-DEC
Rain abates and crowds remain thin. Good shoulder season.

GETTING AROUND

Bus Frequent buses run along the coastal road, making these the quickest and easiest ways to get along the coast. Weligama and Matara are transport hubs.

Train Trains run from Colombo/Galle to Matara, with stops at coastal stations in Thalpe, Ahangama and Weligama.

Tuk Tuk & Scooter The easiest way to get around towns and to local beaches, temples and tea estates is by tuk tuk, and many offer sightseeing tours. For freedom nothing beats travel by scooter, though the main coastal road can be busy.

TOP: STYLE_TTT/SHUTTERSTOCK
BOTTOM: FANFO/SHUTTERSTOCK

EATING & DRINKING

The south coast's ever-growing community of surfers, digital nomads and foreign entrepreneurs means that it offers some of the best international cuisine on the island. If you are hankering for a matcha latte (pictured top right), avocado toast or a poke bowl, this is your place. Enjoy the hipster vibes, but try also to track down locally owned restaurants and especially the region's *ambul thiyal* (pictured bottom right), a distinctive sour fish curry, which gets its tang from *goraka* (dried tamarind-like fruit).

Best cocktails
Smoke & Bitters (p108)

Must-try Lankan fusion
Sama (p109)

CONNECT & FIND YOUR WAY

Wi-fi The South is digitally well connected, with co-working spaces catering to the many digital nomads who set up base here.

Navigation Easy – just follow the single coastal road – save for a few unmarked turnoffs to beaches around Hiriketiya and Tangalle.

WHERE TO STAY

Accommodation for all budgets is easy to find throughout the South. Where to stay depends on your reason for coming: surfing, beach-bumming or wildlife-spotting.

Town	Pros/Cons
Ahangama & Midigama	Hostels, surf camps and designer digs, aimed at surfers; few local amenities.
Weligama	Sociable hostels in the bustling town, luxury villas in nearby countryside.
Tangalle	Family-run guesthouses and midrange resorts; beachside but spread out.
Yala National Park	Luxury (but remote) tented camps on the park's edge; decent guesthouses in Tissamaharama require an earlier start.

PADI CARD

Bring your PADI scuba-diving card if you plan to dive, though operators can often find your accreditation online.

MONEY

Most places take cards and contactless payments, though you'll need cash for smaller guesthouses and restaurants. Look for ATMs in towns like Ahangama, Matara and Mirissa.

12 Find Your PERFECT BEACH

PALM TREES | BEACH BARS | SUNSET STROLLS

The south coast is blessed with some of the island's best beaches – some wild and empty, hidden down nondescript dirt roads; others in perfect palm-fringed bays with a single seafood restaurant. Find the beach that's just right for you.

LEONID RADASHKOVSKY/SHUTTERSTOCK

Stilt Fishermen

Along the south coast you'll see stilt fishermen (pictured) perched precariously like storks above the waves at high tide. Stilt locations are passed down from father to son and are highly coveted, though many fishermen today earn more from tourism, so expect to be asked for payment if taking photos.

Trip Notes

Getting around Buses plying the coastal road reach most beaches, or at least get you within 1km of the sands, but nothing beats the freedom of a scooter when beach hunting.

Go exploring The stretch of coast between Matara and Tangalle offers the best scope for exploring.

Dangers Not all beaches are safe for swimming, with strong undertows and reefs, so get local advice before taking the plunge.

01 Quiet **Wijaya Beach** has a calm, reef-fringed lagoon ideal for families and a palm-tree swing at its western end that's a perfect sunset selfie spot.

02 The beach at little-known **Madiha** offers surfers some intermediate waves and brings big weekend parties, while nearby **Polhena** (pictured) has a small, sandy, reef-sheltered cove for snorkelling.

03 The quiet 1km curve of sand at **Talalla** (pictured) is only lightly touched by tourism, with just a couple of restaurants and a beach bar at one end and bathtub-warm waters.

04 **Blue Beach** is a photogenic bar of sand (and actual bar) linked to a promontory and lapped on both sides by sea waves, east of Hiriketiya; no longer a secret but still charming.

05 **Goyambokka** has two secluded sandy coves separated by a headland; the eastern beach offers lovely strolls but the western **Silent Beach** is the real stunner, dominated by the Amanwella Resort but open to all.

FROM TOP: ALEXANDR SUKHARENKO/SHUTTERSTOCK, AURORE KERVOERN/GETTY IMAGES

13 Tea & CINNAMON

TEA | SPICES | CINNAMON

Few things are more representative of Sri Lanka than its tea and its world-class cinnamon. Add some spice to your trip by touring a tea estate to learn about the different types of tea, see some of the island's famous spices and learn about how cinnamon is harvested, using traditional methods that have changed little in centuries.

IAN PETER MORTON/SHUTTERSTOCK

How to

Getting here Handunugoda Tea Estate is 6km inland from the coastal highway and best visited in a tuk tuk or your own transport. Mirissa Hills is 5km north of Mirissa, up a steep access track.

When to go Handunugoda and Mirissa Hills are open year-round, though there's not much production to see on Sundays.

Top tip White tea is expensive, but it can be brewed four times from one bag.

TRABANTOS/SHUTTERSTOCK

BRADLEY MAYHEW

Far left Handunugoda Tea Estate
Bottom left Cinnamon bush at Mirissa Hills
Left Virgin White Tea buds, Handunugoda Tea Estate

Sri Lanka's Best Tea

The **Handunugoda Tea Estate** (hermanteas.com) in the hills above Koggala is one of the best places on the island to learn about its famous tea production. The hour-long tour takes you through the manicured fields of the estate to the main planter's bungalow for a cup of oolong tea and slice of chocolate cake. It then visits the factory's 150-year-old machinery, and ends up in the tasting room, where you can sip 42 different types of tea by the spoonful. The estate is famed for its fabled Virgin White Tea, a delicate, unfermented brew made from young unopened leaves plucked before dawn.

The World's Best Cinnamon

As you tour Handunugoda you'll see the odd rubber tree, pepper plant and cinnamon bush, but to learn more about cinnamon production head to **Mirissa Hills** (mirissahills.com) to join a tour of its 24-hectare estate. You'll get to examine bushes that can be up to 40 years old, and see how a skilled worker removes the bark by hand using a specialist brass instrument. It also has a small museum explaining how during its heyday Sri Lanka's famous cinnamon, long considered the world's best, was literally worth its weight in gold.

You can taste Sri Lankan spices across the South, from cinnamon-cooking demonstrations in Hikkaduwa (p85) to the award-winning botanical- and spice-infused cocktails of **Smoke & Bitters** (p108), named one of Asia's 50 Best Bars.

Tea Fit for an Emperor

Handunugoda's flagship Virgin White Tea traces its origin to 6th-century imperial China. Back then, virgins harvested the purest leaves with golden scissors, offering the tea exclusively to the emperor untouched by human hands.

Revered for its rarity and purity, it has been found by SGS Switzerland to have remarkable health benefits. Our white tea contains over 10% antioxidants, helping slow aging and promote overall wellness.

Following the same ancient method, we hand-pluck just 150g daily – compared to 25kg to 30kg for regular tea – preserving its imperial heritage and exceptional quality.

Herman Gunaratne, *author and owner of Handunugoda Tea Estate.*

14 Learn to SURF

SURFING | SWIMMING | BEACH BARS

Sri Lanka's south coast is a magnet for surfers from across the globe. There are waves for all skill levels here, from sandy beach breaks to hollow A-frames, and dozens of surf schools, instructors and surf camps to help you on your way. Throw in the region's hippest surf cafes and liveliest bars and the allure is clear.

GORAN_SAFAREK/SHUTTERSTOCK

How to

Getting here Frequent buses connect towns all along the coastal road. Tuk tuks can take you to individual beaches (some have surfboard racks attached).

When to go November to March brings the best surf, with December and January considered the peak months.

More information Pick up the locally published *The Surfer's Guide* (thesurfersguide.com) for the lowdown on the region's best breaks, or visit Rich Francis' thesurfatlas.com.

DUDAREV MIKHAIL/SHUTTERSTOCK

Weligama If you fancy learning how to surf, the long, uncrowded beach break of Weligama is the single best place to do it, with perfect, consistent swell, dozens of surf schools and a host of sociable surf hostels and swanky surf camps. Even better, it feels like a proper Sri Lankan town, not just a surfer enclave.

Ahangama and Midigama In recent years this 4km-long collection of surf breaks has become one of the most popular surfing spots for intermediate or experienced surfers keen to hone their skills. Kabalana Beach, west of Ahangama, is best for beginners, while intermediates looking for a reef break should head to Marshmallow or Lazy Left. For something more challenging, try Sticks (a reef break), Plantations or Coconuts (with left and right breaks). Only the experienced should tackle Ram's barrel waves.

Don't expect to have the waves to yourself here. At peak season it's not unusual to find 50 people battling it out on a single wave. Ahangama boasts the hippest accommodation and surf camps in the region and the best nightlife, while smaller Midigama is more laid-back.

Hiriketiya The perfect horseshoe-shaped cove at Hiriketiya is another popular place to learn (or just hang out) thanks to its central beach break, although there's less space here, so expect some dropping in.

Top left Surfers, Hiriketiya
Bottom left Midigama

Surf Camps

If you're serious about learning to surf, a string of slick, mostly foreign-run surf camps offer five- to seven-day packages, inclusive of accommodation, food and even post-instruction video analysis.

In a colonial mansion in Weligama, there's the well-organised **Kima Surf** (kimasurf.com). In Ahangama you'll find the stylish and female-friendly **Sunshine Stories** (sunshinestories.com); and the upmarket **Soul & Surf** (soulandsurf.com), which combines surf instruction with yoga and massage therapy.

For locally owned budget options in Weligama, try six-roomed **Lucky's Surf Camp** (luckyssurfcamp.com), operated by Sri Lanka's most famous surfer; or **Layback** (layback.lk), catering to budgets from dorms to private rooms.

15 Dive the SOUTH COAST

SCUBA | SHIPWRECKS | HISTORY

The waters off the south coast offer wreck diving, some of it world-class, with excursions offered by a dozen dive schools in Unawatuna, Weligama and even remote Kirinda. Newcomers can learn to dive on a half-day introduction to scuba or a full PADI course. Either way, a dive here will open up a whole new world.

TIMOFEEV VLADIMIR/SHUTTERSTOCK

How to

When to go November to April is the diving season, when the sea is calm and visibility best. February to April are the best months for Kirinda.

Freshen up If you haven't been diving for a year or more, brush up your skills on a two-hour refresher dive, before opting for something more adventurous.

Learn to dive Get PADI certificated on a four-day Open Water course. Dive centres often offer discounted accommodation during the course.

OLEG SHULDIAKOV/GETTY IMAGES

NICK HOBGOOD IMAGES/SHUTTERSTOCK

Far left Diving trip
Bottom left Weligama
Left Lionfish, Unawatuna

Unawatuna Dive centres such as **Diving Guru** (divinguru.com) and **Pearl Divers** (pearldiverslk.com) offer a wide range of sites. The *Lord Nelson* is a cargo-ship wreck with a 15m-long cabin that can be explored at a depth starting at 8m, and so is accessible to snorkellers and anyone doing a half-day Discover Scuba course. The remains of a century-old British steamer, the *Rangoon,* are a 30-minute boat ride away, in 30m of water. Less visited is the *SS Oristes,* a steamship complete with an intact boiler.

Also just off the coast of Unawatuna is the photogenic **Underwater Chess Set**, unveiled in 2026. It features life-sized Sri Lankan and Portuguese warriors as pieces, in a re-creation of the 1559 battle of Mulleriyawa. It's just 500m off the coast in about 8m of water.

Weligama Further along the coast, Weligama is the place for reef dives, with a rock wall and several pinnacles attracting abundant fish life. Experienced divers might even see whale sharks in the deeper waters of Dispa Rock in January or February. Try **Weligama Bay Dive Center** (scubadivingweligama.com), which also runs snorkelling excursions.

Kirinda The most unique dive site in Sri Lanka is Great Basses Reef, where the Mughal-era ship of Emperor Aurangzeb sank centuries ago with its cargo of silver coins, brought to purchase war elephants. The only way to dive here is through the Coastguard's **Malima Diving Centre** (coastguard.gov.lk/diving-center.html).

Diving at Great Basses

The most important dive site at Great Basses is definitely the Aurangzeb Silver Coin wreck, but there is also a 'Bottle Wreck', full of soda bottles, and a 'Copper Wreck', which has a massive propeller. There are also some beautiful limestone underwater caves.

Only the Coastguard is allowed to bring divers to Great Basses, to protect the wrecks from treasure hunters, and no fishing is allowed, so the marine life is excellent. Conditions are often dangerous, though, with huge swells, so only morning dives are possible.

Namal Kumara, *Lieutenant Commander of the Sri Lanka Navy in Kirinda.*

16 Whale-Watching in MIRISSA

WHALES | NIGHTLIFE | FAMILY BEACHES

Mirissa is the brashest party destination along the south coast, but out of earshot of the thumping techno lies a gargantuan secret: one of the world's largest populations of blue whales. Head out on a dawn whale-watching trip to come face to fin with the largest species that has ever existed. Only in Sri Lanka can you spot the world's largest land and sea animals on one trip.

CURIOSO.PHOTOGRAPHY/SHUTTERSTOCK

How to

Getting here Buses run frequently from Galle and Matara. Morning trains run from Mirissa to Colombo, with more services from Weligama, just 5km away.

When to go Blue whales can be spotted throughout the year, but December and April seem to be peak months. Avoid the rough waters of May to July.

Top tip Avoid Mirissa's noisy main road and seek out accommodation and restaurants in back lanes.

TRAVEL FAERY/SHUTTERSTOCK

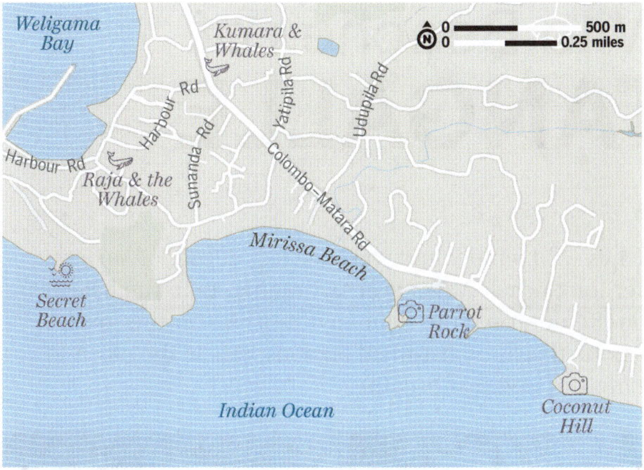

Whale Trips

The waters off Mirissa and Dondra Head are home to large numbers of blue whales, the world's largest animal species (larger than the largest dinosaur). Besides the big blues, look out for their (slightly) smaller cousins: fin whales, sperm whales and Bryde's whales, along with mega pods of spinner dolphins. The early bird spots the whale, so get to the dock by 6am for the half-day boat trip.

Watching whales can be a powerful experience, but bear in mind that it's very rare to see the whales leap photogenically out of the water. Normally you'll only get a quick glimpse of a whale coming up for air or a tail rising in the the sky as it starts to dive. That said, the scale and power of these leviathans is truly impressive.

Mirissa Beach

Recover from a turbulent morning of whale-spotting on Mirissa's family-friendly stretch of beach. **Girigala**, or **Parrot Rock**, is a tiny island with a much-photographed sandbar that you can walk across with care at low tide. At the far eastern end of town is **Coconut Hill**, which offers the most photogenic sunset views in town, if you can battle your way through the selfie sticks.

Hidden in the headland west of town is the perfectly framed micro-cove of **Secret Beach**, where three bar-restaurants offer sunset views from a tiny collection of sun loungers.

Top left Coconut Hill
Bottom left Whale-watching trip, Mirissa

Whale-Watching Tips

- When choosing a tour, look for companies that respect international conventions about approaching whales; for example, boats should always maintain a 100m distance from whales. Ask companies directly and read reviews online.
- Recommended operators include **Raja & the Whales** (rajaandthewhales.com) and **Kumara & Whales** (kumaraandwhales.lk).
- Avoid chartered fishing boats or anyone that advertises 'swimming with whales', as many of these harass whales by boxing one animal between two boats.
- The long day and potentially rough seas mean this is not a suitable trip for children under 10. Pack anti-sea-sickness medication if you have it.

17

Wild Beaches of TANGALLE

SOLITUDE | NATURE | SAND

If you like your beaches wild, empty and wave-lashed, devoid of surfers and dive schools, and prefer long beach walks over swimming, then the beaches around Tangalle are for you. Remoter feeling than anything else on the south coast, complete with nesting turtles and bird-filled lagoons, this is the place to find your deserted section of sand and just breathe.

TRABANTOS/SHUTTERSTOCK

How to

Getting here Tangalle has frequent bus services to Galle, Matara and Tissamaharama, plus several direct air-con expressway buses to Colombo. Trains run to Colombo and Galle from Beliatta, 9km from Tangalle.

Beware Tangalle's beaches have steep drop-offs, strong currents and heavy shore breaks, making them dangerous for swimming and unsuited to families.

Detours Tangalle is the base for several excursions, including to Mulkirigala Rock Temples (p108), Ussangoda National Park (p109)and Kalametiya Bird Sanctuary (p109).

JAKLZDENEK/SHUTTERSTOCK

Top left Medaketiya Beach
Bottom left Rekawa Beach

Beach Bliss

Medaketiya is the closest beach to Tangalle town, lined with a sprinkling of guesthouses and restaurants but still refreshingly undeveloped. Further east the guesthouses turn to midrange mini-resorts, excellent for a quiet few ̧quiet days of R&R. For a sublime sunset stroll take a tuk tuk 2km east, past the guesthouses, to the end of the road at Ganesh Garden, and walk back to town, stopping for a drink at **Secret Tide** (secrettide.lk), the best beach restaurant in the region. Alternatively, walk out along the beach and find a place for a lamplit oceanside dinner, as you wiggle your toes contentedly in the sand. Several operators and guesthouses offer birdwatching and kayaking trips on the mangrove lagoon here.

The further east you walk the wilder and more deserted things become. Continue along palm-fringed **Marakolliya Beach** or take a tuk tuk along the main coastal road to Mangrove Beach Cabana and walk from there.

Rekawa Beach

Another 4km along the coast, 10km east of Tangalle, is **Rekawa Beach**, a key turtle-nesting site where turtles lurch ashore at night to lay their eggs on the same beaches where they were born and hatchlings take their first hesitant steps. For ethical viewing, join tours hosted by **Turtle Watch Rekawa** (turtlewatchrekawa.org), a community project that involves locals who previously relied on poaching to support their livelihoods. Small group guided tours begin at 8.30pm daily, with the peak nesting season from April to July.

Ethical Turtle-Watching

Baby sea turtles have a hard life. Faced with the threats of illegal poaching, habitat loss and the dangers of the ocean, only one in 1000 hatchlings survive until adulthood. So if you do come across turtles laying eggs, give them plenty of space, and avoid flash photography and flashlights as turtles are sensitive to brightness. Noise can also scare away turtles. Never touch adult turtles, nests or hatchlings, even at a turtle hatchery.

A rash of commercial turtle hatcheries litter the coast around Rekawa (and Kosgola on the West Coast), cashing in on tourism. Visit only vetted organisations.

18 Explore the Ruins of RUHANA

BUDDHISM | RUINS | STUPAS

East of Tangalle the beachside cafes and surf schools peter out and something unexpected takes their place: an ancient city of 2000-year-old white stupas, monasteries and lake-sized water reservoirs that once made up the mysterious ancient kingdom of Ruhana, today located in the town of Tissamaharama (Tissa). Explore monastic ruins, then use Tissa as a base for trips to Yala and Kataragama.

MARIUSLTU/GETTY IMAGES

How to

Getting here Buses run from Matara and Tangalle to Tissamaharama. From Tissa, travel on to Ella and the Hill Country is more convoluted; catch a through bus at Wirawila or Pannegamuwa junctions west of town to Wellawaya and change there.

Top tip Head at dusk to the southeastern corner of **Tissa Wewa** to watch hundreds of roosting bats and egrets as the sun sets.

What to wear Cover your legs and remove your shoes when visiting the Tissa Dagoba.

TRABANTOS/SHUTTERSTOCK

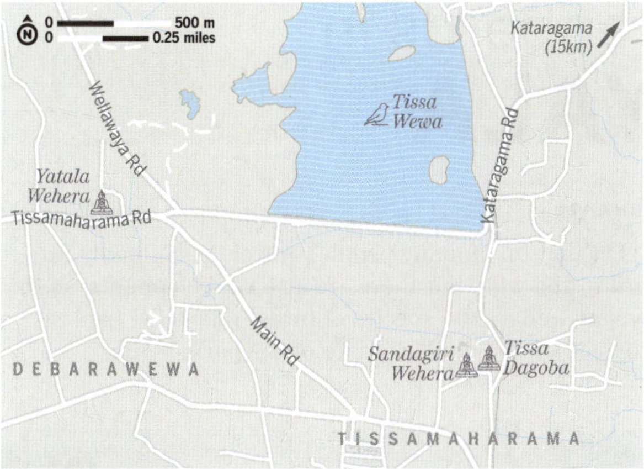

Ancient Ruhana

The ancient kingdom of Ruhana long acted as a rival power base and place of exile or refuge for kings from the central plains. The main vestige of this kingdom in Tissamaharama is the 56m-tall **Tissa Dagoba**, said to have been built around 200 BCE by King Kavantissa to hold the sacred tooth and forehead-bone relics of the Buddha. Also here is the smaller brown-brick stupa **Sandagiri Wehera**, from where you can explore the remains of the 2000-year-old monastery complex.

Another stupa worth seeing is the small but charming **Yatala Wehera** (pictured pp86–7), surrounded by a carved wall of elephants. It was built 2300 years ago by King Mahanaga, the founder of Ruhana, in thanks for the birth of his son and his escape from an assassination attempt by his brother.

Sacred Kataragama

An easy excursion 18km north of Tissa is Kataragama, a holy pilgrimage centre for Buddhists, Muslims, Hindus and Veddahs (Sri Lanka's indigenous people), whose shrine to Kataragama Deviyo has existed here for well over 2000 years. Watch pilgrims smash burning coconuts against boulders while reciting prayers at the main **Maha Devale** temple, then join them in offering lotus flowers at the 29m-high Kiri Vehera dagoba. With its Muslim healing stone, which is said to suck bad spirits out of anyone who touches it, the entire site has an air of magic and mysticism.

Top left Sandagiri Wehera
Bottom left Maha Devale

Kataragama Festival

Kataragama swells with pilgrims, spectacle and sanctity during July's full-moon Kataragama Festival. In the 45 days leading up to the festival some devotees walk the length of Sri Lanka to reach Maha Devale temple, transiting Yala National Park on foot.

During the festival elephants are paraded, drummers whip the crowds into ecstasy and devotees swing from hooks in their skin or walk on beds of red-hot cinders – 'treading the flowers' as it's called. It's the kind of chaos and spectacle that only a South Asian festival can deliver, and it's an unforgettable time to visit the temple.

19 Leopards in YALA

LEOPARDS | SAFARIS | ELEPHANTS

Yala National Park is at the top of many people's travel lists, notably for the chance to spot a leopard in the wild, but there are also wild elephants, sloth bears and sambar deer here, as well as 200 species of birds. Yala is Sri Lanka's most visited park, so try to visit a less popular corner of the park, if your budget allows.

DILLRO HUB/SHUTTERSTOCK

How to

When to go The end of the dry season in March and April, before animals disperse during the rains, is the best time to visit Yala. That said, any time from February to July is good.

Park entry fees US$30 to US$36 per person, depending on the number of people in a jeep.

Safari lodges A handful of luxury lodges on the fringes of Block I offer fabulously atmospheric tented accommodation and employ expert nature guides.

POYLOCK19/SHUTTERSTOCK

SVITLANANIKO/SHUTTERSTOCK

Far left Yala National Park
Bottom left Pheasant-tailed jacana, Bundala National Park
Left Leopard, Yala National Park

Yala National Park

With its trumpeting elephants, monkeys crashing through the canopy and cunning leopards slinking like shadows through the undergrowth, the woodlands, grasslands and watering holes of **Yala National Park** are *The Jungle Book* brought to glorious life. Yala is famous for boasting the world's densest concentration of leopards, with the local subspecies unique to Sri Lanka.

Most people join a half-day safari to Block I, known as Yala West, which was a hunting reserve until 1938. It's the closest entrance to Tissa and so the busiest, with long queues of jeeps here at 6am. Serious wildlife enthusiasts should instead charter their own (pricier) jeep and experienced guide to enter the park's quieter northern part of Block I or southern part of Block III, via Kataragama, or the even-less-visited northern section of Block III, via Galge. You'll pay for your solitude with rougher roads, but it's worth it.

Bundala National Park

Much less visited than Yala, the Ramsar wetland site of **Bundala National Park**, 18km southwest of Tissa, is a particularly good early-morning choice for birders. The maze of waterways, lagoons and dunes glitters in the rising sun, revealing around 200 species of birds, from diminutive bee-eaters to crested hawk eagles and open-billed storks, many of them journeying from Siberia to winter here between August and April. Organise a jeep tour from Tissamaharama and come at dawn for the best sightings.

Jeep Safari Tips

- Most accommodation in Tissa can arrange jeep safaris. Don't arrange anything with people you meet on the bus or in the street, as travellers have been cheated this way.
- Half-day tours depart around 5am, returning at lunchtime. Dusk tours run from 3pm to 7pm.
- Be sure your vehicle has forward facing, preferably banked, seats and open sides.
- Ask your driver to turn off the engine when the jeep is not moving.
- Budget guesthouses offer group trips for up to six people, which solo travellers can join, starting at around US$55 per person, including park entry fees.

Listings

BEST OF THE REST

Buddhist Temples

Kataluwa Purwarama

A 13th-century Buddhist temple that feels a million miles (but actually just over 1km) from the coast, featuring some fabulous 19th-century murals; east of Koggala Lake.

Kushtarajagala Statue

Ignored by all the partying surfers in Weligama, this ancient rock-cut structure of a standing Bodhisattva in the west of town by the railway tracks is an unexpected delight.

Mulkirigala Rock Temples

Climb up 500 steps to view six caves full of stunning 18th-century murals, clearly showing European influence. The summit has fine views over the green coconut forest; 16km northwest of Tangalle.

Rumassala Peace Pagoda

Japanese-built pagoda offering fine sunset views from the Rumassala headland, a 20-minute walk west of Unawatuna; visitors can join the 4.30pm prayers and meditation.

Culture & History

Martin Wickramasinghe Folk Art Museum

Exhibits on masked dances, puppets and carriages in the traditional house in Koggala where Sinhalese author Martin Wickramasinghe (1890–1976) was born.

Star Fort

Small but atmospheric six-pointed 1763 Dutch fort in bustling Matara, featuring a drawbridge, VOC insignia and a small local history museum in former soldiers' quarters. Closed Tuesday.

Dondra Head Lighthouse

This British-built lighthouse (not open to visitors) marks the southernmost point of Sri Lanka. Look out to sea here: the nearest land mass south is Antarctica, 8000km away.

Beach Bars & Nightlife

Smoke & Bitters $$$

Award-winning cocktails, bitters and syrups infused with local spices and botanicals, plus barbecued meats and roasted jackfruit. Located in Dikwella and in a league of its own.

Trax $$

Renovated villa and garden venue beside the railway tracks in Ahangama, with international DJs and live music making things lively on Friday and Saturday nights.

Hakuna Matata $

A dreamy beachside location in Ahangama, with good jackfruit burgers and a late-night Thursday after-party that continues until the sun rises over the Indian Ocean.

JOHN ELK III/GETTY IMAGES

Star Fort, Matara

Doctor's House $$

Energetic bar-restaurant in a former Dutch hospital in Madiha that draws hundreds from along the coast to its famous Saturday-night parties, with good food options.

Tiki Bar & Kitchen $$

Fabulous clifftop location 3km outside Weligama, serving a great tuna steak and with Friday-night parties that are popular with the surfing crowd.

Beach Brunches

Nomad $$

Hip foreign-run bakery-cafe in Weligama serving all-day brunch and healthy lunch options until 6pm, with good coffee and vegan options from smoothies to poke bowls.

Kip $$

Mediterranean menu and all-day brunch in a stylish cafe and guesthouse away from the beach in Ahangama.

Shanti Shanti $$

Charming beachside bar-restaurant in Thalpe, offering sun loungers, pizzas, smoothies and seafood, including a fine tuna *tataki* (lightly seared).

Wijaya Beach $$

Renowned for its wood-fired pizza, ceviche, tuna wasabi wraps and seafood, even fresh oysters, right on the beach, near Thalpe.

Skinny Tom's Deli $$

Your best bet in Unawatuna for good coffee, lazy brunches and tapas-style small plates. Until 4pm.

Sama $$$

One of south Sri Lanka's best meals. Chef Anilka Amarasekara's fusion menu includes Turkish eggs flavoured with *kithul* treacle and yellowfin tuna crudo in chilli oil; in Ahangama.

GORAN_SAFAREK/SHUTTERSTOCK

Birdwatching tour, Kalametiya Bird Sanctuary

Zephyr $$$

Fine seafood and island-rooted cocktails at this laidback local-run bar-restaurant on a powdery beach in Kamburugamuwa, east of Mirissa. Book a table in the sand.

Natural Highs

Koggala Lake

This huge lake is alive with birdlife and sprinkled with islands, including one producing cinnamon and another housing a Buddhist temple linked by a causeway. The lake is best seen on a 90-minute boat tour.

Ussangoda National Park

This coastal plateau east of Tangalle with its ochre iron-rich earth seems otherworldly, which local stories put down to a 2000-year-old meteorite. The coastal views and colours are beautiful.

Kalametiya Bird Sanctuary

Punt through this peaceful marshy lagoon, 20km east of Tangalle, on a two-hour sunrise or sunset tour (kalametiyabirds.com) and you'll spot kingfishers, purple swamp hens and the occasional eagle.

GALLE

HISTORICAL CHARM | SHOPPING | HERITAGE ACCOMMODATION

RESEARCHED BY BRADLEY MAYHEW

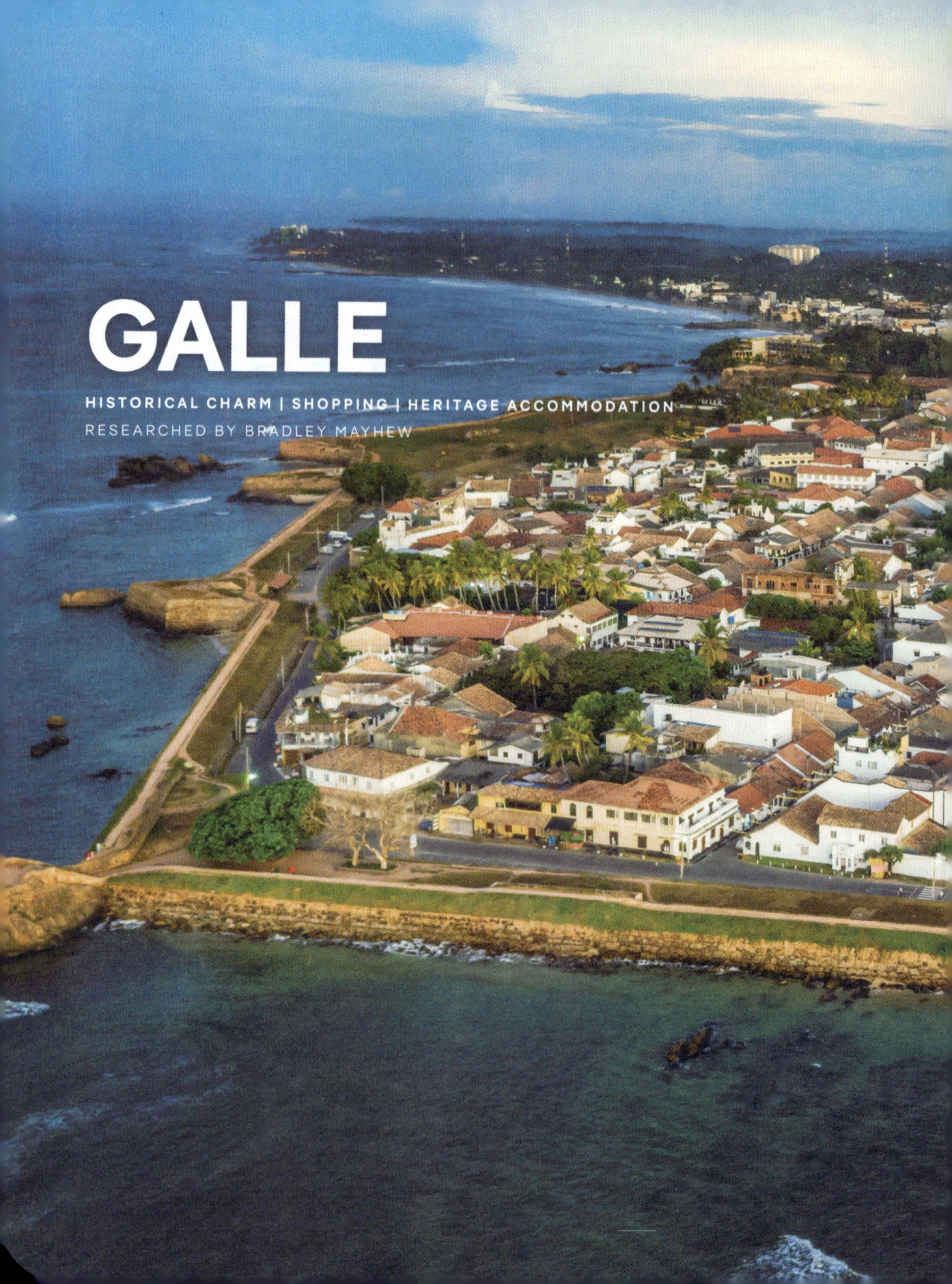

GALLE
Trip Builder

Galle is unmissable for its historical charm, colonial architecture and magnificent fortifications, but budget time also to wander its backstreets, browse some of Sri Lanka's coolest boutiques and indulge in one of its stylish restaurants.

Peek at views of the Galle International Cricket Stadium from **Moon Bastion** (p117)

Imagine what life was like for Dutch traders while visiting the **Dutch Reformed Church** (p115)

Linger over a pot of Sri Lankan tea on the terrace of a historic hotel such as **Fort Bazaar** (p119)

Learn about Sri Lanka's favourite spirit, arrack, at the Rope-walk bar at **Galle Fort Hotel** (p119)

Look for feeding turtles and watch the sun set at **Neptune Bastion** (p117)

Enjoy the ocean views and daredevil locals diving off **Flag Rock** (p117)

Practicalities

ARRIVING

Trains from Colombo arrive at **Galle Railway Station**, 400m north of the fort. Buses leave from **Express Bus Stand** at 7.30am and 4.30pm for Colombo Bandaranaike Airport.

FIND YOUR WAY

The fort is very compact and has only half a dozen roads, but you can also walk the ramparts.

MONEY

Major restaurants, hotels and shops accept international cards. Family-run places prefer cash; the fort has ATMs.

WHERE TO STAY

Area	Pros/Cons
Galle Fort	Historical charm, authenticity and maximum atmosphere; higher prices.
Outside the fort	Less touristy and a wider range of accommodation; less style.
Outside Galle	A wider range of beach resorts, historical properties and budget accommodation within 10km of town.

GETTING AROUND

Tuk Tuk These wait for tourists at the northern end of the fort, but you'll get much better fares through an app like PickMe.

Walk Easily the best way to get around the fort, though it gets very hot in the afternoons.

TOP: AARKADIJ SCHELL/SHUTTERSTOCK
BOTTOM: LOOMO DIGITAL/SHUTTERSTOCK

EATING

Seafood (pictured top left) is a popular option, with the better restaurants getting their daily catch from Galle fish market, 1.5km east of town. Galle's historical connections with Indian and Arab traders are visible in local biriyani dishes (pictured bottom left) and Middle Eastern flavours at restaurants like Chambers.

Best seafood
Elita Restaurant (p121)

Must-try arrack sour
Galle Fort Hotel (p119)

MID-DEC–APR
High season with low rainfall and peak crowds; make reservations.

JAN
Galle Literary Festival (galleliteraryfestival.com) and Gourmet Galle (gourmetgalle.com).

MAY–SEP
The southwest Yala monsoon brings rain and rough seas.

NOV–MID-DEC
Some rain but fewer crowds; dinner reservations easier.

20 Galle's HISTORY

COLONIAL HISTORY | ARCHITECTURE | BACKSTREETS

The historic fort of Galle, encased by powerful walls and jutting into the Indian Ocean, is easily the South's most absorbing human-made attraction. For centuries it was a strategic and cosmopolitan home to Portuguese soldiers, Dutch bureaucrats and Arab traders. It's stuffed full of colonial-era mansions, churches and historic hotels, making it a fascinating and deeply atmospheric place to explore.

RUWAN WALPOLA /SHUTTERSTOCK

How to

Getting around Galle Fort is best navigated on foot. Tuk tuks wait for passengers at the northern end, but cars are discouraged.

When to go Avoid Galle's heat by exploring in early morning or late afternoon. Most shops stay closed until 10am.

Top tip Galle has some of the country's most stylish shops (p120). Mix in a couple while exploring the town.

TRUBA7113/SHUTTERSTOCK

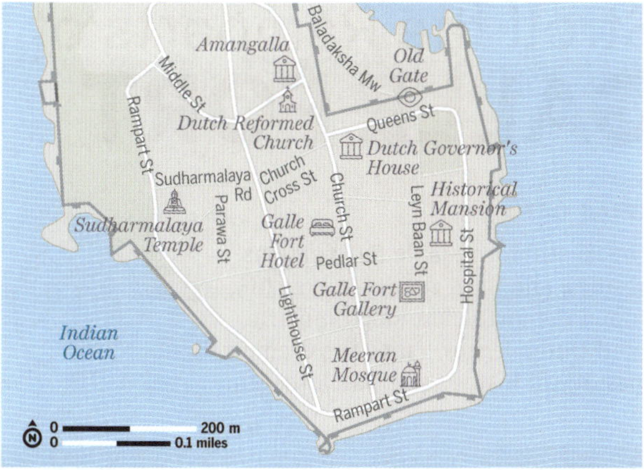

Dutch legacy It is said that Portuguese sailors founded Galle after they were blown off course and landed here by mistake. That may be so, but today it is the Dutch legacy that dominates the fort (pictured pp110–11). Enter the 1755 **Dutch Reformed Church**, or *Groote Kerk*, and you'll see the floor paved with Dutch gravestones. At the the nearby former **Dutch Governor's House** (1683) you can spy the symbol of the city (a rooster – *galo* in Portuguese), while just downhill are several huge former Dutch spice warehouses and the **Old Gate**, inscribed with the letters 'VOC' for *Vereenigde Oostindische Compagnie*, or Dutch East India Company.

Fort by foot Head down **Leyn Baan**, or Rope Walk, where visiting ships would lay out their ropes for repair, and a different face of the city reveals itself – a traditional street of artisans. Pop into the **Galle Fort Art Gallery** here to connect with the city's art scene or join an art class (p121). This is also the heart of the town's Muslim population, centred on the white **Meeran Mosque**.

Wind your way north to Pedlar St, past inviting cafes and gelato shops, and swing north on tiny **Parawa St**, with its Dutch-style shaded porches called *stoep*. In residential corners like this, you can still find locals doing their shopping, playing football in the street or heading to prayers at the nearby 19th-century Buddhist **Sudharmalaya Temple**. Behind the tourist facade, local life in Galle continues as it always has.

Top left Galle Fort wall
Bottom left Dutch Reformed Church

Galle Secrets

As you walk around Galle, notice that several historic buildings and even the fort walls are made from corals and shells – the former ballast of trading ships. You can see examples in the facade and interior well of the **Historical Mansion** museum and the **Amangalla** hotel.

If you are near the **Galle Fort Hotel**, pop into the central colonnaded courtyard, designed by the notorious Comte de Mauny, and notice how the spaces between the columns narrow, creating a forced perspective that makes the space seem grander than it actually is.

Juliet Coombe, *Galle-based author and photographer*

21 Stroll the Ramparts of GALLE FORT

CITY WALLS | SUNSETS | OCEAN VIEWS

Galle is dominated by its still formidable fortifications. As Galle's daytime heat subsides, join local residents, courting couples and visitors alike upon the fort's 3km-long ramparts to ponder the Portuguese and Dutch legacy. Enjoy the evening breezes, contemplate the passage of history and watch the sun set over the Indian Ocean.

SON OF THE MORNING LIGHT/SHUTTERSTOCK

How to

Getting here You can climb on to the fort walls at several locations, but the best section to walk is from the lighthouse to the Sun Bastion.

When to go Sunset is the most popular time to stroll the ramparts, for both locals and visitors.

Top tip Look for sea turtles grazing the seaweed in the waters off the Neptune Bastion.

KENGOO/SHUTTERSTOCK

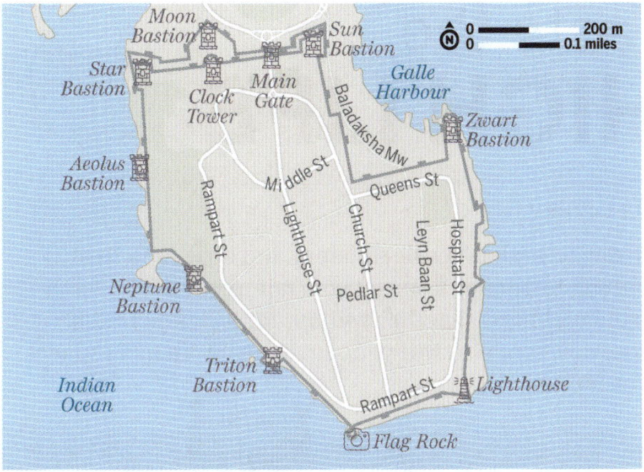

Top left Sun Bastion
Bottom left Triton Bastion

North Several sections of fort wall are worth exploring. The strongest fortifications are on the land-facing northern side, whose ramparts were first built by the Portuguese, then enlarged by the Dutch into the current **Moon** and **Sun Bastions**. Look north to the Galle International Cricket Stadium, a former race course, to see if a match is playing. The British legacy here goes well beyond cricket, with the nearby 1873 **Main Gate** and **Clock Tower** still providing the main access into the fort.

Another place to check out is the northwestern **Zwart Bastion**, the oldest of the remaining Portuguese structures (1580), where you can explore old gunpowder stores, tunnels and gunsmith workshops.

Southeast The best section for strolling starts in the southeast corner of the fort, at the still-functioning British-era **Galle Lighthouse**. Head along the ramparts to **Flag Rock**, where approaching boats were signalled, warning of dangerous rocks. Buy some chilli-sprinkled papaya and watch local daredevils dive off the bastion walls into the waters below.

West The western walls offer the best sunset views. You'll pass the **Triton Bastion**, once topped with a Dutch windmill used to flush out Galle's streets; and then the **Neptune** and **Aeolus Bastions**, named for the Greek gods of the sea and wind, essential support for sailors everywhere. Finish your walk back at the formidable northwestern **Star Bastion**, once a Dutch barracks and later a British-era duelling ground.

Galle Timeline

10th century BCE Some scholars think Galle is the ancient port of Tarshish, which exported ivory, peacocks and silver to King Solomon.

1344 Moroccan traveller Ibn Battuta arrives in Galle, as part of the monsoon trade that operated between Southeast Asia and East Africa.

1505 A Portuguese fleet bound for the Maldives is blown off course by a storm and arrives in Galle by mistake.

1524 The Portuguese build Galle's first fortifications, eventually wresting control of the port from the Sinhalese kings of Kandy.

1640 The Dutch take Galle from the Portuguese.

1796 The British take Galle from the Dutch, ruling for 150 years, as Galle gradually cedes importance to Colombo.

22 Taste the HIGH LIFE

HISTORIC CHARM | DESIGN | LUXURY

The most indulgent way to soak up Galle's history and style is to treat yourself to a high tea, an arrack tasting or a sunset cocktail in one of the fort's beautifully restored heritage hotel bars. Whether you opt for a classic Dutch, British or art deco backdrop, nowhere else will you find so many chances to feel like a million bucks, for considerably less.

GEOGRAPHY PHOTOS/GETTY IMAGES

How to

When to go Make dinner reservations during the high season of mid-December to April. Check what special events are planned during January's **Galle Literary Festival** (galleliteraryfestival.com) and **Gourmet Galle** (gourmetgalle.com) food week.

What to wear This is one place where you should consider pulling out your last uncrumpled outfit for a romantic dinner.

Top tip Several bars (eg at Fort Bazaar and Galle Fort Hotel) offer happy-hour discounts (5pm to 7pm).

DOV MAKABAW/ALAMY

IMAGE PROFESSIONALS GMBH/ALAMY

Far left Galle Fort Hotel terrace
Bottom left Clan House
Left Amangalla hotel

High tea The most indulgent way to spend a couple of hours in Galle is the afternoon high tea (from 3pm) at the five-star **Amangalla**, originally home to the Dutch governor in 1684, and later the New Oriental Hotel, when it was the lodging of choice for discerning 1st-class cruise passengers. The band Duran Duran shot scenes for *Hungry Like the Wolf* and *Save a Prayer* here; pack a linen suit and lip gloss and create the 1980s New Romantic vibe in the hotel bar.

For similar style at a fraction of the price, snag a table on the terrace of the 17th-century **Fort Bazaar** hotel and linger over a pot of golden pekoe tea, grown in the nearby highlands. The next-door **Clan House** still boasts its original arrival board, announcing steamers from around the world.

That's the spirit For something stronger, the nearby **Galle Fort Hotel** has a particularly good bar and terrace offering a wide range of arracks and cocktails infused with local spices. End a sweaty day with a refreshing arrack sour with lime, ginger and lemongrass, or sign up for the US$50 arrack tasting, during which you'll try five different types of arrack and make your very own arrack cocktail.

For the classiest sunset cocktail head south to the art deco cool of **Charlie's** bar in the Charleston hotel, whose breezy open-air terrace overlooks the fort's western ramparts.

Arrack

Sri Lanka's favourite tipple, arrack is made from the sap of coconut-palm blossoms, syphoned early in the morning by daredevil toddy tappers navigating the palm trees on high-wire ropes. After about an hour the sap ferments naturally to produce *raa* (toddy, or palm wine), a cloudy, slightly fizzy drink of about 5% alcohol.

Arrack is then distilled from the toddy, finally reaching about 40% proof, with different palm trees (such as the palmyra) giving slightly different flavours. Arrack is naturally clear; dark arracks get their colour from barrels made from teak or *halmilla* (Trincomalee wood).

Listings

BEST OF THE REST

Museums

Historical Mansion

Rambling Aladdin's Cave-style collection of treasures unearthed from shipwrecks and houses across Galle, from ceramics to porcelain, in an 18th-century mansion. Free.

National Museum

Dusty displays in an 1865 Dutch building, including on Galle's Portuguese-inspired tradition of lace-making. Features a copy of the the famous trilingual stele brought here by Chinese admiral Zheng He in 1409.

National Maritime Museum

This museum housed in a former Dutch spice warehouse is worth a look for its skeleton of a Bryde's whale and model explaining how tsunamis occur. Closed Monday.

Maritime Archaeology Museum

Upper-floor museum details the ancient port of Godawaya and its various foreign shipwrecks, including a replica of the 17th-century Dutch East India Company *Avondster* wreck, discovered in Galle harbour in 1993.

Best Boutiques

Withered Leaves

A non-pushy specialist store selling 50 types of top-quality green, white and single-estate teas, on the upper level of the Old Dutch Hospital.

Stick No Bills

Super-stylish reproductions of vintage Sri Lankan tourism posters, in both poster and postcard sizes, properly sourced without ripping off artists.

Barefoot

Galle's single best store, founded by designer Barbara Sansoni, with handwoven cloth, home decor, bags, fashion, books and pretty much everything else.

Olanda Antiques

Large antiques, some from shipwrecks, and smaller repurposed pieces in a former cinnamon warehouse that's great fun to browse; notice the cable that holds the building together.

Karma Collection

Women's fashions, using locally designed and produced fabrics, strong on sundresses and pyjamas. Does alterations on the spot or makes items to order.

Walking Tours

Ceylon Soul

Bespoke Galle Fort walks that will take you beyond the facade of the city to reveal traditional local life, plus biriyani cooking classes, family treasure hunts and more. Contact Atheeq Ifthikar (ceylonsoul.com).

TRABANTOS/SHUTTERSTOCK

National Maritime Museum

Galle Fort Walks

Shanjei (gallefortwalks.com) runs entertaining walking tours catered to your interests, with lots of potential add-ons from arrack tasting to a home-cooked lunch in a local's house.

Juliet Coombe

The author and photographer (julietcoombe@yahoo.com.au) runs a range of well-researched walking tours, focusing on everything from supernatural myths to local artisans. Look for her book *Around Galle Fort in 80 Lives*.

Coffee & Stories with Fazal

The owner of the Royal Dutch Cafe (72 Leyn Baan) has hundreds of stories to tell about Galle, either on a morning walk or a moonlit stroll that includes coffee on the ramparts.

Fine Dining

Elita Restaurant $$$

The freshest seafood in town, with fabulous octopus salad, yellow fish curry and snapper in lime cream sauce.

Puppets $$

Great for brunch croissants and French-inspired dishes like prawn curry cassoulet, calamari provençale and chocolate mousse.

Chambers $$

Middle Eastern dishes like tajines, kebabs, mezze and North African chermoula prawns reflect Galle's long Arab-influenced history.

Aqua Forte $$$

Perhaps the best Italian restaurant on the island, recommended by none other than Italy's Ambassador to Sri Lanka.

Coconut Sambol $$

Superior buffet of excellent Sri Lankan curries, including some local Galle specialities and even a sweet and spicy fruit curry, washed down by house-made ginger beer.

Take a Break

Kaffi $$

Quiet and stylish cafe in the quiet northeast section of the fort, inside an interior decor shop and boasting a Nordic twist.

Dairy King $

House-made ice cream at this old-school, family-run venture; try a tamarind or mango scoop and take it onto the nearby ramparts.

Coffee Brunch $$

Excellent coffee, matcha and cinnamon-dusted French toast at this charming courtyard cafe behind Stick No Bills. Closed Monday.

Get Creative

Mask Carving

Janaka De Silva, the curator of Galle Fort Art Gallery (p115), offers mask-carving and mask-painting classes above the gallery, which are great for families (ages 10 and older); US$50 per person.

Jewellery Making

Bring a design, stone or piece of jewellery you want to copy and the jewellers below the Antic Guesthouse will help you make a unique silver keepsake (US$75).

Chilli Dragon Spice Shop

Travellers rave about the cookery classes here, where you'll learn to make coconut sambol and curries from scratch using home-roasted spices.

THE HILL COUNTRY

HIKING | WILDLIFE | LANDSCAPES

RESEARCHED BY ANNA KAMINSKI

THE HILL COUNTRY
Trip Builder

With its mist-shrouded, waterfall-washed mountain ranges and emerald-green tea estates rising above the southern heartlands, the Hill Country is Sri Lanka at its most scenic. Spectacular train rides, endless hiking opportunities in cooler climes, elephant-spotting in national parks and Kandy's timeless culture are highlights.

0 20 km
0 10 miles
Mahiyangana
Learn about tea cultivation at the **Somerset Tea Estate** (p135)
45min from Nuwara Eliya
Behold the majestic (Sri Lanka's highest!) **Bambarakanda Falls** (p139)
50min from Haputale
Gampola
Pussellawa
Kotmale Reservoir
Tawalantenne
Nawalapitiya
Pidurutalagala (Mt Pedro)
Pundaluoya
Ragala
Badulla
Uma Oya
Nuwara Eliya
Talawakelle
Nanu Oya
Hakgala
Welimada
Passara
Ride the train across the iconic **Nine Arches Bridge** (p128)
15min from Ella
Hatton
Dikoya
Badalkumbura
Ella
Thotupolakanda
Pattipola
Maskeliya
Ohiya
Bandarawela
Kirigalpotta
Bogawantalawa
Idalgashinna
Horton Plains National Park
Haputale
Koslanda
Buttala
Look down upon the misty mountains from **Lipton's Seat** (p153)
45min from Haputale
Wellawaya
Belihul Oya
Kalu Ganga
Balangoda
Pelmadulla
Kahawatta
Madampe
Kuda Oya
Yala National Park
Uda Walawe National Park
Lunugamvehera National Park
Rakwana
Uda Walawe Reservoir
Thanamalwila
Hinipitigala
Gongala
Deniyaya
Hike to World's End in **Horton Plains National Park** (p144)
45min from Nuwara Eliya
Gaze upon elephants in **Uda Walawe National Park** (p142)
2hr from Ella

Practicalities

SAIKO3P/SHUTTERSTOCK

ARRIVING

Nanu Oya Railway Station Nuwara Eliya's closest train station, Nanu Oya, is 9km along the road towards Hatton and Colombo. Most Nuwara Eliya accommodation will pick you up if you have already booked. A taxi from the station is around Rs 1500 and a tuk tuk is around Rs 800.

Ella Railway Station Just north of central Ella, the pretty train station is within walking distance of much accommodation; otherwise, tuk tuks charge Rs 500.

HOW MUCH FOR A

High tea spread Rs 4800

Rice and curry Rs 1000

Cup of tea Rs 100

WHEN TO GO

JAN–APR
Dry, sunny days and cool nights, perfect for highland trekking.

MAY–SEP
Wetter, warmer season, with afternoon downpours; best for white-water rafting.

OCT–NOV
Maha monsoon brings heavy and frequent rains.

DEC
Rains ease and pilgrimage season to Sri Pada begins.

GETTING AROUND

Bus Frequent buses connect Colombo and Kandy with Hill Country towns. There are also good bus links with coastal towns such as Galle, Tissamaharama and Matara, plus Anuradhapura, Dambulla and Polonnaruwa.

Train Four daily trains link Colombo and Badulla, all passing through Kandy, Hatton, Nanu Oya, Haputale and Ella – a slow but incredibly scenic journey that for many travellers is one of the highlights of their time in Sri Lanka.

Tuk Tuk & Car Some travellers hire a car and driver, or else a tuk tuk, to reach remoter destinations at their leisure. You can hire tuk tuks locally for anything from short jaunts to inter-city rides.

EATING & DRINKING

TOP: BADAI/SHUTTERSTOCK
BOTTOM: ENSWIZ/SHUTTERSTOCK

Hill Country cuisine is shaped by the region's cool climate, multicultural history and local vegetables and dairy products, including buffalo curd. In tea country, tea is still king, though coffee is returning. British colonial influence is still making itself felt (and high-end restaurants have a dress code) in Nuwara Eliya, where roast dinners, scones and high tea are menu staples alongside rice and curry. Street foods including *kotthu rotti* (pictured top right), string hoppers and fiery *sambols* reflect Tamil and Malay influences.

Best curry spread
House of Kitchen (p153)

Must-try lamprais (pictured bottom right)
Cafe Samsara (p153)

CONNECT & FIND YOUR WAY

Wi-fi Most accommodation has wi-fi. Stay connected by buying a SIM card (data and unlimited local minutes) at Colombo airport upon arrival.

Navigation Google Maps is reasonably reliable for getting around. During monsoons, when some roads are blocked by landslides, you'll need to ask locals how to detour, as Google Maps won't show the obstacles.

WHERE TO STAY

Pick your bases according to your interests: some are better for hiking and tea estate visits, while others are best for water sports or elephant safaris.

Place	Pros/Cons
Ella	Accommodation for all budgets, varied dining scene, hiking, temples, tea factories, waterfalls. Touristy; can be noisy.
Haputale	Great for tea country trekking and birding; fabulous views. Limited dining.
Hatton and Around	Proximity to Sri Pada, hiking trails, waterfalls. Limited lodging and dining.
Kitulgala	Good for rafting, jungle trekking and birdwatching.
Nuwara Eliya	Vestiges of 'Little England', tea estates, botanical gardens, high tea, international restaurants. Can be cold and rainy.
Uda Walawe National Park	Ideal for early morning/late afternoon elephant safaris.

WILDLIFE

If you spot a wild elephant or a leopard while cycling or scootering on a remote road, give them a wide berth.

MONEY

Carry plenty of rupees (particularly smaller denominations) to pay in shops and restaurants, and also to pay tuk tuk drivers in locations where Uber Tuk Tuk/PickMe don't work.

23 Sri Lanka's Most SCENIC TRAIN

RAILWAY | MOUNTAINS | LANDSCAPES

The hugely popular eight-hour train journey from Kandy to Badulla is one of the most beautiful in the world, taking you through dramatic valleys and ravines, and showing off misty mountain ranges, greenery-clad hills and endless tea estates.

SURANGALK/SHUTTERSTOCK

Snapping a Pic

Looking to photograph Sri Lanka's most scenic railway? Walk from Ella through the Ella Forest Reserve for 2km to the **viewpoint** overlooking the **Nine Arches Bridge** (pictured) and/or take a tuk tuk to the lofty **Demodara viewpoint** to watch the Ella–Badulla train navigate the Demodara Loop by the Demodara railway station.

Trip Notes

Getting around This train connects the Hill Country's most popular destinations, including Nuwara Eliya, Hatton, Haputale and Ella.

When to go For the driest, sunniest weather, opt for the January-to-April dry season. December can be mistier and rainier, but also offers fantastic photo opportunities.

Top tip Purchase tickets several weeks in advance (seatreservation.railway.gov.lk). A seat in 1st class costs only a little more than 2nd class and has viewing windows.

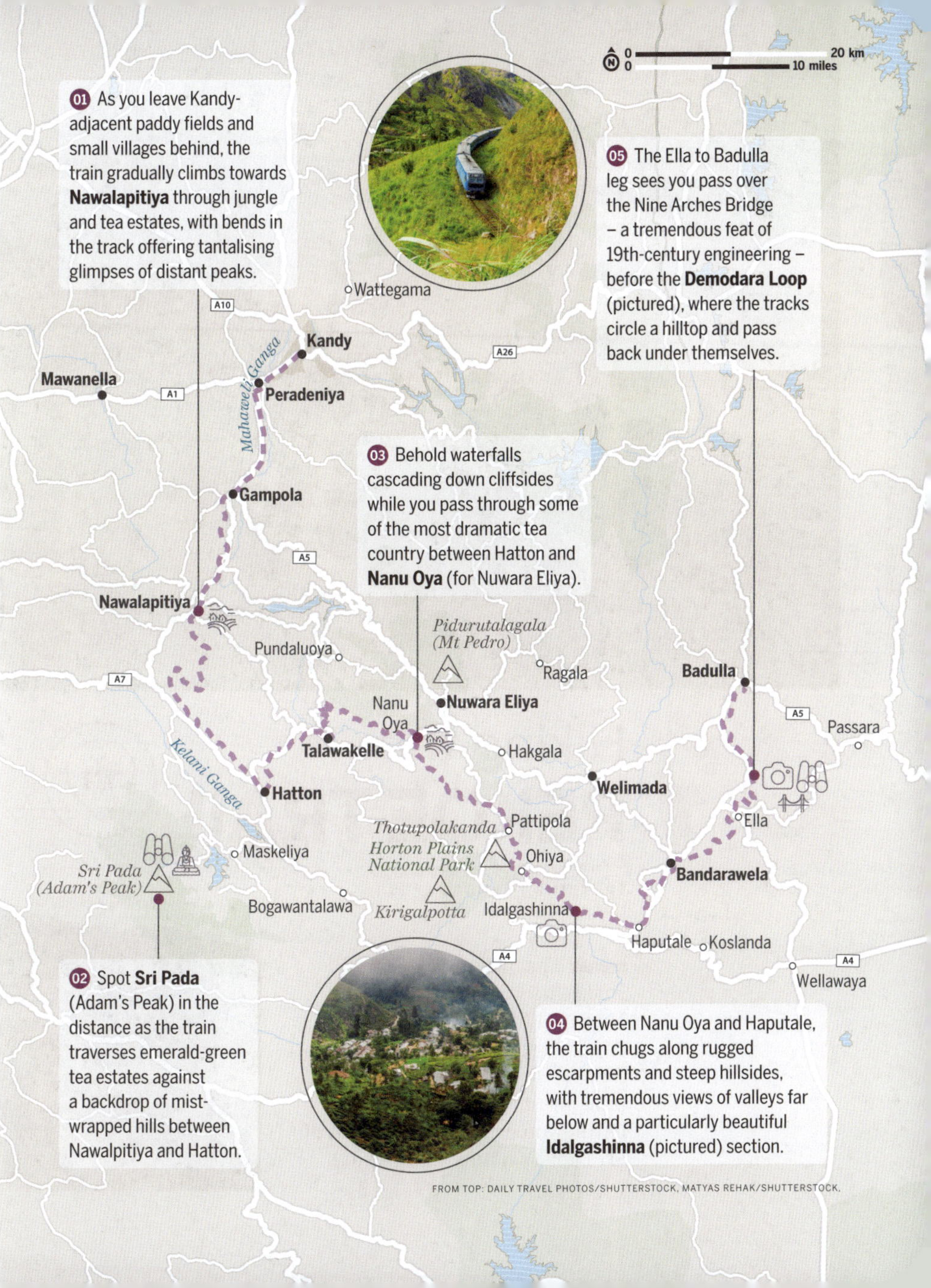

01 As you leave Kandy-adjacent paddy fields and small villages behind, the train gradually climbs towards **Nawalapitiya** through jungle and tea estates, with bends in the track offering tantalising glimpses of distant peaks.

05 The Ella to Badulla leg sees you pass over the Nine Arches Bridge – a tremendous feat of 19th-century engineering – before the **Demodara Loop** (pictured), where the tracks circle a hilltop and pass back under themselves.

03 Behold waterfalls cascading down cliffsides while you pass through some of the most dramatic tea country between Hatton and **Nanu Oya** (for Nuwara Eliya).

02 Spot **Sri Pada** (Adam's Peak) in the distance as the train traverses emerald-green tea estates against a backdrop of mist-wrapped hills between Nawalpitiya and Hatton.

04 Between Nanu Oya and Haputale, the train chugs along rugged escarpments and steep hillsides, with tremendous views of valleys far below and a particularly beautiful **Idalgashinna** (pictured) section.

FROM TOP: DAILY TRAVEL PHOTOS/SHUTTERSTOCK, MATYAS REHAK/SHUTTERSTOCK.

24 Hiking the PEKOE TRAIL

TREKKING | LANDSCAPES | LOCAL CULTURE

The 323km Pekoe Trail snakes its way from Kandy to Nuwara Eliya. Divided into 22 day-hike sections, it takes you through tea estates, cloud and pine forest, towns and villages, letting you experience the best of Sri Lanka's nature and culture.

SAIKO3P/SHUTTERSTOCK

How to

Getting here Trailheads in main towns can be reached by train; for remoter ones, take a tuk tuk.

When to go Weather conditions depend on specific elevation and microclimate. Hike the trail year-round; January to April and July to September are driest.

Essential info The trail pass (US$10 per day) must be purchased online in advance. Download maps and detailed trail descriptions ahead of time using the Pekoe Trail app.

VIDATH AMARASEKARA/SHUTTERSTOCK

The Trail Experience

The Pekoe Trail takes 16 to 22 days to hike in its entirety, depending on your fitness and how long you choose to spend in each locale. Each trail section is designed to be walked independently, so many hikers choose sections that interest them the most. Wild camping is not permitted along the trail, but hikers can stay in designated eco-campsites and glamping sites, as well as in guesthouses, homestays, eco-hotels and boutique hotels, located along or near most trail sections. The Pekoe Trail website (thepekoetrail.org) has a comprehensive accommodation directory.

CHES86/SHUTTERSTOCK

Scenic Jaunts & Cultural Attractions

Kick things off at Stage 1, which stretches from the Ceylon Tea Museum on the Hanthana Estate to the town of Galaha. Passing through

Guided Hikes

The trail is well marked and can be hiked without a guide. That said, guides provide invaluable cultural context and insight into local life. Main guides are Sarath Wijayawardane (+94 71 115 1717) for Kandy; Amit Jayasundara (+94 77 351 9152) for Haputale and Ella; Ramith (+94 77 888 5011) for Hatton; and Lal Rathnayake (+94 77 770 1288) for Nuwara Eliya.

Top left Lake and tea estate at Maskeliya Valley
Above Railway hike (part of Stage 15) to Ella Rock (p152)
Left Horton Plains National Park (p133)

prime tea country, the moderate four-hour trail was used by Scotsman James Taylor (p136) to transport tea to Kandy. A gentle ascent gives you fantastic views of Kandy, Hantana Mountain Range, Victoria Reservoir and the Knuckles Mountain Range. Stage 2, the moderately demanding 14.7km, five-hour jaunt from Galaha to the Loolecondera Tea Estate via the lively market town of Deltota, features stretches of dense forest, some wonderful rock formations and mountain views, plus remnants of Taylor's original cottage.

Spectacular Views

Stage 8 is a moderately challenging 16km stretch that leads you from Norwood through the beautiful Bogawantalawa Valley – 'the Golden Valley of Tea'. Besides views of rolling misty hills and of Castlereagh Lake, you experience tremendous vistas of the Sri Pada–dominated Maskeliya Valley – considered the most beautiful tea-growing valley along the Pekoe Trail – once you climb the ridge that separates the two. The tougher 17km trek to Dayagama (Stage 9)

Trail Tips

- Pack light but smart: good hiking shoes with grip, breathable clothing, sun protection, a raincoat, plenty of water.
- A walking pole is surprisingly useful on tea-estate paths and uneven descents.
- Start early to avoid the midday heat and allow time for encounters with people along the way.
- Carry some rupees to buy bananas from a roadside stall, incense for village kovils... These exchanges are the best way to support local communities.
- Pace yourself. The trail isn't about speed, but about slowing down and enjoying the conversations and landscapes that unfold.

Miguel Cunat, *Pekoe Trail's creator. These are his top tips for trekkers.*

THETRIGGERHAPPYDOC/SHUTTERSTOCK

Far left Devil's Staircase
Left Stage 1, through tea estates
Below Stage 21, through a eucalyptus forest

FROM LEFT: ISURU MADUSANKHA/SHUTTERSTOCK, ANNA KAMINSKI

gives you plenty of opportunities to photograph mist-shrouded mountains, plus the dramatic change from tea country to rolling grasslands.

Physical Challenges

The demanding 16km hike between the secluded village of Dayagama and Horton Plains National Park (Stage 10) has an overall ascent of over 700m, with the stiffest climb beginning once you enter the cloud forest of Horton Plains National Park. Stage 11 – the 14km trek from Horton Plains to Udaweriya – involves the Devil's Staircase: the Pekoe Trail's steepest descent from its highest point (2170m) along a woodland trail that zigzags its way into the spectacular Udaweriya Valley.

Sitting between Ella and Nuwara Eliya, Stages 18 to 20 are remote and physically challenging, with the biggest ascent of around 500m between the towns of Hali-Ela (730m) and Ettampitiya (1246m), where the landscapes alternate between tea country, pine and eucalyptus forest, terraced fields and rice paddies. You'll encounter few other hikers here. Highlights include a gentle descent from Ettampitiya to Uma Oya river, a gradual ascent towards Nuwara Eliya through unspoiled tea country, and the myth-rich Sthripura Caves, which lie between the towns of Lunuwatte and Uda Pussellawa.

25 Nuwara Eliya's TEA ESTATES

TEA ESTATES | WATERFALLS | LANDSCAPES

The highland town of Nuwara Eliya sits among Sri Lanka's most prolific tea country. Hire a tuk tuk, a car and driver or scooter for a 100km spin through the hills carpeted in tea bushes and sip superlative cuppas at tea factories en route.

SERGII FIGURNYI/SHUTTERSTOCK

Trip Notes

Getting around Budget around Rs 12,000 for a tuk tuk (pictured above) or around Rs 20,000 for a car and driver.

When to go The dry season of January to April, with its cool, clear days, is the best time for touring Nuwara Eliya's tea country.

Best views The most scenic part of the drive is the switchbacking stretch between Pundaluoya and Talawakelle. The St Clair Tea Centre provides waterfall vistas.

Making a Perfect Cup of Tea

Boil a fresh pot of water. Use one teaspoon of loose-leaf tea for an average-sized cup. Let the tea brew for three to five minutes to allow the flavour to blossom. Toss the tea leaves straight after to avoid bitter, over-brewed tea. Pour the milk first, then the tea.

01 At the 1885-founded **Pedro Tea Factory**, just east of Nuwara Eliya, take a 20-minute guided tour of the factory with its 19th-century processing equipment.

02 Be greeted with a cup of freshly brewed, delicate highland tea at the **Damro Labookellie Tea Factory** – one of Sri Lanka's oldest tea centres (1841) – and tour the facilities.

03 Stroll through the 1840-established **Bluefield Tea Estate** before indulging in Sri Lankan and European cuisine at the on-site restaurant and shopping for award-winning Pekoe and black-and-green tea blends.

04 Admire the Devon Falls cascades and choose from a wealth of regional teas (including white tea) at the **St Clair Tea Centre** before taking in the estate's own St Clair Falls.

05 Pick tea leaves alongside estate workers, sample the wares and delve into the history of Sri Lanka's tea cultivation during an absorbing two-hour tour of the **Somerset Tea Estate**.

FROM TOP: EXTRADEDA/SHUTTERSTOCK, SAMANWEERATUNGA/SHUTTERSTOCK

Steeped in Heritage

TEA CULTIVATION HAS PROFOUNDLY SHAPED THE HIGHLANDS

'Ceylon' has long been synonymous with some of the world's best tea, even though the plant was introduced to the island fairly recently. The first recorded tea plant was brought to Sri Lanka from China in 1824 by the British; in 1867, the first commercial tea farm was established, altering the highlands for good.

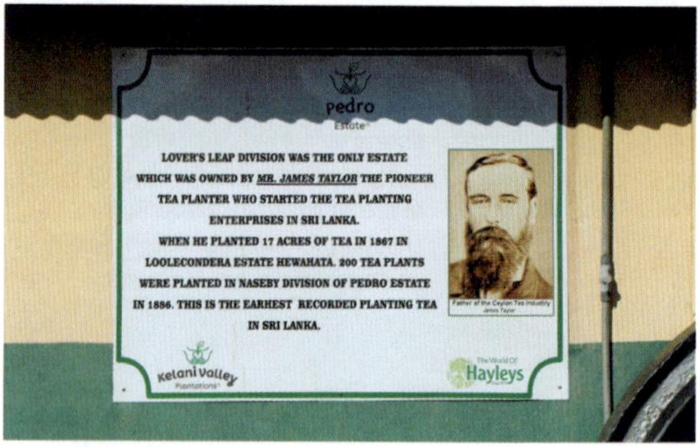

JACKIE ELLIS/ALAMY

A Tradition Is Born

The origins of tea planting in Sri Lanka are to be found on the Loolecondera Estate, 35km south of Kandy, where in 1867 Scotsman James Taylor planted the first Assam hybrid tea seedlings on a coffee estate he'd purchased 15 years prior as a mere 16-year-old. In 1866, Taylor learned the basics of tea cultivation in India; in Sri Lanka, his 19-acre experiment bore fruit. When in 1869 coffee plantations across the island were devastated by the fungal disease coffee leaf rust, Taylor found himself ahead of the game. By 1875 his tea factory was exporting Ceylon tea to the London Tea Auction.

The Hill Country's rugged topography, combined with humidity and ample rainfall, proved ideally suited to tea cultivation, with faster-growing, bolder-flavoured varieties favouring lower altitudes (up to 600m); and higher altitudes (up to 2000m) nurturing the slower-growing, delicate *Camelia sinensis* with its complex bouquet. Soon vast swaths of the highlands were carpeted with tea estates, the range of tea-growing zones – with their own distinctive characteristics – resulting in extraordinary diversity of flavours.

Following the abolition of slavery across the British Empire in 1834, Sri Lanka's British tea magnates – who quickly forced out small tea cultivators like James Taylor – initially struggled to find a labour force to work on their burgeoning estates. Local Sinhalese agricultural workers refused to work for the low wages on offer, so the planters brought in Tamil labourers from impoverished parts of India, such as Tamil Nadu, luring them with promises of a better life and then exploiting them by binding them to the estates with the *kangany* (indentured labour) system.

Left Sign at Pedro Tea Factory (p135)
Centre Tea leaves and bud
Right Tea pickers, Loolecondera Estate

EYETRAVELPHOTOS/SHUTTERSTOCK

ANNA KAMINSKI

From Leaf to Cup

Today, tea remains one of Sri Lanka's biggest exports and the billion-dollar industry employs over 5% of the country's population, with the descendants of the original Tamil labourers playing a key part. Tea cultivation is labour-intensive and physically demanding. Tea bushes are pruned to waist height to make hand-picking easier; only the tender top two leaves and a bud are plucked by hand from tea bushes every seven to 14 days – a meticulous process usually carried out primarily by skilled women workers. During 10-hour working days, the pickers must reach a quota of 20kg per day to earn the full daily wage of around US$3, and are penalised if they fail. After being picked, the leaves are withered, rolled, fermented, dried and graded in tea-estate factories before being sent to Colombo to be auctioned.

> The Hill Country's rugged topography, combined with humidity and ample rainfall, proved ideally suited to tea cultivation

Challenges Ahead

Tea is deeply woven into the fabric of Sri Lankan culture, yet tea cultivation is facing more challenges than ever. Erratic rainfall and rising temperatures caused by climate change threaten harvests, as does a shortage of workers (which might be partially solved by using tea-cutting machinery instead of plucking and by using drones for spraying insecticide). It remains to be seen whether the tea industry can embrace sustainable practices to ensure its long-term survival.

Sri Lanka's Tea-Growing Regions

Sri Lanka has six main tea-growing regions, each defined by the unique taste and aroma of its tea. Nuwara Eliya is responsible for light, floral teas with complex bouquets, grown at the highest elevations. Robust, full-flavoured teas grown at mid-elevations are the pride of Kandy. Dimbula bridges the gap between Kandy and Nuwara Eliya with its flavoursome, medium-bodied teas. If you're after a cup of dark and strong pick-me-up tea, then low-elevation breakfast blends from Ruhuna hit the spot. Sabaragamuwa is known for its smooth, almost sweet teas – an international hit – whereas Uva's teas are particularly aromatic, making them a favourite in blends.

26 Do Go Chasing WATERFALLS

WATERFALLS | SWIMMING | LANDSCAPES

Fed by the Yala (Southwest) and Maha (Northeast) monsoons, the Hill Country's majestic waterfalls are among Sri Lanka's most arresting natural spectacles. Swim in some, admire the rainbows playing on the water vapour and hear legends behind the creation of the falls.

M.L.NUWAN/SHUTTERSTOCK

Diyaluma Falls

Trip Notes

Getting around Ravana Ella Falls and Devon Falls are easily reached by public buses; for the rest, you'll need your own wheels.

When to go Waterfalls are at their most spectacular during the October-to-December rainy season. The January-to-March dry season is better for swimming in the falls.

Best refreshing dip A stiff 45-minute ascent gets you to the crystal-clear pools at the top of the Diyaluma Falls.

Legend of the Diyaluma Falls

According to local lore, a prince fell in love with a young woman belonging to a lower caste. Their union was forbidden, so they climbed the cliff to flee together. The young woman tripped over a creeper and fell to her death. The gods then created the waterfalls from the prince's tears.

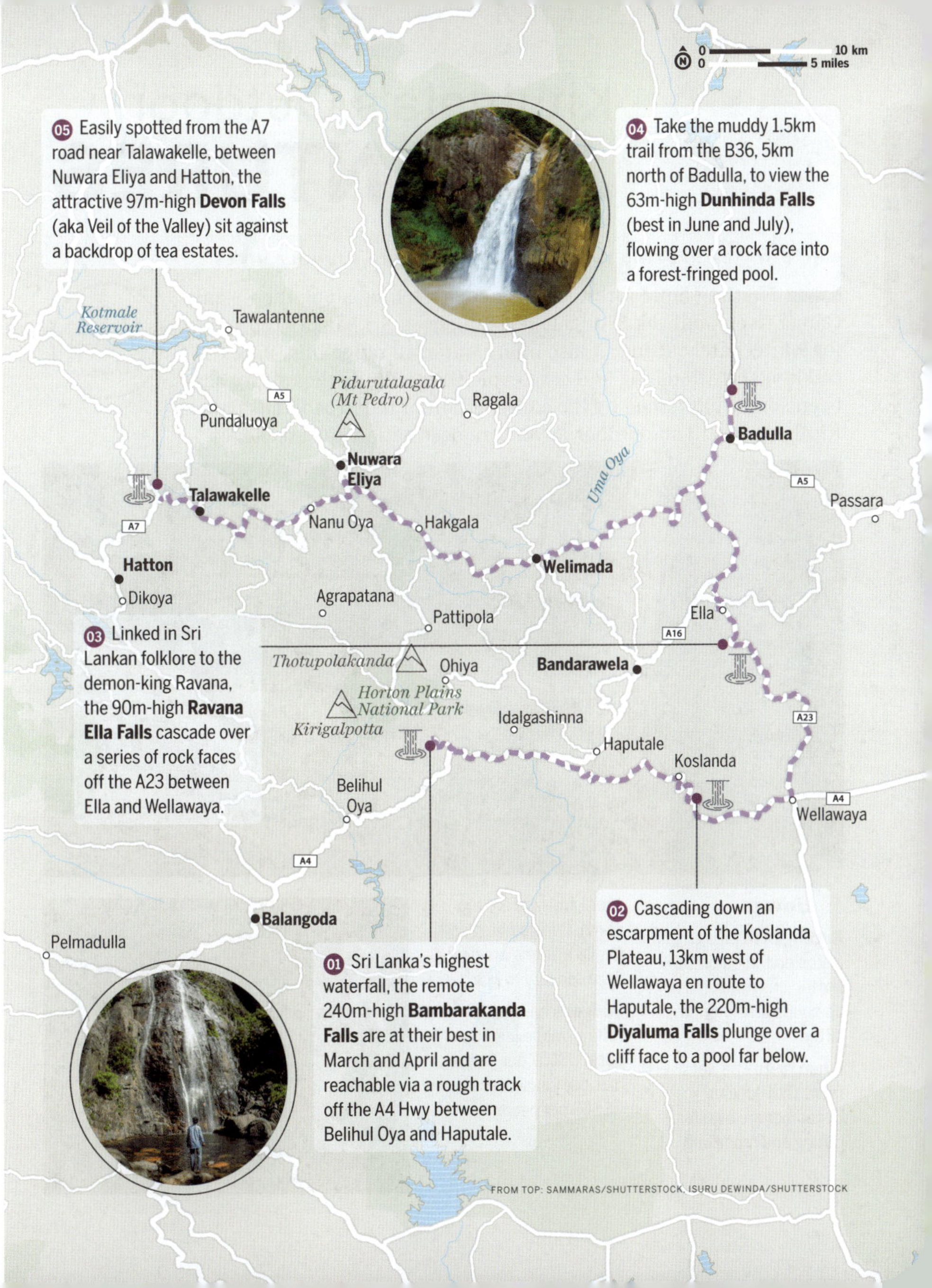

05 Easily spotted from the A7 road near Talawakelle, between Nuwara Eliya and Hatton, the attractive 97m-high **Devon Falls** (aka Veil of the Valley) sit against a backdrop of tea estates.

04 Take the muddy 1.5km trail from the B36, 5km north of Badulla, to view the 63m-high **Dunhinda Falls** (best in June and July), flowing over a rock face into a forest-fringed pool.

03 Linked in Sri Lankan folklore to the demon-king Ravana, the 90m-high **Ravana Ella Falls** cascade over a series of rock faces off the A23 between Ella and Wellawaya.

02 Cascading down an escarpment of the Koslanda Plateau, 13km west of Wellawaya en route to Haputale, the 220m-high **Diyaluma Falls** plunge over a cliff face to a pool far below.

01 Sri Lanka's highest waterfall, the remote 240m-high **Bambarakanda Falls** are at their best in March and April and are reachable via a rough track off the A4 Hwy between Belihul Oya and Haputale.

FROM TOP: SAMMARAS/SHUTTERSTOCK, ISURU DEWINDA/SHUTTERSTOCK

27 Kitulgala's Outdoor ADVENTURES

WHITE-WATER RAFTING | WATERFALL RAPPELLING | JUNGLE HIKES

Nestling amid forested hills and stretching along the Kelani Ganga river, laidback Kitulgala has long been Sri Lanka's top spot for white-water rafting; it also offers waterfall rappelling, jungle trekking, birdwatching and cave exploration. While the rafting has been somewhat tamed by the construction of the Broadlands dam, Kitulgala is still an outdoor-adventure destination par excellence.

M A PUSHPA KUMARA/EPA-EFE/SHUTTERSTOCK

How to

Getting here Kitulgala is a stop on the Colombo–Hatton bus route and is an hour's drive from the latter.

When to go The wet months of June to December are best for rafting and rappelling (April and May are too rainy). Birdwatching and jungle trekking are best from January to March.

Budget A half-day rafting/rappelling tour costs US$57 per person; half-day jungle treks are US$50 per person.

MATT DEAKIN/SHUTTERSTOCK

INTREEGUE PHOTOGRAPHY/SHUTTERSTOCK

Far left Belilena Cave
Bottom left Kelani Ganga river
Left Rafting, Kelani Ganga river

Watery Adventures

Kitulgala is Sri Lanka's go-to destination for white-water rafting, and the Kelani Ganga's Class II and III rapids are suitable for first-timers and swimmers over the age of 10. The 5km journey down the Kelani takes 90 minutes; rafting guides call out rowing commands as you traverse the five larger rapids, whereas the four minor ones are a sedate float. Abseiling (rappelling down waterfalls using a rope and safety harness) is also hugely popular in Kitulgala; the best place to do it is at Sandun Ella, a 32m (105ft) highland waterfall. Combine abseiling with canyoning – using small waterfalls as natural slides and leaping into deep swimming holes. **Kitulgala Adventures** (kitulgalaadventures.com), **Rapid Adventures** (rapidadventures.lk) and **Rafting Club Kitulgala** (WhatsApp +94 77 517 4704) all offer wet 'n' wild fun.

On Dry Land

The rainforested hills surrounding Kitulgala offer jungle treks ranging from moderate to demanding. Most lodgings can arrange a guide. If you want to visit a site of remarkable archaeological significance, enquire about **Belilena Cave** treks. In the 1970s, a Sri Lankan palaeontologist discovered the skeletons of 10 prehistoric ancestors of indigenous Sri Lankans in said cave, around 8km from Kitulgala. Using the bone and stone tools found with the human remains, archaeologists were able to date the era of these 'Balangoda Men', Sri Lanka's oldest human inhabitants, to around 28,500 years ago.

Birding in Makandawa Forest

The protected **forest** across the river from Kitulgala village is one of Sri Lanka's top birdwatching spots – home to 23 of Sri Lanka's 27 endemic bird species, including the Sri Lanka blue magpie, chestnut-backed owlet, Serendib scops owl, green-billed coucal and Sri Lanka grey hornbill. Bring your birding binoculars for a glimpse of the red-faced malkoha, Layard's parakeet, Sri Lanka hanging parrot, orange-billed babbler and Sri Lanka crested drongo.

Some of Kitulgala's lodges, including **Rafter's Retreat** (www.raftersretreat.com), have excellent ornithological guides, who greatly increase your chances of avian encounters. Arranged by your accommodation, tours (US$40) include forest entry, guide fees and boat transport.

28 Elephant-Spotting in UDA WALAWE

ELEPHANTS | BIRDLIFE | SAFARI

Centred on the vast Uda Walawe Reservoir – the main watering hole – the savanna and scrubland forest of the 308-sq-km Uda Walawe National Park are among the best places in the world to see wild elephants. The park is home to over 600 pachyderms, who roam in herds of up to 50; see them up close on a jeep safari.

LUBAN71/SHUTTERSTOCK

How to

Getting here Day tours are offered from Ella and south-coast resorts. Stay overnight in Uda Walawe village to avoid daytime crowds and see the animals at their most active around dawn or dusk.

When to go The park can be visited year-round; the dry periods (May to September and December to March) are the best times for elephant-spotting.

Budget Park entrance costs US$25/15 per adult/child; a safari vehicle will set you back Rs 10,000.

EFIMOVA ANNA /SHUTTERSTOCK

ANNA KAMINSKI

Far left Elephants, Uda Walawe National Park
Bottom left Buffaloes, Uda Walawe National Park
Left Safari vehicle and elephant, Uda Walawe National Park

The Safari

You enter **Uda Walawe National Park** 12km from the Ratnapura–Hambantota road turnoff, which is, in turn, 12km from Embilipitiya. Purchase tickets in a building a further 2km on. Park gates open at 6am, and the last entrance is 5pm. Book your safari for the early morning or late afternoon; the best time to observe elephant herds is from 6.30am to 10am and again from 4pm to 6.30pm. The price of admission includes a driver who acts as a guide, and who'll point out animals during the safari.

To make the most of your time, explain to the driver beforehand that you don't want to rush from one elephant herd to the next, as many visitors seem to do. Due to the park's popularity, there are issues with drivers crowding around flagship pachyderms; if there are more than five vehicles, ask you driver to wait or find something else to admire.

Not Just Elephants

Tours booked beforehand through accommodation may be more expensive, but they can be personalised so that you get the experience you want. Uda Walawe is beautiful. Slow down to take in the soaring highlands to the north, the vast expanse of grasslands, dotted with small lakes, and other wildlife – wild buffaloes wallowing in mud, fleet-footed sambars and spotted deer, crocodiles visible in the water, monitor lizards basking in the sun, and over 210 species of colourful birds.

Elephants Under Threat

Uda Walawe's elephants face numerous challenges. Illegal settlement and the associated grazing of cattle encroach upon the grasslands, the elephants' main food source. Some elephants get injured by explosive devices planted by poachers targeting wild boar.

The park is largely surrounded by an elephant-proof fence that prevents free movement to waterholes and grazing sources; the access road to the park is lined with shops selling fruit to motorists who then try to feed the elephants through the fence, encouraging dependence and eroding the elephants' fear of humans, thus leading to human-elephant conflict in which the elephants are the losers.

29 Hike to WORLD'S END

MAJESTIC VIEWS | WILDLIFE | MOUNTAINS

Midway between Nuwara Eliya and Haputale, the 32-sq-km **Horton Plains National Park** is a starkly beautiful highland plateau. Overlooked by Sri Lanka's second- and third-highest mountains, Kirigalpotta (2395m) and Thotupolakanda (2357m), the park may only be explored on foot along the 9km loop trail leading past the plateau's edge, where cliffs dramatically plunge to the lowlands below.

VLADYSLAV TRAVEL PHOTO/SHUTTERSTOCK

How to

Getting here Tours are easily organised from Nuwara Eliya or Haputale, with a 45-minute drive to the park from either.

When to go January to March and August and September are the driest months. Aim to reach the park entrance by 7am as mist pulls in around 10am.

Budget Tours cost around Rs 4500 per person; otherwise, pay the entry fee (adult/child US$25/15) and vehicle charge (Rs 150) at either park entrance.

M.L.NUWAN/SHUTTERSTOCK

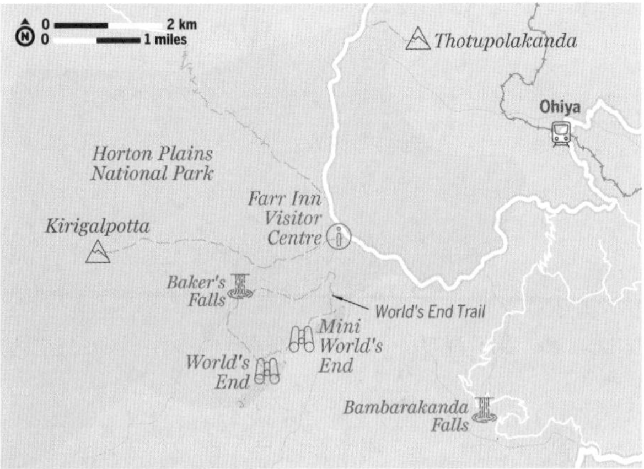

Top left World's End
Bottom left Baker's Falls

World's End Trail

This 9.5km loop trail, walkable in three hours, begins by the **Farr Inn Visitor Centre**. Proceed at a leisurely pace, since the altitude of 2000m may leave you breathless, and take layers, since it can be cold and wet on the plateau.

The first 500m takes you through *patana* grasslands, before you plunge into a 2km stretch of cloud forest – distinctive umbrella-shaped *keena* trees draped in old man's beard lichen. Another 2km or so gets you to the first viewpoint – **Mini World's End**, with glimpses of the lowlands below. Continue through another 1.5km of cloud forest and thickets of dwarf bamboo to the show-stopping **World's End** (2140m), a viewpoint where cliffs plunge 825m, granting you incredible views of Sri Lanka's south, all the way to the coast. Some 2km further along, the trail shadows the Belihul Oya river, and you pass **Baker's Falls**, reachable via a steep scramble. A final stretch through more *patana* grasslands brings you back to the trailhead.

The Wildlife

The major fauna in the park, such as leopards, can be elusive, though you're likely to spot herds of sambar deer and bear monkeys. If you're a birdwatcher, bring your binoculars: Horton Plains is one of Sri Lanka's best birding destinations, featuring highland endemics that are not found elsewhere on the island, such as the Sri Lanka bush warbler, dull-blue flycatcher, and Sri Lanka white-eye.

Choose Your Mountain

Kirigalpotta (2395m) is a moderately strenuous, 11km return hike that begins from Farr Inn and takes around five hours, passing through a landscape of high grasses, twisted dwarf forests festooned with lichens, and squelchy bogs. After a steep final section, you're rewarded with expansive views of the lowlands.

Since the trail is indistinct, a guide is essential: Lal Rathnayake (+94 77 770 1288), Nimal Herath (+94 77 618 9842) and Kaneel Rajanayeka (+94 77 215 9583) charge around Rs 15,000, including transport from Nuwara Eliya.

More straightforward is the two-hour, 6km return hike up **Thotupolakanda** (2357m); the trailhead is near the Pattipola park entrance.

30 Ascending SRI PADA

MOUNTAIN | SHRINES | TREMENDOUS VIEWS

A pilgrimage site for over a thousand years, Sri Pada (Adam's Peak; 2244m) is the most famous mountain in the Sri Lankan highlands. A sacred site for Buddhists, Hindus, Muslims and Christians, it's also an excellent hike with fantastic summit views.

VIKHESSE_PHOTOGRAPHY/SHUTTERSTOCK

How to

Getting around Frequent buses and tuk tuks link Hatton (nearest train station) and Nallathanniya (Dalhousie), where the most popular trail up Sri Pada begins.

When to go During pilgrimage season (December to May), the weather is better but the trail is crowded. Bring a head torch if hiking between May and November.

Tea stops Take it easy during the hours-long ascent and stop at any of the numerous teahouses en route for refreshments.

SAIKO3P/SHUTTERSTOCK

The Climb

Most travellers and pilgrims opt to summit **Sri Pada** via the Nallathanniya route, which begins from the west end of the eponymous village, at the **makara thorana** – a beautiful stone archway with carved bears and motifs of Kala (a ferocious monster from Hindu mythology personifying time and death).

As the path runs gently uphill, you'll walk through a tea estate and past a waterfall viewpoint, arriving at the foot of the first of the 5500 concrete stairs, marked by the **Sama Chitiya Japanese Peace Pagoda** (1976). From there, the sheltered footpath steepens in earnest as you trek through Sri Pada's Wilderness Sanctuary, home to the world's rarest toad, the *Adenomus kandianus*. A small bridge takes you over a river, marking the beginning of a more intense stair climb to the summit.

BATSAC/SHUTTERSTOCK

Trails up Sri Pada

There are six summit trails: the little-trodden Kuruwita, Malimboda, Murraywatte and Mookaywatte routes require a guide. The 7km route from Nallathanniya (Dalhousie) is the most popular; it takes 2½ to four hours to reach the top. The tough Ratnapura–Palabaddala route (15km, around seven hours) is the second most popular.

Top left Sri Pada, Nallathanniya route
Above Makara thorana
Left Sama Chitiya Japanese Peace Pagoda

Here, the trail is lined with rest stops and small shops selling tea and refreshments (although bathroom options are limited). As your calves and thighs burn from the strain, the trail suddenly ascends near vertically, with handrails to help you up. This is the *mahagiri damba,* the great rock climb, which takes you up the last 750m to the summit along the final 1500 or so steps.

The Summit

As you reach the top of Sri Pada, which is dotted with pilgrim huts, ring one of the two bells to announce your arrival – it's a tradition to ring it the number of times you've reached the summit. Then head inside the **Sri Padaya temple** to see a shrine to Samantha, the mountain deity. As dawn breaks, the views of the surrounding mountains are as spectacular as they come before the clouds begin to pull in shortly after sunrise. Face west from

Hiking Tips

- Stay at a guesthouse near the trailhead to get some sleep before starting the hike.
- Start climbing after dark and take a sleeping bag to snooze in a pilgrim hut upon summitting, or else begin around 2.30am to reach the summit for sunrise.
- Don't underestimate the cold at the summit. During pre-dawn hours at the peak it can be as low as 5°C. Pack extra layers so that you can swap your sweaty gear for some warm, dry threads.
- Take hiking poles or a sturdy stick; your knees will thank you on the descent.

SHUTTERLK/SHUTTERSTOCK

Far left Sri Pada
Left Sunrise, Sri Pada summit
Below Shrine along the trail

FROM LEFT: DILLRO HUB/SHUTTERSTOCK, IWCIAGR/SHUTTERSTOCK

the back of the mountain at dawn, and if you're lucky, you'll see a mysterious phenomenon: a triangular shadow of a peak that doesn't correspond to the relief of the actual summit, suspended in mid-air for around 20 minutes.

The Sacred Footprint

At the summit sits a large rock with an indentation 170cm long and 46cm wide (67in and 18in) that vaguely resembles a **giant human footprint** (Sri Pada translates as 'the sacred foot'). It's painted in gold and sheltered beneath a tiny pavilion (closed outside pilgrimage season). Christians and Muslims believe that this is where the biblical Adam first set foot on earth. Buddhists believe it is Buddha's footprint, while Hindus claim it belongs to Shiva.

Pilgrimage on Poya Days

Climbing Sri Pada on a *poya* (full moon) day or weekend is quite the experience. A carnival-like atmosphere reigns, the trailside tea shops are packed to the brim, and you're climbing cheek by jowl with thousands of others, including Hindu pilgrims dressed up as the deity Shiva. You may not even reach the summit due to the queues, but it'll be one of the most memorable things you do in Sri Lanka.

31 Birding in SINHARAJA

JUNGLE TREKKING | BIRDWATCHING | WILDLIFE

Sri Lanka's top birdwatching destination, the UNESCO-recognised, 89-sq-km Sinharaja Forest Reserve protects the largest remaining tract of lowland rainforest in Sri Lanka's southwest. Remote and tricky to access, this is a humid wilderness with prodigious rainfall year-round. Here you'll find over 860 species – plants, birds and animals – unique to the island, and very few visitors.

ANTON_IVANOV/SHUTTERSTOCK

How to

Getting here There are two entrances: Deniyaya in the south (easier to reach by public transport) and Kudawa in the northwest (your own wheels necessary).

When to go The park is easiest to access and birdwatching is best during dry periods (January to March and August to September).

Budget Entry is Rs 1500 for foreigners; hiring a (mandatory) guide at the gates for a half-day guided jungle walk costs around Rs 3000.

NILANKA SAMPATH/SHUTTERSTOCK

LAUBERGERIE/SHUTTERSTOCK

The Jungle Hike

Unlike most Sri Lankan national parks, access to **Sinharaja Forest Reserve** is only on foot, accompanied by a ranger or guide. While operators in south-coast resorts offer day trips to Sinharaja, it's best to base yourself in basic accommodation in either Deniyaya and Kudawa. That way, you can be at the park gate when it opens at 7am, when the birds and other wildlife are more active, rather than spend hours in a vehicle and visit the reserve in the middle of the day.

The mandatory guides are indispensable, since the dense rainforest canopy lets in limited daylight and wildlife-spotting isn't particularly easy. The two- to three-hour rainforest treks are incredibly worthwhile if you're a keen walker unperturbed by regular tropical downpours, muddy forest tracks, leeches (bring leech socks) and other denizens of the forest floor, including fist-sized arachnids, plus the venomous krait and hump-nosed viper.

The Wildlife

Sinharaja's largest carnivore is the leopard, although you're more likely to see its droppings and tracks than to catch sight of its majestic feline form. Also seldom seen are rusty-spotted cats and fishing cats. You're more likely to spot a sambar deer, barking deer or wild boars in the undergrowth, or perhaps see the canopy above you move, betraying the presence of a group of purple-faced langurs. Other notable mammals include mongooses, porcupines, pangolins and three kinds of squirrel.

Far left & left Sinharaja Forest Reserve
Bottom left Sri Lanka grey hornbill

Birds of Sinharaja

If you're a dedicated birdwatcher particularly interested in birds unique to Sri Lanka, you've come to the right place!

Some 147 species have been recorded here, including 32 of the island's 34 endemic bird species. In the rainforest, you may spot the Sri Lanka grey hornbill, red-faced malkoha, Sri Lanka scimitar babbler, Legge's flowerpecker and Laynard's parakeet, among others. With a good birding guide, you might even be lucky enough to glimpse the elusive Serendib scops owl and the Sri Lanka blue magpie.

Other fascinating feathered creatures to watch out for include the Sri Lanka frogmouth and the Malabar trogon.

Listings

BEST OF THE REST

Historic Tea Bungalow Stays

Planter's Bungalow $$

Ten miles south of Ella, this converted 19th-century tea-planters' bungalow is fringed by beautifully tended gardens with a swimming pool, while the rooms are decked out with carefully chosen antiques and art.

Kelburne Estate $$$

White-suited staff provide superb service at this clutch of immaculate former tea-planters' bungalows (for four to six people) near Haputale, surrounded by rolling tea estates. Home-cooked meals available.

Heritance Tea Factory $$$

Inside a century-old tea factory amid mist-shrouded hills near Kandapola, this intimate luxury hotel retains original tea-processing machinery. Dress up to dine inside an old steam-train-carriage restaurant.

Thotalagala $$$

Seven individually styled suites, named after tea-industry pioneers, await at this sensitively updated 19th-century bungalow adjoining the Dambatenne tea estate. Candlelit barbecues, high tea and birdwatching excursions are perks.

Strathisla Guest House $$

Near Matale, this 1860-built coffee-turned-tea-estate bungalow has morphed into a boutique B&B featuring mountain views and a pool. Activities include guided hikes, cooking classes and Hatale Tea Factory tours.

Royal Majesty Bungalow $$

One of Sri Lanka's oldest tea-estate houses, this intimate bungalow in Norton comprises four characterful rooms with four-poster beds. It's a fantastic base for hiking the Pekoe Trail; local guides arranged.

Fabulous Day Hikes

Ella Rock

A 10km roundtrip (three to four hours), this moderately strenuous loop hike involves following railway tracks from Ella, a ramble through tea estates and a steep final ascent, with 360-degree views your reward.

Single Tree Hill

Take two hours (6km roundtrip) to climb Single Tree Hill (2100m) near Nuwara Eliya via tea estates and eucalyptus and pine groves for expansive vistas of Horton Plains and Pidurutalagala peak.

Caves

Nil Diya Pokuna

The largest cave system discovered in Sri Lanka, one of Ella's most spectacular sights, features a vast, boulder-strewn main cave and an underground lake that's accessed via an 800m-long tunnel.

Botanical Gardens

National Spice Garden of Sri Lanka

Stroll the trails, fragrant with cinnamon, cardamom, pepper and cloves, and learn about the vital role spices have played in shaping Sri Lanka's trade for centuries. Just outside Matale.

Hakgala Botanic Gardens

Some 10km southeast of Nuwara Eliya, these beautifully landscaped gardens feature a fine rose garden, a Japanese garden, an orchid collection, cedars and giant cypresses. Visit outside planting season (January to March).

Scenic Viewpoints

Lipton's Seat

Get to Lipton's Seat from Haputale at sunrise to view a rolling sea of tea estates, verdant valleys and mist-shrouded mountains before the morning cloud rolls in.

Little Adam's Peak

A stroll through a tea estate, followed by an ascent up concrete steps gets you to Ella's Little Adam's Peak, with wonderful views of Ella Rock and the Ravana Ella Falls.

Temples & Buddhas

Dowa Temple

The highlight of the Dowa Temple, 6km east of Bandarawela, is a 4m-high standing Buddha carved into a rock face. According to legend, King Valagamba took refuge here in the 1st century BCE.

Buduruwagala

Some 10km southwest of Wellawaya stand the beautiful, 1000-year-old rock-cut Buddha figures of Buduruwagala. The 16m-tall central figure, carved into a vast rock outcrop, is Sri Lanka's largest standing Buddha carving.

Maligawila

At verdant Maligawila lie the remains of a 7th-century Buddhist monastery. A shady avenue of magnificent banyan trees leads you to Sri Lanka's tallest free-standing Buddha, 11m tall.

Rice & Curry Meals

Dushan's Home Kitchen $

A homey Nuwara Eliya eatery where rice and curry and other Sri Lankan dishes are made to order – which means longer waits, but fantastic quality. Excellent vegan options.

ANNA KAMINSKI

Buduruwagala

Forest Feast $

Each dish at this friendly Nuwara Eliya spot, including rice and curry spreads, is crafted from organic ingredients from the restaurant's own garden and greenhouses.

Green Paradise $

Traditional multi-curry spreads vie for your attention alongside excellent fried rice, *kotthus* and *rottis* with dhal and *sambol* at this cosy Haputale spot.

Mint of the Mist $$

Wonderful views halfway along the Haputale ridge are complemented by breakfast dosas and rice and curry meals made with vegetables grown on site.

House of Kitchen $

At this small, family-run spot in Ella, a friendly chef prepares heaped platters of rice, surrounded by five veggie curries-of-the-day, ranging from aubergine to pumpkin.

Cafe Samsara $$

Get a bellyful of *lamprais* (rice cooked with curry in a banana leaf), *kotthu rotti* or devilled chicken served in what resembles a Rastafarian's breezy living room in Ella.

KANDY

TEMPLES | MOUNTAINS | ANCIENT RELICS

RESEARCHED BY MARISA MEGAN PASKA

KANDY

Trip Builder

Tucked away in a cosy valley you'll find the Central Highlands' most important city – and not just because of its size. Kandy was once the throne of ancient kings, and remains a spiritual and cultural hub, preserving traditional culture and perhaps the country's most important Buddhist relic.

Take a hike in the pristine **Knuckles Conservation Forest** (p162)
1hr 40min from city centre

Enjoy expansive views over the valley at the **Bahirawakanda Buddha** (p165)
5min from city centre

Marvel at the incredible Kandyan dancers and drummers at the annual **Esala Perahera festival** (p161)
1min from city centre

Pay your respects at the UNESCO Temple of the Tooth, inside of Kandy's **Sacred City** (p158)
10min from city centre

Buy everything from unique foods to souvenirs at Kandy's bustling **Central Market** (p164)
4min from city centre

FROM TOP: MARTIJN VAN DEN ENK/SHUTTERSTOCK, DENIS COSTILLE/SHUTTERSTOCK
PREVIOUS SPREAD: MIKADUN/SHUTTERSTOCK

Practicalities

ARRIVING

Take a train from Colombo or Ella to **Kandy Railway Station,** or a bus to **Bogambara Bus Station**. Comfortable mini-buses are available along common routes such as to the Ancient Cities.

FIND YOUR WAY

Kandy has a central and helpful **Tourist Information Centre** open daily from 8.30am to 7pm.

MONEY

You'll need cash for tuk tuks, market stops and temple entrance fees. There are plenty of ATMs in town.

WHERE TO STAY

Area	Pros/Cons
Downtown Kandy	Close to the action; noisy at night.
Kandy Hills	Quiet, chic and with stunning views; a short tuk-tuk ride to the centre, but not walkable.
Kandy Lake Area	Lake views; walking distance to attractions; sometimes noisy.
Northern Kandy	Residential area; short drive from the city; far from the sites.

GETTING AROUND

Walking Despite the hills, Kandy Old Town is walkable.

Tuk tuk Negotiating hills, or travelling to/from hotels outside the centre, is best done by tuk tuk.

Car If you're going further afield, opt for a ride-sharing car. Both Uber and PickMe work.

TOP: SANDARU MADHAWA/SHUTTERSTOCK
BOTTOM: MIHIDUM JAYASINGHE/SHUTTERSTOCK

EATING

Follow the taka-taka sound of spatulas on the griddle to your local *kotthu rotti* (pictured top left) street stall to taste Kandy's spicy, savoury stir-fried street food.

If curry is your game, check out a Polos curry, a Central Province specialty featuring young jackfruit (pictured bottom left). It's creamy, labour-intensive and delicious.

Best kotthu rotti
Cafe 1886 (p164)

Must-try Polos curry
Kandy Muslim Hotel (p164)

DEC–APR
The driest, sunniest and coolest months of the year.

MAY–SEP
The southeast monsoon keeps scenery lush and tourist numbers down.

JUL–AUG
Festival season. Expect crowds.

OCT–NOV
Rainiest months of the year; no crowds.

32 Temple RITES

CULTURE | RITUAL | DRUMMING

The UNESCO-listed Temple of the Tooth, inside Kandy's Sacred City, is a must on any Hill Country itinerary. For a truly unique visit, schedule your tour during one of the thrice-daily *pujas*. These are sacred rituals filled with chanting and drumming, when the faithful make offerings to Buddha's tooth relic.

LINDA_K/SHUTTERSTOCK

How to

When to go Services start at 5.30am, 9.30am and 6.30pm and usually last around 90 minutes. Arrive early, as lines can be lengthy.

How to go Enter with your normal temple ticket (price varies based on nationality), and bring a small donation for when you visit the inner chamber.

Special services Wednesday at 9.30am there is a special symbolic bathing (Nanumura Mangallaya) of the relic.

Inner Workings

A **puja** offers a look into the inner sanctum of a Buddhist temple – as long as you have a bit of patience for crowds.

Starting with a procession from the lower level of the **Temple of the Tooth**, *puja* worshippers follow the Hewisi drums up the stairs, passing through first the silver, then the golden door to the inner chamber where the tooth relic is held. The faithful wait in long lines to be allowed into the sacred inner room, where one by one they lay their down offerings while prayers, rhythmic drumming and song fill the air.

Time to Pray

There are three daily *pujas*. While each is a bit different, all are wonderful to witness.

The early-morning service feels more solemn, while the midmorning service brings more lively chaos. The midmorning service is also when food is brought in to

symbolically 'feed' the Buddha, adding an extra layer of ceremony. The evening service, however, is by far the most animated, with old flowers switched for fresh ones, and offerings of food, palm syrup, honey, ghee and more lotus flowers.

The space is tight, and it can get quite hot inside. You'll need to be patient if you want to get your turn. If you're just interested in witnessing the spectacle, arrive early so you're not stuck behind the long line of worshippers and grab a spot along the wall near the inner chamber where you'll have a clear view of the processions.

Holy Water

On Wednesdays, a special symbolic bathing of the relic, called the Nanumura Mangallaya, takes place during the midmorning *puja* (the 9.30am service). During this ceremony, a silver replica of the tooth's casket is symbolically 'bathed' in herbal water – a ritual that's considered to have southern Indian influence.

The remaining *nanu* (holy water), which is believed to have healing powers, is then distributed among the worshippers present. If you feel driven to participate in this deeply spiritual experience, bring a flower offering and wait in line with the other worshippers for your turn to enter the inner sanctum.

Left and above Temple of the Tooth

33 Festival NIGHTS

PARADES | PERFORMANCES | ELEPHANTS

Esala Perahera is a 10-day celebration in the streets of Kandy every July or August (auspicious dates are chosen each year). The festival pays homage to the sacred tooth relic of the Buddha with parades, drumming, music, dancing, fireworks and cannon fire. This celebration is an offshoot of ancient parades held to ensure rainfall for a good harvest.

THOMAS WYNESS/SHUTTERSTOCK

How to

Street views To watch for free, arrive early for a good spot on the street. Police close the Old Town's entrance when it's too crowded (as early as 3pm on the final night). Arrive by 2pm.

Paid seats Book a balcony spot at the Queen's Hotel (p165) or in the front row at a local shop.

Clothing The event is religious, so wear clothing that covers your shoulders and knees – and abstain from alcohol.

Elephants and animal welfare Elephants are an integral and revered part of this festivity. However, the 2019 collapse of one elephant and the 2023 repatriation of another to Thailand following abuse claims has seen their role in festivities become a point of controversy between festival adherents and animal-rights advocates.

PHOTO WICKY/SHUTTERSTOCK

THOMAS WYNESS/SHUTTERSTOCK

Far left and bottom left Kandy Esala Perahera
Left Temple of the Tooth (p158)

Ancient Processions

The **Kandy Esala Perahera** dates back to the Kingdom of Kandy, when the faithful put on elaborate *peraheras* (parades) to appease the gods, pray for adequate rainfall and ward off disease. Later, similar celebrations were held in honour of the Buddha's tooth relic, which combined with the earlier *peraheras* to create today's festival extravaganza.

Parades for days Modern-day Esala Perahera begins with five days of private processions inside the *devalayas* (temples), of the island's four guardians – Natha, Vishnu, Kataragama and Pathilini – before hitting the streets for 10 days of public parades that will have culture-lovers swooning. Each day's parade follows a different route through Kandy Old Town, with the size and scale of the parades gradually ramping up. Nights one to five, known as Kumbal Perahera, are smaller in scale but just as rich in tradition. These nights are perfect for those keen to experience the festival without the dense crowds.

The grand finale Nights six to nine offer grander parades with elephants in full regalia and dancers, drummers and fire performers filling the streets. The final night's parade – the Randoli Perahera – runs through nearly every street in the Old Town, lasting over five hours and attracting tens of thousands of spectators. During the Randoli Perahera, over a hundred elaborately costumed elephants guide the Maligawa Tusker, the most sacred elephant, which carries the golden casket that holds the sacred tooth relic as it's paraded through the streets.

Restoring Balance

The day after the Randoli Perahera, priests and the faithful make one last procession down to the banks of the Mahaweli River to close the Esala Perahera festival with a sacred water ritual. The crowd sets out before dawn, gathering on the riverbanks where the priests ceremonially 'cut' the water three times with a sword, a gesture meant to 'sever misfortune and restore balance'. They then collect holy water and carry it back to the temple.

This ceremony isn't open to the public. However, early risers can see the procession make its way to and from the river.

34 Conquer the KNUCKLES

NATURE | HIKING | VALLEY VIEWS

The Knuckles Conservation Forest is home to some of Sri Lanka's most spectacular mountain scenery. These UNESCO-protected mountains are replete with breathtaking views and rife with biodiversity – including some of the country's rarest wildlife. And if you're a true adventurer, you'll want to see it all by toiling your way up to the summit.

ALEXIS DUBAN/SHUTTERSTOCK

How to

Get a guide Hiking in the Knuckles Conservation Forest is prohibited without a registered guide. Talk to **Knuckles Adventure** (knucklesadventure.com) or **Nipuna Knuckles Trekking** (+94 72 121 0172) to arrange hikes.

Leech protection This is leech territory. Don your leech socks and spray Dettol on your shoes before hitting the trail.

Pack it in There are no services offered in the park, so bring snacks and water for your trip.

JASENTHU/SHUTTERSTOCK

MATT DEAKIN/SHUTTERSTOCK

Far left and bottom left Hiking trails, Knuckles Conservation Forest
Left Knuckles Mountain Range

Sky High

The Knuckles Mountain Range (Dumbara Kanduvetiya; 'mist-laden mountain range') climbs to nearly 1900m above sea level and offers extensive panoramic views, but they're views you'll have to earn. Reach the first summit by hopping on the **Dawatagala Trail** (aka the Knuckles Five Peaks Trail). This involves between two and three hours of uphill hiking with a 600m (2000ft) change in altitude. Once you're at the top, you can continue along the ridge to see peaks two through five, although most stop at the second knuckle, as the trail gets a bit overgrown after that.

Stay a while While you can opt to go up and down in a single day (the 8km hike takes approximately six hours out and back), consider spending an exceptional night under the stars at the summit. Enjoy your morning coffee with amazing mountain views before heading back down, refreshed and renewed. About 300m from the trailhead, you can veer off and visit crystal-clear (and quite cold) **Knuckles Falls**.

Ready for rain Book your hike during dry season (March to October), but remember that it can rain any time in the Knuckles, so always have your rain gear on hand, and leave for your hike as early as possible (6am to 7am is ideal) to avoid the clouds that collect on the peak in the afternoon. Between November and late January, the rainiest time, choose your days wisely, or you might spend the entire trek looking at little more than fog and clouds.

Animal-Spotting

The Knuckles Conservation Forest is one of Sri Lanka's most important biodiversity hotspots, home to 34% of the island's endemic species. A number of them are endangered or threatened, and some species from the Knuckles are found nowhere else on earth.

While you're unlikely to see these endangered animals, keep your eyes peeled for other fan favourites, like wild buffaloes, purple-faced langurs, wild boar, barking deer and the toque macaque. There are also elephants and leopards who call the forest home – another reason trekking with a guide is indispensable in the Knuckles.

Listings

BEST OF THE REST

Caffeine Fix

Cafe Secret Alley $$

Flop on a beanbag chair to enjoy your Turkish eggs, banana pancakes or hummus-avocado toast paired with quality coffee. Ideal for your international brunch favourites.

Roots'n'Beans $$

This thimble-sized lakeside cafe caters to all your chickpea burger, avocado spinach pasta and sweet-potato toast needs. Vegetarians and vegans will happily flock.

Department of Coffee $$

A hip, blond-wood-covered spot serving some of Kandy's best espresso, plus international dishes like baked quinoa with pomegranate and thick, juicy burgers.

Local Eats & Live Music

Cafe 1886 $$

With over 860 years of culinary experience, this historic eatery has had plenty of time to get the recipe for *kotthu rotti* right. Go here for your Lankan staples.

Kandy Muslim Hotel $

There's not much in the way of ambiance, but the food is beyond divine. Try some of Kandy's best samosas, spiced curries and frisbee-sized flatbreads.

Hideout Lounge $$$

Traditional cocktails, boozy brunch options, all-day poke bowls and delectable pizzas define this hipster hideaway. Evenings feature live music.

Sharon Inn $$

A nightly buffet dinner served in the rooftop restaurant includes a feast of lovingly prepared veggie curries, from jackfruit to banana leaf to aubergine.

Slightly Chilled Lounge Bar $$

Western-style bar and lounge with a billiards table, live music and an amazing view from the terrace. The perfect spot for a post-temple sundowner.

Kandyan Arts

Central Market

Inside Kandy's Central Market you'll find shops selling breathtaking batik clothing and beautiful homewares. Don't miss Jayamali Batiks Studio, a tiny shop that has long been a destination for those seeking traditional arts in modern, artistic styles.

Kandyan Arts & Crafts Gallery

Choose between the ubiquitous fire demon masks, woodcarvings of the Buddha and elephants, local jewellery and cosmetics made from jungle plants.

ANNA KAMINSKI

Kandy Lake Club

Waruna Antiques

Antique shopping is a favourite Kandyan pastime, and about 2km southwest of the centre, this warren of an antique shop is a treasure trove of vintage masks, jewellery, coins, textiles, maps and art.

Kandy Lake Club

Get a taste of traditional Kandyan dancing – Sri Lanka's can't-be-missed performing art – at one of the nightly, hour-long performances involving drumming, animal-like movements, acrobatics and fire-eating.

Architectural Gems

Giragama Walawwa

Stop by the town's oldest surviving *walawwa*, a colonial-era mansion with a red roof and wood-lattice details that was once inhabited by a member of the royal court.

Queen's Hotel

The beautifully restored Queen's Hotel was once the mansion of the British governors in Kandy, and while it is a legacy of British occupation, the white-painted facade is a striking example of colonial-era Ceylon architecture.

Red Mosque of Kandy

Built in 1908 for the expanding Muslim community, Kandy's most important mosque features red-and-white tiled designs, candy-cane columns and an elaborate entryway.

Bahirawakanda Buddha

The bright white Bahirawakanda Buddha is one of the tallest in Sri Lanka. This 27m-high statue sits on the top of Bahirawa Kanda hill, offering incredible views over the valley.

A Peek at the Past

Ceylon Tea Museum

Travel 5km south of Kandy to find the 1925-vintage Hantane Tea Factory, now a

SAMANWEERATUNGA/SHUTTERSTOCK

Ceylon Tea Museum

museum where you'll learn about the island's tea history and production.

National Museum of Kandy

Get a glimpse of Sinhalese life before European occupation at this museum where royal relics, folk games and ancient weapons are on display.

Tusker Raja Museum

If you love elephants, this tiny museum can't be missed. 'Raja' was the bearer of the sacred tooth relic for nearly half a century, and a national treasure. The museum has a replica statue of him, as well as photos of the tusker in his glory days.

Glamping in the Mountains

Wild Glamping Knuckles

Luxury, safari-style tented camps (with running hot water showers) in a quiet valley in the Knuckles Conservation Forest are ideal for multi-day hikers or those looking to escape the crowds.

Madulkelle Tea and Eco Lodge

Both traditional rooms and luxury tents are available at this high-end site just outside of the Knuckles Conservation Forest. Expect exceptional service and to-die-for views of mountains and tea fields.

ANCIENT CITIES

LOST CITIES | TOWERING STUPAS | WILD ELEPHANTS

RESEARCHED BY BRADLEY MAYHEW

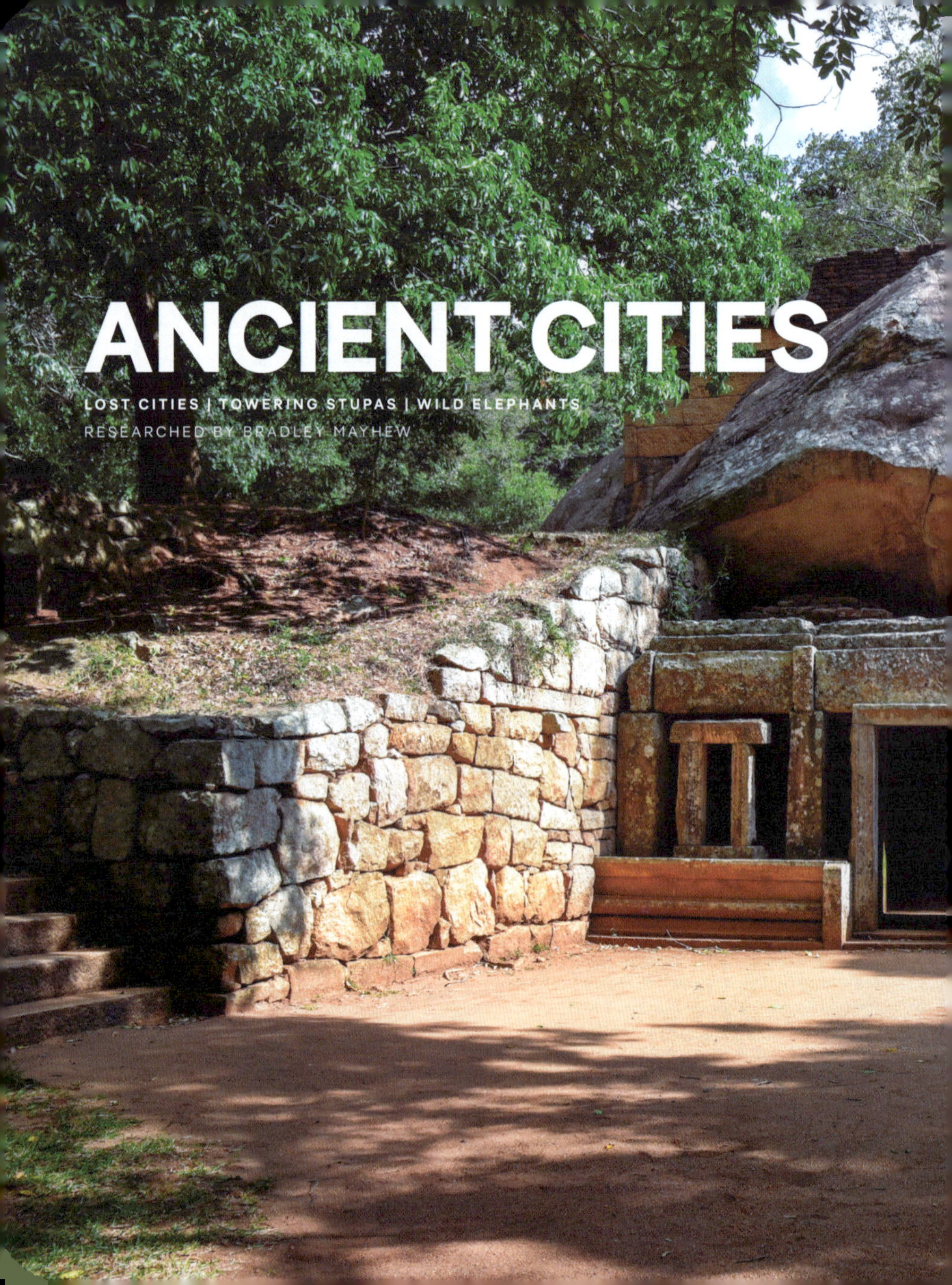

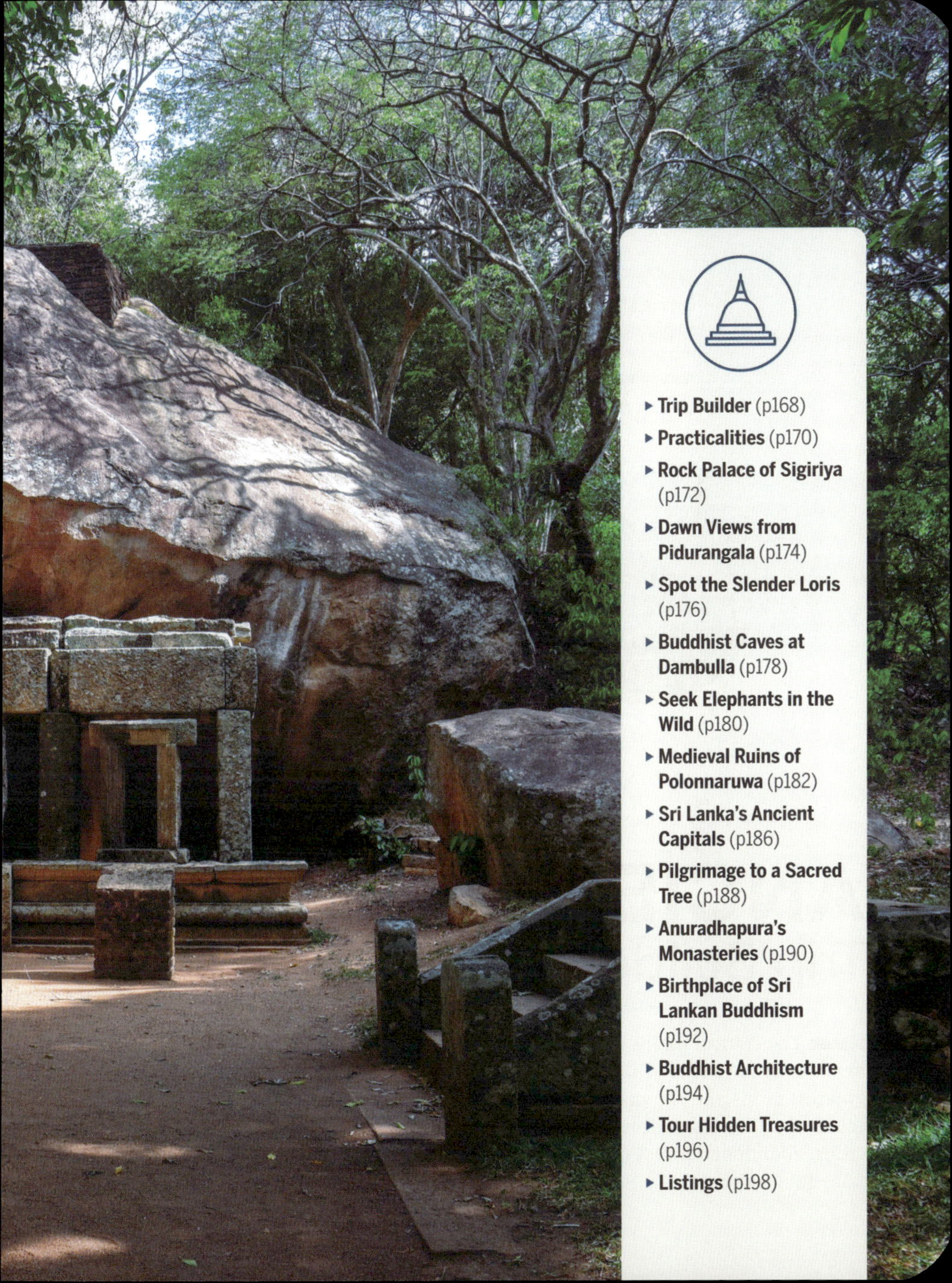

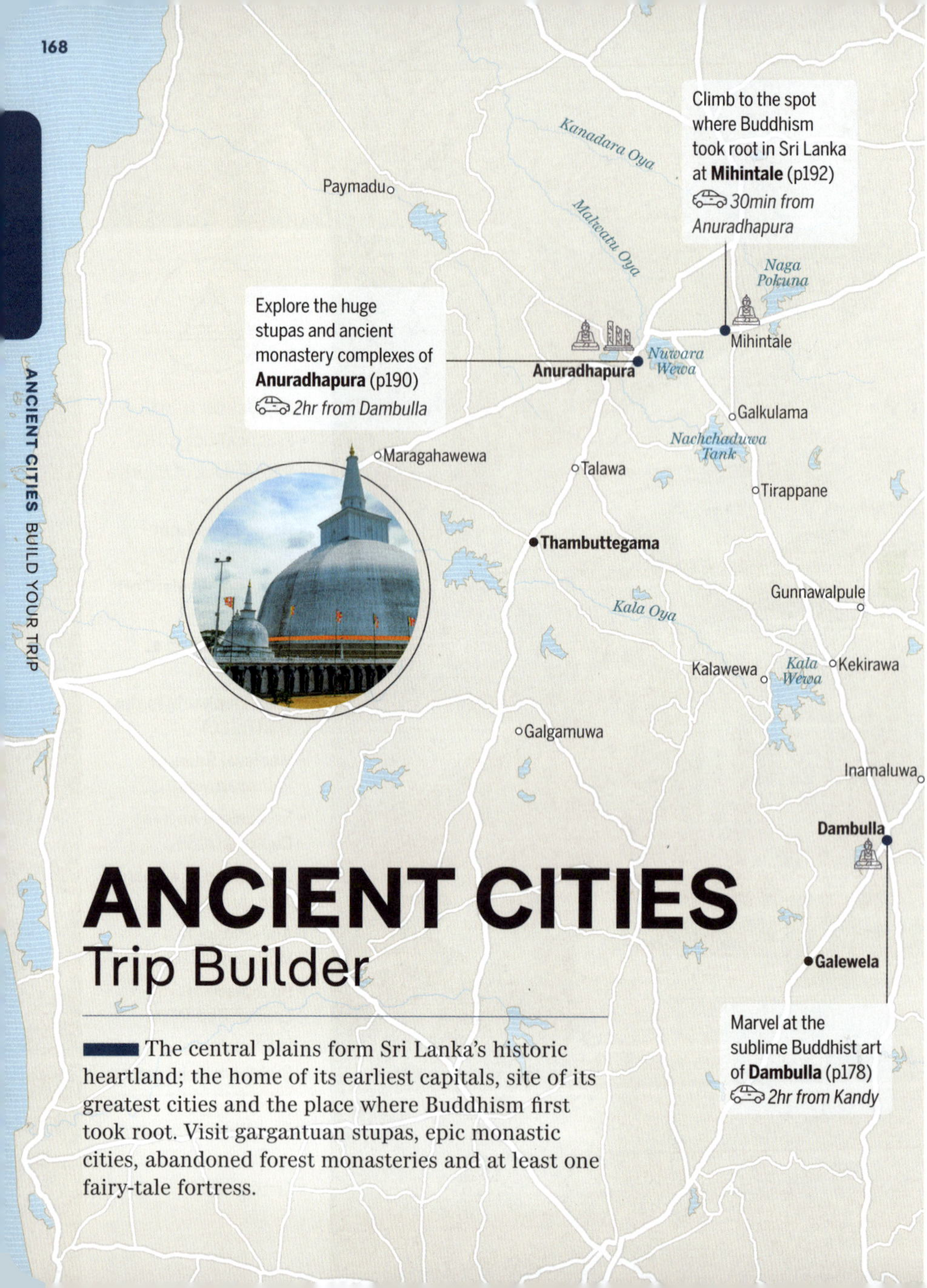

ANCIENT CITIES
Trip Builder

The central plains form Sri Lanka's historic heartland; the home of its earliest capitals, site of its greatest cities and the place where Buddhism first took root. Visit gargantuan stupas, epic monastic cities, abandoned forest monasteries and at least one fairy-tale fortress.

CLOCKWISE FROM LEFT: OSCAR ESPINOSA/SHUTTERSTOCK, WESCHE/SHUTTERSTOCK, PILESASMILES/GETTY IMAGES, IMAGE PROFESSIONALS GMBH/ALAMY
PREVIOUS SPREAD: AJIT WICK/SHUTTERSTOCK

Practicalities

VIRTUALEXPLORING/SHUTTERSTOCK

ARRIVING

Anuradhapura Train Station Air-con rail connections to Colombo, Jaffna and Talaimannar.

Dambulla Lots of highway buses (pictured), especially to/from Kandy, plus through buses to Polonnaruwa and Anuradhapura. Sigiriya is a short bus or tuk tuk ride away via Inamaluwa Junction.

Polonnaruwa Served by the bus and train station at Kaduruwela, 4km to the east. Overnight and daytime trains to Colombo Fort and several services to Batticaloa.

HOW MUCH FOR A

Meal at Hela Bojan Hala US$2

Sigiriya entry ticket US$35

Minneriya park entry approx US$40

WHEN TO GO

MAR–JUN
Hot. Festivals of Vesak (May) and Poson Poya (June) in Anuradhapura.

APR–OCT
Dry season. Good time to spot elephants at Minneriya.

NOV–JAN
Rainy. The Unduvap Poya (last full moon) festival in Anuradhapura.

JAN–APR
Dry, hot weather. High season in Sigiriya and Anuradhapura.

GETTING AROUND

Bus Local buses shuttle between major towns, including to the Minneriya National Park entrance, though you may have to change between Polonnaruwa and Anuradhapura.

Car The best way to reach rural sights and to see multiple sights in one day, for places like Yapahuwa and Aukana.

Tuk Tuk Best for getting to Pidurangala and to spread-out sights and suburban hotels around Sigiriya. Hire one for a day's sightseeing in Anuradhapura or Polonnaruwa.

Scooter Best for short rides and maximum freedom, if you have a license.

EATING

Finding stand-out food is harder in the central plains than on the coasts or even in Jaffna. There are plenty of local places and family-run tourist-oriented restaurants in Sigiriya and Anuradhapura, but little in the way of the international-class restaurants that you'll find on the south coast. There are good opportunities to learn how to prepare food family-style at cookery courses in Sigiriya and Anuradhapura. Top hotels generally have the most interesting food.

Best blowout
Apsara Restaurant at Jetwing Vil Uyana (p177; pictured top right)

Must-try kotthu rotti (pictured bottom right)
Bro Restaurant (p198)

CONNECT & FIND YOUR WAY

Wi-fi Common and free of charge in all hotels, and 4G coverage is generally excellent if you have a local data package.

Navigation Backroads can be confusing, so load up Maps.me beforehand if navigating yourself. Don't trust Google Maps navigation off the main roads.

WHERE TO STAY

The central plains are compact, so some travellers base themselves in one or two hotels and day trip from there.

Town	Pro/Con
Sigiriya	Lots of choice and a good base for Dambulla and Minneriya National Park, but spread out.
Dambulla	Great top-end places in the countryside north and east of town, if you have transport.
Polonnaruwa	Mostly budget options, but overnighting allows a cooler early start.
Anuradhapura	All budgets are covered. Slightly limited choices.

PACK SOCKS

Bring a pair of socks when visiting temples and Buddhist sites, as you need to go shoeless and the stone floors can get burning hot at midday.

MONEY

Entry tickets for Anuradhapura and Polonnaruwa add up, so get an early start and see everything you want to in one day. Accommodation is generally good value. ATMs are common in all towns.

35 Rock Palace of SIGIRIYA

FAIR-TALE PALACE | GARDENS | RUINS

Sri Lanka's most dramatic sight, Sigiriya, is the stuff of legends – a monastery converted by a patricidal king into an impregnable fortress atop an unassailable 180m-high rock. Throw in serene gardens, Sri Lanka's oldest frescoes, a series of cliffside walkways and astonishing views from a seemingly impossible palace in the sky and you have a fairy-tale site that continues to stir the imagination.

AMZ_BORNEO/SHUTTERSTOCK

How to

Getting here Sigiriya is 17km northeast of Dambulla, just north of the village of the same name.

When to go It's worth getting up early to avoid both the heat and the crowds. The ticket office and site opens at 5am.

What to wear Sigiriya is not a religious site, so wearing shorts and a T-shirt is fine. Bring water and a hat, as there is no shade on the summit.

SERGEMI/SHUTTERSTOCK

ROGELIO GOZUM ARCANGEL/SHUTTERSTOCK

Far left Sigiriya
Bottom left Lion's paws
Left Steps up Sigiriya

Climbing the Rock

The approach and ascent of **Sigiriya** (adult US$35) is a series of superlatives. Water defines the lower sections as you cross the city's encircling moat and proceed though **gardens** of cooling water channels, lake pavilions and fountains powered by monsoon rains, before ascending terraces to a side platform. Sigiriya (from *sinha-giri*) means 'Lion Rock' and the epithet becomes clear as you tread gingerly between two gigantic **lion's paws** to ascend steps that would originally have led through the huge lion's open jaws.

Finally, the flat-topped **summit** reveals the foundations of royal palaces and large water tanks that were vital to the site's viability, alongside fabulous views north towards Pidurangala. Pause to consider the audacity and insecurity that motivated King Kasyapa to build his palace in such an impractical spot.

The descent takes you past an iconic series of **frescoes**, Sri Lanka's oldest and most famous, depicting 21 buxom women who scholars believe represent either *apsara* (celestial nymphs), Kasyapa's courtly maidens or images of the bodhisattva Tara. Scholars believe that frescoes once covered the entire cliff.

Finally, back down on ground level you wind past the dramatic boulders and meditation caves of the original **lower monastery**, before exiting the site. If you have time, head back to the museum to learn more about the history and trade connections of the amazing site.

The Story of Sigiriya

Sigiriya likely started life over 2000 years ago as a Mahayana-influenced Buddhist monastery, built around the rock that monks envisaged as a symbolic Mt Potala, the heavenly abode of the bodhisattva Avalokiteshvara. It was King Kasyapa (r 477–95) who reimagined the rock by building his palace and capital here, after killing his father King Dhatusena of Anuradhapura and usurping the throne.

Kasyapa ruled from Sigiriya for 16 years before the past finally caught up with him in the form of his vengeful half-brother (and Dhatusena's designated heir) Moggallana. By the 14th century the monastic site was abandoned.

36 Dawn Views from PIDURANGALA

RUINS | VIEWS | MONASTERY

Once an in-the-know budget-saving backpacker alternative to Sigiriya, the pre-dawn ascent of Pidurangala has become a must-do for its dawn views over the surrounding plains. It's not a replacement for Sigiriya but rather a nice complement, hiking through an ancient monastery that is thought to predate its famous counterpart.

TRAVELWILD/SHUTTERSTOCK

How to

Getting here Pidurangala is 1.5km north of Sigiriya. Guesthouses can arrange a return tuk tuk for Rs 1500, including waiting time.

When to go The clearest sunrises are during the dry-season months of December to April and July to September.

Top tip A rental scooter or self-drive tuk tuk is an enjoyable way to explore the countryside viewpoints around Sigiriya, including Kaludiya Pokuna.

INIGOLAI-PHOTOGRAPHY/SHUTTERSTOCK

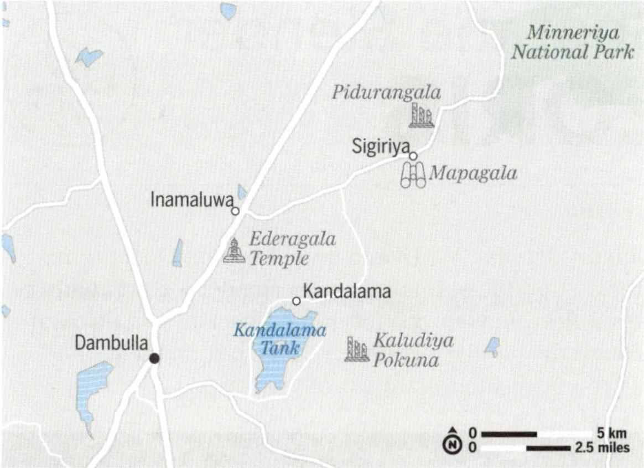

Pidurangala Views

Every day the pre-dawn darkness north of Sigiriya is punctuated by the headlights of tuk tuks dropping bleary-eyed travellers at the base of **Pidurangala** rock. From here, steps lead up past monastery temples, squeezing between house-sized boulders to pass a sleeping Buddha statue. Scholars believe that the monastic ruins are older than Sigiriya, with some monks forcibly moved here when King Kasyapa chose the rock as his royal palace.

A final squeeze and scramble over boulders drops visitors on the wide, sloping summit of Pidurangala, like ants atop a giant molar, high above the emerald jungle. In clear weather, sunrise bathes Sigiriya rock in soft, magical dawn light.

Most accommodation can arrange a pre-dawn tuk tuk. Avoid walking here before dawn; a tourist was killed by a wild elephant while walking to Pidurangala in 2025.

Other Sigiriya Viewpoints

Several other spots in the region offer alternate views of Sigiriya rock without the crowds. The ancient rock of **Mapagala** in the outskirts of Sigiriya village is becoming increasingly popular for its sunset and rock views, and is an easier 10-minute walk (some easy scrambling still required).

If you are heading back to Sigiriya from Dambulla around sunset, be sure to catch the expansive views from the hilltop stupa of **Ederagala Temple**, a monastery nestled among giant boulders 2km southwest of the Inamaluwa junction.

Top left Pidurangala
Bottom left Sleeping Buddha statue

Kaludiya Pokuna

Both Sigiriya and Pidurangala are popular sights. If you want to see a ruined forest monastery in sublime solitude, take a tuk tuk 13km southwest of Sigiriya along dirt backroads to the off-grid **Kaludiya Pokuna** monastery.

Here forest trails wind past caves, rock inscriptions, a stupa and the monolithic stones of a prayer hall, thick with monkeys and fabulously buttressed tree roots, making you feel like the first person to ever explore the site. The ruins lie 3km off the Kimbissa-Kandala road, down a bumpy dirt track.

37 Spot the Slender LORIS

WILDLIFE | NATURE | FAMILY FUN

The grounds of the luxury Jetwing Vil Uyana hotel are home to a group of Sri Lanka's oddest and most adorable animal, the grey slender loris. Catching sight of a loris' disc-like eyes reflecting your red torch-light back at you through the darkness on a walk through the hotel's forested grounds is a moment of wonder that might rank as the unexpected highlight of your trip.

DR. MALALA RAJAPAKSHA/SHUTTERSTOCK

How to

Getting there The Vil Uyana is 7km southwest of Sigiriya Rock; take a tuk tuk.

When to go The dry months of March to April and September to November are best, though loris live here year-round.

Top tip Try to avoid a visit during, or just after, heavy rain, as rain washes away the loris' food supply. They also stay hidden during full-moon nights, fearing the greater visibility.

ARIADNE VAN ZANDBERGEN/ALAMY

SAURABH CHITALE/SHUTTERSTOCK

Far left & left Slender loris
Bottom left Jetwing Vil Uyana

Loris The slender loris is a lovely, bizarre-looking primate about 20cm long with giant eyes, pencil-thin limbs and five frog-like fingers. A five-star resort is probably the last place you'd expect to spot this intriguing animal, but every evening naturalists at the **Jetwing Vil Uyana** lead loris-spotting tours around the hotel grounds, using red light to avoid harming the nocturnal loris' sensitive eyes.

Rewilding The Jetwing-run hotel is a model of environmental stewardship. Over the last 20 years staff have removed invasive grasses and planted 2000 native trees and bushes on the property, turning what were abandoned paddy fields into an island of rich biodiversity. And it's not just loris; the hotel grounds also provide a home to fishing and jungle cats, civets, porcupines, fruit bats, 160 species of birds (up from 24 species in 2004) and even two on-site crocodiles. It's small-scale local rewilding at its best.

Tours The evening **spotting tours** (US$40 per person for non-guests) are particularly good for families, but the hotel also runs a 6.30am spotting walk for birders, as well as night jeep safaris (US$150 per couple) to spot civets and the rusty-spotted cat, the world's smallest feline. For a classy add-on, book dinner at the hotel's **Apsara Restaurant** for before or after a safari.

Loris Lowdown

At the Vil Uyana we have so far identified around 10 individual loris in our 3-acre conservation area, including two babies born in 2025. They are so slender and light that they can sleep deep in the dense undergrowth and bamboo canopy, where predators can't reach them, holding on to branches with their tiny hands as they sleep.

The loris come out hunting just after nightfall. To maximise your chances of spotting one, keep quiet and walk slowly, as loris are very sensitive to sound and vibration. Listen also for their high-pitched whistle-like calls.

WMNW Bandara, *naturalist at Jetwing Vil Uyana. @jetwing.viluyana*

38 Buddhist Caves at DAMBULLA

BUDDHISM | ART | MURALS

The five spectacularly decorated rock caves of Dambulla rank as one of Sri Lanka's great artistic treasures. Every square inch of the caves' interiors is covered in sublime Buddhist murals, depicting everything from serene Buddhas to stories from Buddha's past lives and even demonic temptation, drenching the cool interior spaces in colour and sanctity. Don't miss them.

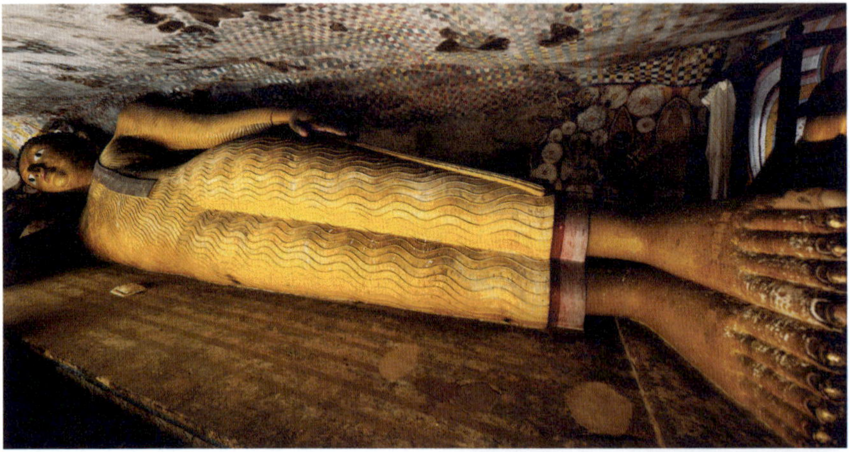

POSZTOS/SHUTTERSTOCK

How to

Getting here Dambulla is easily reached by public transport from Kandy and Sigiriya. Most people visit on a half-day tuk tuk trip from Sigiriya (Rs 3500).

When to go Year-round, though the region's driest weather is February to October.

What to wear Wear a long skirt or long trousers to visit the caves, or rent a sarong at the entrance. Leave your shoes at the entrance.

GUILLAUME ANGLERAUD/SHUTTERSTOCK

TWABIAN/SHUTTERSTOCK

Far left Reclining Buddha
Bottom left Pachima Viharaya
Left Cave temples of Dambulla exterior

The moment you enter the **cave temples** of Dambulla your eyes will widen, trying to adjust not only to the dim light but also to the rich colours that saturate the space. The first murals were painted here almost 2000 years ago, after Anuradhapura's King Valagamba sought refuge in the caves, and further paintings were added by Polonnaruwa's King Nissanka Malla in the 12th century and the Kandy kings in the 18th century. Given the centuries between paintings, the overall impact is remarkably coherent.

The first cave, or **Devaraja Viharaya**, houses a 15m-long reclining Buddha, but it's the second cave, **Maharaja Viharaya** (Temple of the Great King), that really impresses, from its painted stupas and gilded Buddhas to the ornate ceiling murals. A vessel to the right collects sacred water that constantly drips from the ceiling, even during drought. A wooden statue of King Valagamba stands to the left of the cave.

The third cave, **Maha Alut Viharaya**, is more recent, converted into a temple in the 18th century. The small dagoba (stupa) in the fourth cave, **Pachima Viharaya**, was looted by thieves looking for the jewellery of Queen Somawathiya, a 2nd-century BCE royal.

The best way to visit the hilltop temples is to climb the steps for 15 minutes from the ticket office, then afterwards descend gradually eastwards to the kitschy, modern **Golden Temple** and meet your transport there.

Hela Bojan Hala

If you are looking for a cheap, authentic lunch of traditional Sri Lankan snacks, be sure to stop at **Hela Bojun Hala**, a network of women-run food stalls, established by the government to preserve traditional local foods and support female entrepreneurship.

You can load up on everything from *narung kewum* (a rice-flour, coconut and treacle ball) or a cowpea *wade* (fritter) to a full meal of *pittu* (steamed rice flour and coconut) with curry, washed down with *belimal* flower tea, all for pennies. There are branches across Sri Lanka but our favourite is in **Pelwehera**, 3km north of Dambulla.

39 Seek Elephants in THE WILD

WILDLIFE | SAFARI | PHOTOGRAPHY

Every year during the dry season hundreds of wild Asian elephants congregate beside the reservoirs of Minneriya and Kaudulla national parks, drawn to the succulent, fresh grass sprouting on the receding lakeshores. A jeep safari to Minneriya in August and September, and Kaudulla in October, will bring you face to face with this 'gathering', one of Asia's great wildlife spectacles.

AL CARRERA/SHUTTERSTOCK

How to

Getting here Most people organise a jeep safari from Sigiriya or Habarana. Minneriya is on the main road between Habarana and Polonnaruwa; Kaudulla is further north.

When to go The dry season (April to October) is the best time to visit, with afternoon safaris considered best for elephant spotting.

Top tip The elephants move around the region seasonally, so speak to guides and guesthouse owners to find the current best location.

RADOMIR REZNY/SHUTTERSTOCK

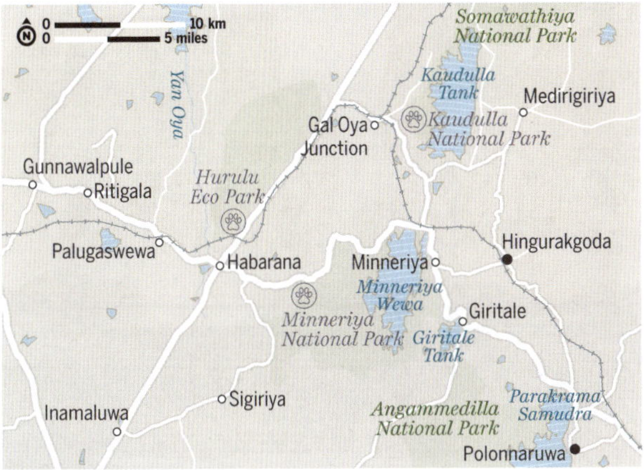

Jeep safari If you fancy a break from peering at archaeological sites and ruined capitals, then sign up for a jeep safari to **Minneriya** or **Kaudulla** national parks for a chance to see wild elephants, toque macaques, sambar deer, crocodiles, painted storks and eagles in their natural environment. If you are lucky, you'll watch spellbound as dozens of elephants graze less than 50m away, as babies shelter shyly by their mothers knees, and juveniles tussle and play in nearby waterholes.

The Gathering Elephants are drawn to Minneriya's lush sprouting grasses in the biggest numbers during the dry season months of August and September, in a seasonal event that has been dubbed 'The Gathering', before moving on to the lakeshores of Kaudulla National Park in October and November.

Hurulu As the rains begin to fill the reservoirs, some elephants move to the higher grounds of **Hurulu Eco Park** further west, near Habarana, so consider a visit there if visiting November to January. Hurulu is smaller and offers a narrower range of habitats than the national parks, but entry fees are cheaper.

The future The recent construction of the Moragahakanda dam has affected Minneriya's water levels and diminished elephant numbers in recent years, so hopefully the local government will find a way to balance the demands of both tourism and agriculture to ensure the future of this remarkable gathering.

Top left Elephants, Minneriya National Park
Bottom left Hurulu Eco Park

Safari Tips

- Ask your driver to keep a safe distance from elephants at all times and turn off the engine when the jeep isn't moving.
- National park fees are complicated, with an entry fee of US$25 per person, plus vehicle charges, a US$10 service charge per group and 18% tax. Hurulu costs less: around US$8 per person.
- Half-day jeep safaris from Sigiriya to Minneriya cost around US$120 for two people, including park fees.
- Budget agencies like **Ceylon Rides** (ceylonrides.com) at ever-popular **Roy's Villa** in Sigiriya arrange regular group safaris starting at US$50 per person.
- Groups normally tip their driver and guide around 10% of the tour cost.

40 Medieval Ruins of POLONNARUWA

ANCIENT CITY | STUPAS | RUINS

Polonnaruwa was Sri Lanka's second major capital, between the 10th and 13th centuries. What remains today are hundreds of temples, royal palaces, towering stupas, ponds and exquisite Buddhist statues, built on a more intimate scale than Anuradhapura. It's a historical highlight.

KHOROSHUNOVA OLGA/SHUTTERSTOCK

How to

Getting here Trains and buses run to stations at Kaduruwela, 4km east of Polonnaruwa.

When to go Visit as early as possible to avoid the heat; the site's ticket office at the Archaeology Museum opens at 7.30am.

Touring Cycling is a good way to tour the archaeological sites. Bicycles are available through vendors and guesthouses for Rs 1000 per day.

Entry tickets US$30 per person; major cards accepted.

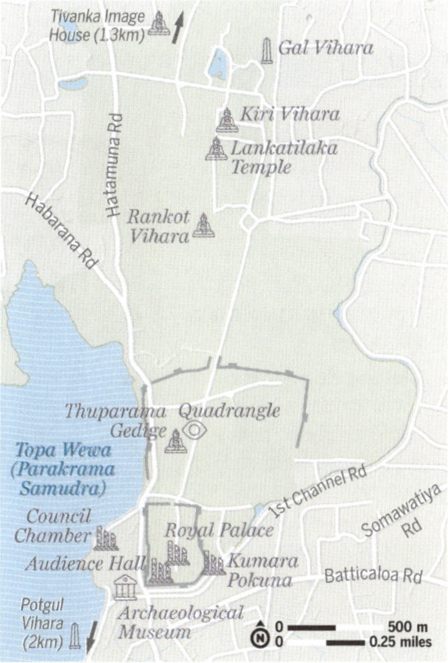

The Ancient City

There's a lot to see in Polonnaruwa, so give yourself most of the day. Start off inside the ticketed ancient city at the 12th-century **Royal Palace**, where you can wander the remains of King Parakramabahu's ruined palace, once seven storeys tall and now resembling a crumbling molar. Run your hand over the impressive stone lions of the king's nearby **Audience Hall** and then head down to the **Kumara Pokuna** royal bathing pool with its lotus island and crocodile-mouth spouts.

ALONANOLA/SHUTTERSTOCK

Top left Royal Palace ruins
Bottom left Audience Hall

The Quadrangle

The densely packed ruins of the **Quadrangle** housed the sacred relic of the Buddha's tooth during Polonnaruwa's heyday, in a series of buildings commissioned by successive kings intent on outdoing their predecessors. Remove your shoes to visit the terraced *vatadage* relic house and its beautiful moonstone.

Polonnaruwa is noted for its Indian architectural influence, which you'll notice at the roofed stone temple of **Thuparama Gedige**. Details are also what separate Polonnaruwa from Anuradhapura; notice the lotus-stalk pillars of King Nissanka Malla's pavilion and the literal 'stone book' *(gal pota)*, whose inscriptions glorify King Nissanka Malla's rule (1187–96).

Aluhana Piravena Group

A short cycle north lies the **Rankot Vihara**, the largest stupa in the city and the fourth-largest in Sri Lanka, at 54m tall. Also in this section of monastery is the city's largest convocation (meeting) hall, the beautiful brick cathedral-like **Lankatilaka Temple**, with its huge headless Buddha, and the milky-white **Kiri Vihara** stupa. This is one place to go exploring, tracking down enigmatic monastic foundations and miniature stupas away from the main paths.

Gal Vihara

Sri Lanka's most stunning Buddhist sculptures are on display in the **Gal Vihara**, cut

Buddhist Temple Etiquette

Whenever visiting active Buddhist sites, or any archaeological site that houses a Buddha image, try to observe the following etiquette:

Clothing Remove your shoes and cap when entering a shrine, temple or stupa courtyard, and wear clothes that cover your knees and shoulders, or bring a sarong to cover yourself. Most Sri Lankans wear white when visiting a Buddhist site, so try to follow suit if possible.

Photos Most temples allow interior photography, but be sure to check. Don't take selfies with a Buddha statue or pose with your back to a statue.

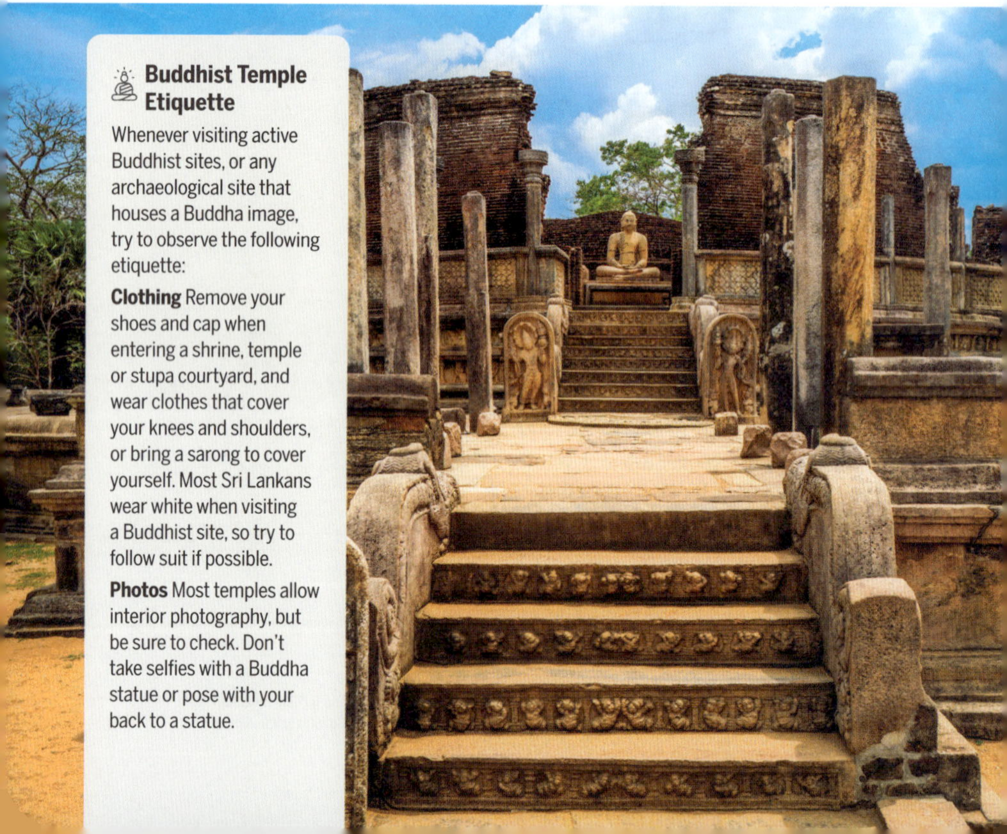

SERGII FIGURNYI/SHUTTERSTOCK

Sea of Parakrama

Polonnaruwa's 25-sq-km water tank is so large that it was named the 'Sea of Parakrama' when built by King Parakramabahu I (r 1153–86). The classiest spot to savour the lake's sunset views is the bar of the **Ekho Lake House**, where Queen Elizabeth II stayed in 1954.

from a long slab of marbled granite. The 7m-tall standing Buddha with unusually crossed arms seems disguised in the rock, while the 14m-long reclining Buddha boasts fabulous toes and a remarkably lifelike stone pillow.

Before leaving the ticketed archaeological site, detour north to see the beautiful Buddhist frescoes of the **Tivanka Image House**, which rival Sigiriya's in their vibrancy and beauty.

Southern Sites

If you fancy some background on Polonnaruwa's ancient architecture, invest an hour in the **Archaeological Museum** outside the main ticketed site, on the banks of the lake Topa Wewa. Just north of here are the ruins of King Nissanka Malla's 12th-century palace, royal baths and **Council Chamber**, whose royal throne atop a stone lion still radiates prestige and power.

Finally head to the south of town to visit the **Potgul Vihara** and its enigmatic 4m-high statue of Parakramabahu I holding the yoke of kinship. Cycle here at sunset to catch beautiful colours over the Topa Wewa.

FROM LEFT: RICHIE CHAN/SHUTTERSTOCK, PAWEL_LUBLIN/SHUTTERSTOCK

Left Quadrangle
Top right Tivanka Image House
Bottom right Gal Vihara

Sri Lanka's Ancient Capitals

TWO CITIES THAT RULED SRI LANKA FOR 1700 YEARS

Sri Lanka's central plains form the cradle of the island's history. Known as Rajarata, the 'Land of Kings', this is where Buddhism took root and where spectacular Buddhist monuments, palaces, monasteries and kingdoms rose and fell, defining Sinhalese culture and leaving a rich, and still relevant, cultural legacy.

Left Kuttam Pokuna, Anuradhapura
Centre Satmahal Prasada, Polonnaruwa
Right Polonnaruwa *vatadage* (circular relic house)

VIDU GUNARATNA/SHUTTERSTOCK

Anuradhapura

Sri Lanka's history emerges from mythology when King Pandukabhaya, an offshoot of the earlier Vijaya dynasty of Tambapanni (p85), established Anuradhapura as his capital in 377 BCE. Around 130 years later the monk Mahinda, son of the Indian emperor Ashoka, converted Anuradhapura's King Devanampiya Tissa (r 307–267 BCE) to Buddhism, setting the direction of both the kingdom and the entire island. The king tied the royal dynasty to the new faith by adopting the title Devanampiya (Beloved of the Gods) and established the first of Anuradhapura's three main monasteries, which would eventually exercise huge influence over the legal, moral and political life of the kingdom. The arrival from India of the sacred Buddha's tooth relic in the early 4th century CE cemented Anuradhapura's rulers as the island's legitimate Buddhist kings.

In return for their aura of semi-divinity, Anuradhapura's kings commissioned a string of spectacular Buddhist stupas: Devanampiya Tissa built Thuparama; King Dutugemunu (r 161–137 BCE) built Ruvanvelisaya and Mirisavatiya; Valagamba (r 103 BCE and 89–76 BCE) built Abhayagiri; and Mahasena (r 276–303 CE), the last 'great' king of Anuradhapura, built Jetavanarama – each king keen to outbuild the last.

Repeated invasions from southern India also shaped the region. Chola kings ruled Anuradhapura several times, including for 44 years under King Elara during the 2nd century BCE, and although kings Dutugemunu, Valagamba and Dhatusena (r 459–77 CE) all managed to overthrow Chola rule and reunify the country from bases in the southern kingdom of Ruhana, the threat remained.

M.L.NUWAN/SHUTTERSTOCK

BOSSA ART/SHUTTERSTOCK

Finally, in 1017, after 1400 years as capital, Anuradhapura was sacked one last time by the Cholas and never recovered. Monks continued to inhabit the city for centuries, until even they abandoned their town-sized monasteries to the jungle.

Polonnaruwa

After overthrowing Chola rule in 1070, Sinhalese King Vijayabahu I (r 1055–1110) shifted his court capital to Polonnaruwa, which served at the island's capital for two centuries.

Under King Parakramabahu I (r 1153–86) the city and indeed country reached its zenith. The king lavished public money on Polonnaruwa, erecting huge buildings, constructing or restoring 165 dams and creating over 1400 reservoirs, including the city's 25-sq-km *wewa* (tank), known as the Parakrama Samudra (Sea of Parakrama).

Parakramabahu I was followed by Nissanka Malla (r 1187–96), who virtually bankrupted the kingdom attempting to match his predecessors' achievements. Much of what you see in Polonnaruwa today dates from these two kings, though you can also spot South Indian influence in the ancient city's half-dozen Shiva and Vishnu *devale* (temples).

A succession of weak rulers, military invasion by the Kalingas of India, and the breakdown of the irrigation system led to the abandonment of the city in 1255, as power and population shifted south and west, away from invading armies from the north. Polonnaruwa was replaced by short-lived capitals at Dambadeniya, Yapahuwa, Kurunegala and Gampola in the 13th and 14th centuries, but none ever again reached the glorious heights of Anuradhapura or Polonnaruwa.

Water Works

Hydraulic engineering may not sound sexy, but it was a science that underpinned the wealth, sophistication and splendour of both Anuradhapura and Polonnaruwa. By the 5th century BCE the central dry zone's many dams, reservoirs and canals had reached such a scale that local legends say they were built with the help of giants and demons.

Through their storage of monsoon rains, the tanks transformed the dry zone landscape, fuelling a second season of food production that in turn spurred massive population growth and boosted revenue for epic construction projects. The irrigation system turbo-charged Sri Lankan civilisation.

41 PILGRIMAGE to a Sacred Tree

BUDDHISM | SPIRITUALITY | ANCIENT STUPA

At its heart Anuradhapura is a sacred Buddhist city whose ancient ruins retain a current sanctity. The spiritual heart of the city is the sacred **Sri Maha Bodhi**, an offshoot of the tree under which Buddha gained enlightenment. Pilgrims flock here to make offerings and recite prayers: join them at dusk for what can be a deeply spiritual experience.

BOYLOSO/SHUTTERSTOCK

How to

When to go Open daily, but *poya* (full moon) nights are most active, especially June's Poson Poya, when thousands of pilgrims come to commemorate the arrival of Buddhism.

What to wear Be sure to wear long trousers or a long skirt, and a top that covers your shoulders. Locals generally wear white. Socks are useful for tender feet.

Cost Free, unlike the main parts of the ancient city, which require a US$30 ticket.

RUWAN WALPOLA/SHUTTERSTOCK

Far left Sri Maha Bodhi
Bottom left Devotees
Left Ruvanvelisaya Dagoba

Sri Maha Bodhi Tree

According to the Buddhist chronicle Mahavamsa, it was in the 3rd century BCE when Princess Sangamitta, daughter of Indian emperor Ashoka, arrived in Anuradhapura carrying a cutting from the original Bodhi Tree at Bodhgaya. The **tree** grown from that cutting has now been tended uninterrupted for 2300 years, making it the oldest tree in the world with a verified planting date, as well as one of the island's most sacred pilgrimage spots.

White-clad pilgrims flock to make offerings of purple lotus blooms on altars here, while orange-robed monks chant at the tree's base and devotees meditate in quiet corners. It's one of the most palpably sacred Buddhist spaces in Sri Lanka, and the quiet devotion on display is moving.

Ruvanvelisaya Stupa

For the full pilgrim experience, continue from the Sri Maha Bodhi compound for five minutes to the huge **Ruvanvelisaya Dagoba**, commissioned by King Dutugemunu (r 161–137 BCE) over two millennia ago as the world's largest stupa, to enshrine a portion of the Buddha's ashes. It remains Anuradhapura's most active Buddhist stupa, and you'll likely be swept along by processions of villagers and traditionally costumed drummers bringing Buddhist texts here for blessing. Dusk is a particularly lovely time to be here, with the stupa spotlit and pilgrims lighting hundreds of oil lamps in the gloaming.

Archaeological Insights

There's nowhere like Anuradhapura. It's partly the city's huge scale and the fact that it was Sri Lanka's first capital, but also that this was the place where Buddhism first took root and was formally taught in Sri Lanka, some 2300 years ago. Ruvanvelisaya is probably my favourite spot – after 2000 years it still has a spiritual feel.

Things are still being unearthed here. Over the last decade we have found over 400,000 beads, which were likely brought as offerings over the centuries by visiting pilgrims.

Lal Dasanayake, *Senior Research Officer of Archaeology at Anuradhapura's Central Cultural Fund.*

42 Anuradhapura's MONASTERIES

GARGANTUAN STUPAS | JUNGLE RUINS | STONE CARVINGS

The sprawling ancient monasteries of Anuradhapura were the island's centre of Buddhist learning for 1300 years, until abandoned to the forest. Visit ruins that once housed thousands of monks and marvel at the ancient world's largest stupas on this tour of Anuradhapura's monastic centres.

EXTRADEDA/SHUTTERSTOCK

Abhayagiri Dagoba

Trip Notes

Getting around Hotels can arrange half-day tuk tuk tours of Anuradhapura's ancient ruins for around Rs 4500.

Cost An Ancient City ticket for Abhayagiri, Jetavanarama and Thuparama costs US$30. Buy tickets at the **Archaeological Museum** or **Jetavanarama Museum**, open 7am to 5pm.

What to bring Hat and water for the heat, plus long trousers or skirt for Buddhist sites. Stands at major monuments sell cold drinks but not much food.

Exploring the Ruins

The various *mula* (colleges) of **Abhayagiri Monastery** cover hundreds of ruined monastic buildings, from meeting halls and refectories (with huge canoe-like troughs filled with rice at meal times) to *bodhigarya* (buildings housing sacred bodhi trees), image houses and even bathing pools and bathhouses. It's a fantastic place to explore.

04 The meeting hall of **Ratnaprasada** is known for its beautiful guardstone, with the nearby semicircular moonstone considered Sri Lanka's finest. Check out the huge nearby **Eth Pokuna** (Elephant Pond).

03 At 75m tall, the **Abhayagiri Dagoba** is the second-largest stupa in Anuradhapura, and marks the epicentre of a monastery once home to 5000 students. Look for the octagonal spire that once topped the stupa.

02 Dating from the 5th century CE, the **Samadhi (Meditation) Buddha** is one of the finest Buddhist statues in Sri Lanka, beloved by Indian prime minister Nehru among others.

05 The oldest stupa in Sri Lanka, the **Thuparama Dagoba** allegedly enshrines the Buddha's collarbone. The concentric circles of pillars surrounding the stupa once supported a conical wooden roof.

01 **Jetavanarama Dagoba**, the world's third-largest monument when built 2300 years ago by King Mahasena, contains 90 million bricks and is surrounded by monastic ruins. The island's first Buddhist teachings took place here.

FROM LEFT: FRANS SELLIES/GETTY IMAGES, TRAVELVIEW/SHUTTERSTOCK

43 Birthplace of Sri Lankan BUDDHISM

PILGRIMS | STUPAS | HISTORY

Mihintale is where Mahinda, the son of Indian emperor Ashoka, converted the king of Anuradhapura Devanampiya Tissa (and by extension the nation) to Buddhism in 273 BCE. The collection of temples and stupas is a great half-day excursion from Anuradhapura, and its Poson Poya festival is a must-attend if here in June.

JAN WILLEM VAN HOFWEGEN/SHUTTERSTOCK

How to

Getting here Mihintale is 12km northeast of Anuradhapura. Buses run frequently, or book a return tuk tuk (Rs 4000).

When to go Poson Poya in June is the most dramatic time to visit. Some backpackers come to watch the sunset from the highpoint of Eth Vihara stupa.

What to wear Long trousers or skirts are required and you should take off your shoes just before arriving at the Ambasthale Dagoba.

HIGH FLIERS/SHUTTERSTOCK

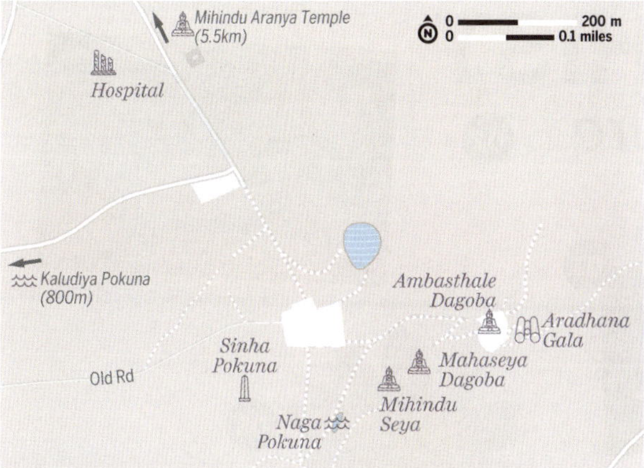

The approach to **Mihintale** is up a wide ceremonial staircase of 2000 steps flanked by beautiful *araliya* (frangipani) trees and is centred around the **Ambasthale (Mango Tree) Dagoba** and **Aradhana Gala** rock, which mark the spots where Mahinda preached to and converted the king.

Further uphill are two ancient stupas: the huge **Mahaseya Dagoba**, said to enshrine the *urna* (third eye) of the Buddha, and the **Mihindu Seya**, thought to contain relics of Mahinda himself.

The real charm of the site comes from its details: the **Sinha Pokuna** (Lion Pool) features a stunning 2m-tall stone lion whose mouth dispensed water for drinking or bathing; while the **Naga Pokuna** (Snake Pool), which feeds it, is named after its decorative cobra carving.

A large monastery complex grew up around Mihintale, meaning there are lots of ruins to explore, including the monks' refectory, meeting hall, relic house and even a hospital, along with many meditation caves.

The site really comes alive during June's **Poson Poya** festival, when thousands of pilgrims stream up the main staircase to pray, chant, make offerings and celebrate the arrival of Buddhism in Sri Lanka. Expect devotional music, a nighttime *perahera* (procession), colourful lanterns and *dansal* stalls offering free food. Free trains normally run from Anuradhapura.

Top left Ambasthale Dagoba
Bottom left Mahaseya Dagoba

Beyond Mihintale

If you have time, be sure to visit **Kaludiya Pokuna** (pictured pp166–7), a lovely artificial pond on the back side of the Mihintale hills, featuring waterside stupas and rock-carved viewing platforms; perfect for a picnic.

Also worth checking out are the remains of Mihintale's 9th-century **hospital**, near the site museum, where monks would have been treated with steam therapy, massages and herbal oil baths.

Half-way between Anuradhapura and Mihintale, the local **Mihindu Aranya Temple** is worth a stop for its astonishing banyan tree and creepy human skeleton in a cage, both used by monks to meditate on the impermanence of existence.

BUDDHIST
Architecture

02

01

03

04

05

06

01 Stupa (Dagoba)
First built to house relics of the Buddha, Sri Lankan stupas come in bubble, bell or 'rice-heap' shapes, below a square top, spire and pinnacle.

02 Sleeping Buddha
Large image of the recumbent, dying Buddha in a state of *paranirvana*, about to enter nirvana.

03 Lotus Flowers
A symbol of purity, given as temple offerings and used as stylised motifs such as the lotus throne of a Buddha statue.

04 Bodhi Tree
Ficus religiosa, a fig tree with heart-shaped leaves under which the Buddha achieved enlightenment.

05 Buddha Feet
The main symbol of Buddhism 2000 years ago, before the now-iconic image of Buddha was created in northwestern India.

06 Buddha Statues
Buddhas come in various positions (sitting, standing) and with various *mudra* (hand positions) indicating protection, teaching or meditation.

07 Sigiriya Frescoes
Iconic female images painted on Sigiriya rock,

07

08

09

10

11

12

depicting either *apsara* (celestial nymphs), courtesans or the bodhisattva Tara.

08 Moonstone
Carved semicircular stone, *sandakada pahana*, at monastery entrances, with concentric bands of elephants, geese and lotus blooms symbolising the cycle of rebirth.

09 Guardstone
A protective figure of Nagaraja (the Snake King) holding a Pot of Abundance *(punkalasa)* and seen at monastery entrances.

10 Squatting Plates
Renunciant monks used these incredibly ornate latrines as a way to show their disdain for life's luxuries.

11 Lion
The symbol of the Sinhalese nation, the lion *(sinha)* is a popular motif of power and protection, commonly seen at royal palaces.

12 Maksara
A mythical protective animal, blending a fish, crocodile and elephant, often on monastery stairways.

01 M.L.NUWAN/SHUTTERSTOCK, **02** ASIF NAWAZ/SHUTTERSTOCK, **03** HYSERB/SHUTTERSTOCK, **04** CK-TRAVELPHOTOS/SHUTTERSTOCK, (LEAF) TASSITA NUMSRI/SHUTTERSTOCK, **05** TAKEPICSFORFUN/SHUTTERSTOCK, **06** JOHN ELK III/GETTY IMAGES, **07** KIRILL SKOROBOGATKO/SHUTTERSTOCK, **08** ALONANOLA/SHUTTERSTOCK, **09** IRYNA RASKO/SHUTTERSTOCK, **10** BRADLEY MAYHEW, **11** GUILLAUME ANGLERAUD/SHUTTERSTOCK, **12** NILA NEWSOM/SHUTTERSTOCK

44 Tour Hidden TREASURES

BUDDHAS | MONASTERIES | FORTRESS

Rent a car or tuk tuk and stop off at a series of little-visited and enigmatic Buddhist and historical sites hidden deep in the forests, mountains and countryside between Anuradhapura and Kurunegala. This is how you get off the beaten track.

HOMO COSMICOS/SHUTTERSTOCK

Aukana Buddha

Trip Notes

Getting around You'll need your own transport to link these historic sites together in one itinerary, though Ridi Vihara and Aukana are accessible by public transport.

When to go Any time. The annual *perahera* (procession; p198) at Ridi Vihara is in August.

What to wear You'll need long trousers or a long skirt to visit Aukana, Sasseruwa and Ridi Vihara; take off your hat and leave your shoes outside when entering a temple.

Offbeat History

There's a lot of history in these offbeat sites. **Yapahuwa** was the island's capital between 1272 and 1284, when King Bhuvanekabahu I of Dambadeniya relocated himself and the sacred Buddha tooth relic here. **Ridi Vihara** (Silver Temple) gets its name from local silver deposits that financed the construction of the **Ruvanvelisaya Dagoba** in Anuradhapura.

01 A deliciously remote-feeling 1100-year-old ruin of a forest retreat, **Ritigala** has a water tank, moat-surrounded meditation hall and monastic bathhouse. It's on the flanks of protected Ritigala peak.

02 The **Aukana Buddha** is a magnificent, 12m-high standing Buddha in *ashiva* (blessing) pose, cut from the surrounding rock face but with a free-standing lotus plinth. Aukana means 'Sun-Eater'.

03 Aukana's twin, **Sasseruva Buddha (Res Vihara)**, is a standing Buddha that was created at the same time and marks a little-visited monastery, whose monks will unlock two chapels with fine Kandy-style murals.

04 A moat-surrounded monastic centre and fleeting 13th-century capital, **Yapahuwa** has an impressive ornamental staircase leading to the summit of a mini-Sigiriya-style rock fortress.

05 For fabulous murals, Buddhist sculpture, an ancient stupa and a short hike to forest views, visit **Ridi Vihara**, a welcoming, active monastery that also offers free accommodation.

FROM TOP: FRANK GOMA/SHUTTERSTOCK, SAIKO3P/SHUTTERSTOCK

Listings

BEST OF THE REST

Archaeological Sites off the Beaten Path

Mandalagiri Vihara

Impressive 7th-century monastic *vatadage* (circular relic house) and hospital ruins, 30km north of Polonnaruwa and a fun half-day excursion from there.

Somawathiya Stupa

Sacred stupa, rarely visited by foreign tourists but said to enshrine another tooth relic of the Buddha. It's 40km northeast of Polonnaruwa and inaccessible during the rainy season.

Aluvihara

Kitsch but historically important group of rock temples, between Dambulla and Matale, where Buddha's teachings were first written down from oral and Sinhalese sources.

Sri Magallena Rajamaha Viharaya

Little-visited rock monastery, 9km from Sigiriya, featuring fabulously exuberant murals inside its two main cave chapels and views towards Pidurangala and Sigiriya from its rock summit.

Something Special

Ridi Vihara Perahera

The lovely Ridi Vihara monastery (p197) celebrates an annual elephant-led *perahera* (procession) in August with dancing and drumming that draws pilgrims up the traditional eastern stairway.

Poson Poya

June's Poson Poya festival celebrates the introduction of Buddhism to Sri Lanka and draws thousands of pilgrims to Mihintale and nearby Anuradhapura, with processions and devotional music.

Sunrise Ballooning

For something special take a dawn balloon flight (srilankaballooning.com) over Kandalama Lake, just east of Dambulla, followed by a post-flight glass of champagne. You might just see elephants from the air.

Rice 'n' Curry

Roy's Villa $$

Food nights at this incredibly popular Sigiriya guesthouse feature regular rice and curry buffets and string-hopper dinners, with a Sri Lankan cooking display every other day.

Hela Bojun Hala Anuradhapura $

Branch of the excellent-value group of food stalls set up by the government and run by local female entrepreneurs (p179), serving traditional local snacks for pennies. It's near the Sri Maha Bodhi car park.

Jaga Food $$

The region's best lunch buffet, including jackfruit, pumpkin, wild mango and meat curries, a few spicy, and excellent for vegetarians; west of Polonnaruwa town.

Bro Restaurant $

A welcoming place in Anuradhapura that serves fabulous 'dolphin *kotthu*', a creamier, tastier, supercharged version of *kotthu* made with paratha bread, milk and cheese.

Rasa Gedara (House of Taste) $

Join Anuradhapura locals for authentic (spicy) Sri Lankan breakfasts and lunchtime rice and curry, served on a lotus leaf. Point to what looks good.

Polonnaruwa Extras

Menik Vihara

Little-visited 9th-century monastery ruins that are fun to track down, including a stupa, relic house, refectory and monk's cells, near the ancient city's main gate.

Pabulu Vihara

The third-largest stupa in Polonnaruwa, built on the orders of Queen Rupavali, wife of Parakramabahu I, and deriving its name from the beads *(pabulu)* found nearby.

Damila Thupa

This gargantuan 12th-century stupa was planned as the world's largest but never completed. It's under excavation and is slowly emerging from the hillside. This is what Polonnaruwa's other stupas looked like two centuries ago.

Anuradhapura Extras

Isurumuniya Vihara

Charming ancient rock temple south of the main ancient city, with pond-side carvings of stone elephants, and famed for its 'Lovers' sculpture and rock-top stupa.

Royal Pleasure Gardens

More charming elephant carvings in two water pools here, and don't miss the enigmatic geometric mandala rock carving claimed by some to be one of the earliest world maps.

Western Monasteries

The scattering of moated *padhanagara* (meditation centres) west of the city was once home to an order of ascetic monks famed for their spectacularly carved squat toilets.

TRABANTOS/SHUTTERSTOCK

Menik Vihara

Citadel

A largely neglected collection: including a monk's refectory, a ruined temple that once held the Buddha's tooth relic, and the royal complex where King Vijayabahu I was crowned in 1055.

Archaeology Museums

Archaeological Museum

This colonial building northwest of the Sri Maha Bodhi Tree is worth a visit for its collection of finds from across the ancient city, including photos of Anuradhapura's stupas before renovation.

Jetavanarama Museum

British colonial building (1937) in Anuradhapura that provides a suitably regal venue for everything from ancient carved urinals to sublime gold and ivory decorations.

Abhayagiri Museum

Commemorates the stay of Chinese Buddhist monk Fa Xian in Anuradhapura (412–13 CE), translating Buddhist texts that he later carried back to China along the Silk Route.

THE EAST

BEACHES | WILDLIFE | SURFING

RESEARCHED BY ANNA KAMINSKI

THE EAST
Trip Builder

Interspersed by white-sand beaches and turquoise lagoons, Sri Lanka's quieter, less-trodden east coast gives you millennia-old seaports, superb surfing, wildlife-rich national parks, mighty centuries-old forts and ancient Hindu temples. The unhurried pace of life adds to the appeal.

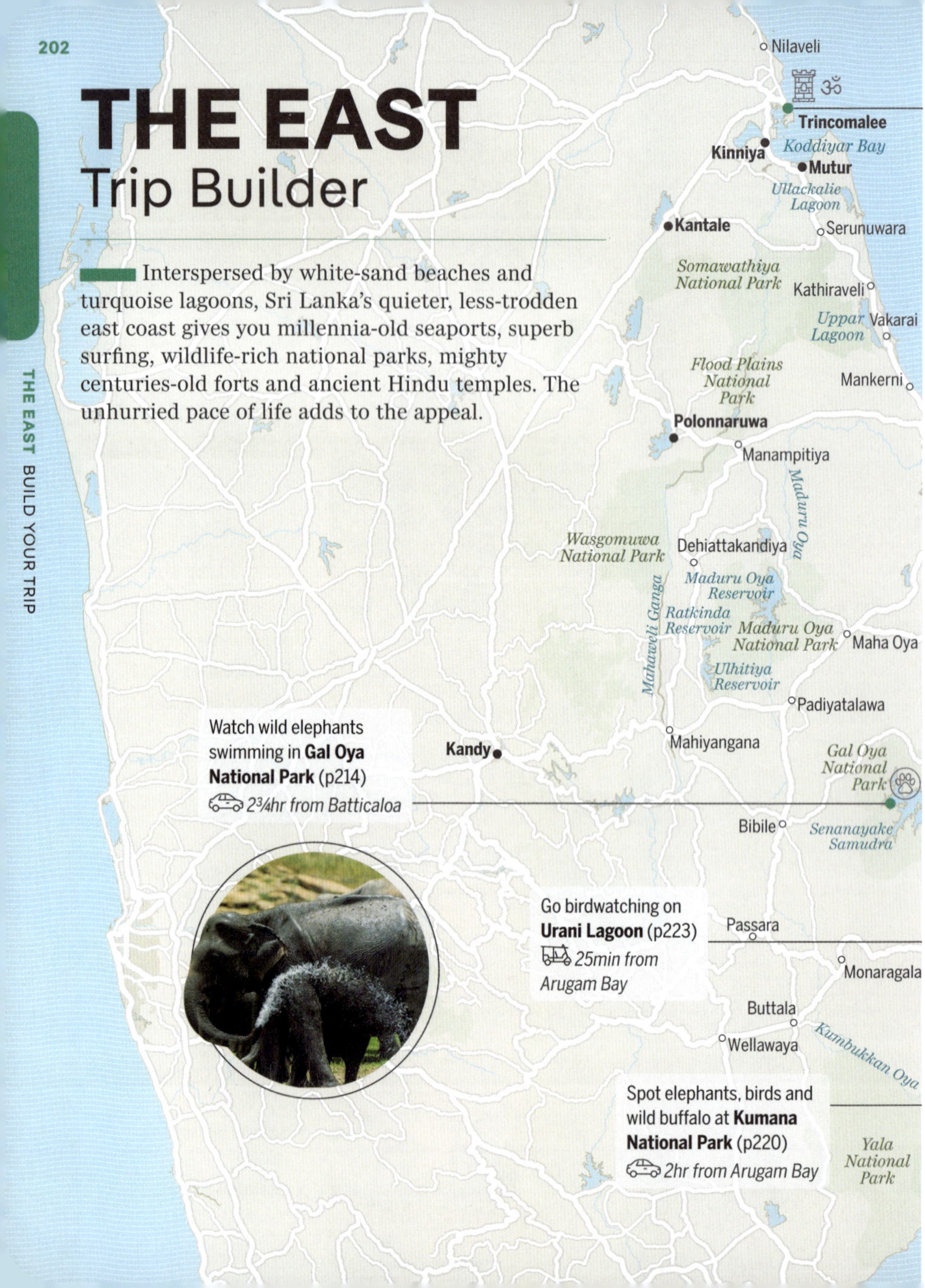

Watch wild elephants swimming in **Gal Oya National Park** (p214)
2¾hr from Batticaloa

Go birdwatching on **Urani Lagoon** (p223)
25min from Arugam Bay

Spot elephants, birds and wild buffalo at **Kumana National Park** (p220)
2hr from Arugam Bay

Wander around Fort Frederick and Koneswaram Kovil in **Trincomalee** (p206)
2½hr from Batticaloa

Laze on the white-sand beaches of **Kalkudah** (p222) and **Passekudah** (p222)
30min from Batticaloa

Explore the Dutch Fort and Heritage Museum in **Batticaloa** (p213)
2½hr from Trincomalee

Ride world-class waves around **Arugam Bay** (p216; pictured pp200–1)
2¾hr from Batticaloa

Contemplate the jungle-fringed **Kudumbigala Monastery** (p218)
1hr from Arugam Bay

CLOCKWISE FROM LEFT: PHOTOS BRIANSCANTLEBURY/SHUTTERSTOCK, JARRETERA/SHUTTERSTOCK, SAIKO3P/SHUTTERSTOCK, MILES ASTRAY/SHUTTERSTOCK
PREVIOUS SPREAD: FRANCESCO RICCARDO IACOMINO/GETTY IMAGES

Practicalities

KARASEV VIKTOR/SHUTTERSTOCK

ARRIVING

Trincomalee Railway Station This central Trinco train station (pictured) receives an overnight train from Colombo. Tuk tuks charge Rs 1500–3500 to take you to your accommodation, depending on whether you're staying in Trinco, Uppuveli or Nilaveli.

Batticaloa Railway Station Centrally located; three daily trains from Colombo. Batti's historic centre is a 10-minute walk away. Tuk tuk fares are around Rs 1500.

HOW MUCH FOR A

Crab curry
Rs 3500

Dosa
Rs 400

Breakfast hoppers
Rs 2500

WHEN TO GO

FEB & MAR
Monsoon gives way to drier, hotter days, ideal for beaches.

APR–JUL
Peak surfing; calm seas for diving and snorkelling.

JUL–SEP
Hot, dry days gather elephants at national park waterholes.

OCT–JAN
Rain and rough seas; many businesses close.

GETTING AROUND

Bus The bus network is extensive and frequent buses connect all the major coastal destinations – Trincomalee, Batticaloa, Arugam Bay – and also smaller inland villages and towns.

Train Trains connect Trincomalee and Batticaloa (via Valachchenai, handy for Kalkudah and Passekudah beaches) to Colombo but not to each other. The Colombo–Trinco train (eight hours) runs overnight, and there are three Colombo–Batti trains (7½ hours), including one overnighter.

Tuk Tuk & Car No matter if it's a five-minute jaunt to a local beach or a two-hour intercity hop, local tuk tuk drivers are always ready to oblige. Visiting Kumana National Park requires a 4WD; tours are easy to arrange in Arugam Bay.

TOP: SANTHOSH VARGHESE/SHUTTERSTOCK
BOTTOM: CHARITH JAYATHILAKE/SHUTTERSTOCK

EATING & DRINKING

Shaped by its deep ties to the sea, spice-rich traditions and centuries-old Tamil, Arab and Sinhalese influences, Sri Lanka's east-coast cuisine is dominated by fresh seafood, with prawns, crabs and cuttlefish appearing in aromatic curries infused with coconut milk, curry leaves and tamarind, alongside grilled fish. Trincomalee and Arugam Bay feature inexpensive beachside restaurants, where you can wash down seafood curry with fresh fruit juices, while Trinco and Batti are renowned for crab curry (pictured top right). Street food includes string hoppers (pictured bottom right) with spicy *sambols*.

Best crab curry
Crab (p223)

Must-try grilled prawns
Nilaveli Moon Restaurant (p223)

CONNECT & FIND YOUR WAY

Wi-fi There are few hotspots, though most accommodation has wi-fi. Stay connected by buying a SIM card (data and unlimited local minutes; at Colombo airport upon arrival).

Navigation Google Maps is reasonably reliable for getting you around. During monsoon season, when some streets and roads in the region get flooded, you'll need to ask locals how to bypass flooded areas.

WHERE TO STAY

Trincomalee, Batticaloa and Arugam Bay are the main urban hubs. Opt for the beaches or national park if you are after tranquillity or wildlife, respectively.

Place	Pros/Cons
Trincomalee	Major city, historical attractions, good transport connections, varied dining. Uninspiring lodgings.
Nilaveli and Uppuveli	Great beaches, snorkelling, diving, whale-watching, seafood restaurants.
Batticaloa	Major city, museum, historical buildings. Dining surprisingly low-key.
Kalkudah and Passekudah	Beautiful beaches. Short on attractions; large, generic resort hotels.
Gal Oya National Park	Wild elephant sightings, boat safaris, birding. Remote; expensive accommodation.
Arugam Bay	Surfing, dining, nightlife, ample lodgings, convenient for Kumana National Park. Can be noisy at night.

WILDLIFE

If cycling long distance on remoter country roads, you might spot a wild elephant (solo elephants are males). Give them a wide berth, as they occasionally charge.

MONEY

Carry plenty of rupees in cash (particularly smaller denominations) to pay in shops and restaurants, and also to pay tuk tuk drivers in locations where Uber Tuk Tuk doesn't work.

45 Secrets of SWAMI ROCK

FORT | TEMPLE | WHALE-SPOTTING

A narrow peninsula separates Trincomalee's Back Bay from Dutch Bay and Koddiyar Bay with its prized Inner Harbour, which European colonial powers fought over for centuries. The peninsula is accessed via 17th-century Fort Frederick, and culminates in the Koneswaram Kovil, sitting atop Swami Rock's 120m cliffs. Dedicated to the deity Shiva, it's among Sri Lanka's most important Hindu temples.

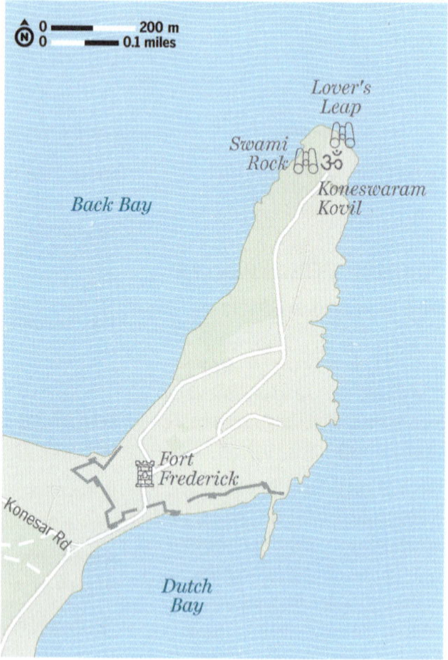

How to

Getting here A paved road runs for 800m from Fort Frederick's gate to the tip of the peninsula; tuk tuks may park some 100m from Koneswaram Kovil.

When to go Trincomalee's dry season is from April to September, when warm and sunny weather makes culture vulturing a pleasure.

Lover's Leap access If the gate near the temple is locked, ask the temple caretaker for the key to access the viewpoint.

A Formidable Fortess

Constructed in 1623 by the Portuguese and seized by the Dutch in 1638, **Fort Frederick** changed hands between the French, the Dutch and the British between 1782 and 1796, and was taken over by the Sri Lankan military post-independence.

To reach Swami Rock's tip, enter through the stone gateway, emblazoned with a British coat of arms and the 'Dieu et Mon Droit' inscription, and proceed past military barracks in the shade of mighty banyan trees, before running the gauntlet of souvenir shops.

A Clifftop Temple

Koneswaram Kovil is the most visited of Sri Lanka's *pancha* (five) *ishwarams*, Hindu temples dedicated to Shiva. Mentioned in Hindu texts around 400 BCE, this place of pilgrimage for the Chola, Pandyan and Pallava dynasties of southern India

PILESASMILES/GETTY IMAGES

consisted of three separate temples and a remarkable thousand-columned hall until its destruction by the Portuguese in 1622 (p209).

Today's temple is a 1963 incarnation with multicoloured *gopuram* (towers), fronted by a massive statue of Shiva. Billowing clouds of incense smoke and rhythmic drumming issues from within. The interior is painted with stories of Shiva, and pride of place is given to the Swayambhu *lingam* – a metre-high circular stone obelisk – reputedly brought here by the demon-king Ravana from Mt Kailash. The 11th-century statue of Shiva's bull, Nandi, stands on the right side of the temple courtyard.

Nearby, a fenced-off walkway leads to **Lover's Leap** with its tremendous coastal views.

Trinco's Whale-Watching Rock

Besides being the location of Trincomalee's two key sights, Swami Rock is also one of the world's best vantage points for spotting sperm whales, spinner dolphins and blue whales. The latter are sighted year-round, but are most likely to be spotted between March and September.

Get up close with the leviathans of the deep by taking a three- to four-hour boat tour (from US$60 per person), typically departing around 6am and organised by various diving outfits (p208). If you're lucky, you'll catch sight of a vast flipper or a giant head, a 30-minute ride from the coast.

Above Swami Rock, near Lover's Leap

46 Underwater WORLDS

SNORKELLING | BEACHES | SCUBA DIVING

The waters of the Indian Ocean around Trincomalee offer some of the best diving and snorkelling in Sri Lanka. At the heart of Pigeon Island National Marine Park lies the eponymous tiny island, around 1km offshore from Nilaveli. It's fringed by the country's healthiest coral, and diving outfits based in Nilaveli, Uppuveli and Trinco itself run daily diving trips there in season.

MATYAS REHAK/SHUTTERSTOCK

How to

Getting here To reach Pigeon Island, hire a boat (Rs 2000 for up to eight people). Reputable diving outfits include DivinGuru (divinguru.com), Poseidon Diving Centre (divingsrilanka.com) and Sri Lanka Diving Tours (srilanka-divingtours.com).

When to go Diving season is from April to September, when the weather is hot and dry, and the waters are calmest.

Budget Snorkelling equipment costs around Rs 1000. Two dives with full equipment rental cost around US$95.

CARLOS J SIERRA/SHUTTERSTOCK

FRANCESCO RICCARDO IACOMINO/GETTY IMAGES

Far left Snorkellers, Pigeon Island
Bottom left Blacktip reef shark
Left Sea turtle

Snorkelling at Pigeon Island

Pay the entry fee (US$45) at the wooden hut on the beach, then choose a boat. Boatmen rent snorkelling equipment of varying quality; alternatively, buy good snorkelling gear from one of Nilaveli's diving outfits. Pigeon Island has no facilities (no toilets!), so bring food and water with you. Use 'sea safe' sunscreen and avoid the roped-off area beyond the beach with its regenerating coral.

Diving Around Trincomalee

Pigeon Island's dive sites are suitable for beginners and are great for spotting abundant sea life, including occasional blacktip reef sharks and green and hawksbill turtles. Highlights include East Rocks, with eel and ray sightings; the North Reef, with Christmas tree tube worms; and the South Reef, with its darting schools of reef fish.

Beyond Pigeon Island, popular dive sites include Coral Island, particularly the leather and sponge corals and anemones of North Reef, home to numerous clownfish; White Rock, replete with different types of stingrays; the beautiful wall of Swami Rock, with its stingrays and groupers; Coral Bay Rock, with its barracuda, stone fish and lion fish; and the advanced cave dives of Navy Island.

Advanced divers may also wish to arrange wreck dives at the 'Underwater Dive Museum' in Trincomalee harbour, featuring the purposely sunk Sri Lankan Navy's *Jagatha* and *Weeraja* gunboats, as well as the wreck of the 18th-century *SS Ava* steamer.

Underwater Treasures

When the Portuguese used **Koneswaram Kovil** as building material for their fort, they unceremoniously dumped temple remains into the sea below Swami Rock. These were discovered in 1957 by sci-fi-maestro-turned-scuba-explorer Arthur C Clarke (author of *2001: A Space Odyssey*) and his diving partner Mike Wilson, who came to Sri Lanka to film marine life.

Clarke chronicled the objects they recovered in his book *The Reefs of Taprobane*. These objects included original stone columns, statues of Ganesh, Chola-era flower friezes and the venerated Swayambhu *lingam* (subsequently enshrined in the present-day temple). Divers are finding temple fragments to this day.

47 Driving North of TRINCOMALEE

TEMPLES | BEACHES | BIRDWATCHING

North of Trincomalee, you encounter the remotest part of the east coast, where crocodile-patrolled lagoons give way to salt pans and dense coastal jungle. Explore its attractions, from hot springs to ancient temples, half-hidden by the limbs of gnarled banyan trees.

LUST N SOUL/SHUTTERSTOCK

Velgam Vihara

Trip Notes

Getting around A leisurely tuk tuk tour from Trincomalee is the easiest way and will set you back around Rs 3000.

When to go April to September is Trincomalee's dry season; hot and sunny days make coastal exploration straightforward. During monsoon season, access roads may be flooded.

Top tip Bring binoculars since there are plenty of opportunities for bird-spotting both at jungle and coastal stops.

Meal Stops

The beachside **Uga Jungle Beach Resort**, 25km north of Trincomalee, makes an excellent stop: non-guests can call ahead to enjoy a set-menu breakfast in a woodland glade. Coming back, opt for a bounty-of-the-sea lunch of giant prawns, crab and grilled fish at the **Nilaveli Moon Restaurant**.

01 Just northwest of Trinco, begin with a local health routine: ablutions at the **Kanniya Hot Springs** – seven pools allegedly created by the sword of demon-king Ravana.

02 Detour into the jungle to behold the 2300-year-old Buddhist complex of **Velgam Vihara**, with its moss-covered stupas and daylight filtered through a canopy of giant fig trees. Fantastic birdwatching, too.

03 Explore the ruins of the promontory-top **Samudragiri Pichchamal Viharaya** Buddhist temple, dating to the 7th century CE, by scaling rock-cut steps, then swim in the shadow of the stupas.

04 Perched on a hilltop offering tremendous coastal vistas, and reachable via zigzagging stone staircases, **Girihandu Seya**, built in the 3rd century BCE, is the oldest Buddhist complex in Sri Lanka.

05 Spy a wealth of pelicans, egrets, herons, the rare black-necked stork and other wader bird species, including migratory visitors from September to April, at the **Kokkilai Bird Sanctuary**.

FROM TOP: PACO COMO/SHUTTERSTOCK, SAIKO3P/SHUTTERSTOCK

48 Historic Sights in BATTICALOA

FORTS | TEMPLES | CHURCHES

Home to Batticaloa's atmospheric old quarter, the island of Puliyanthivu is ideal for exploring on foot or by bicycle. It's where you'll find the city's impressive centuries-old fort and a medley of other historic buildings, including Batti's finest Hindu temple.

PAUL GAPPER/ALAMY

Batticaloa Gate, Mahatma Gandhi Park

Trip Notes

Getting around Walking or cycling is the best way to explore this compact island. If coming here from another part of Batti, take a tuk tuk.

When to go April to September is Batti's dry season, though these summer months can be very hot.

Best view The best lagoon vistas are to be had from the ramparts of the Dutch Fort, accessed via a ladder to the left of the entrance.

Batticaloa's Beginnings

Batticaloa's origins are pretty hazy. It was allegedly settled by the Mukkuvar (Tamil fishermen) from southern India between the 2nd century BCE and the 2nd century CE. According to the *Mattakallappu Manmiyam*, a Tamil historical text, 'Puliyanthivu' refers to the Veddah chief Puliya, who predated the Mukkuvar.

03 Behold the eye-catching bright-blue facade and bell towers of **St Mary's Cathedral**, founded in 1808 by Paschal Mudaliyar, and renovated in 2004 following partial destruction during the civil war.

02 Strung out along Puliyanthivu's north waterfront, **Mahatma Gandhi Park** in centred on the 19th-century Batticaloa Gate, a monument commemorating the 1814 arrival of the first Methodist missionary in Batti.

01 Rebuilt successively by the Portuguese, the Dutch and the British, the 17th-century **Dutch Fort** is renowned for its colonnaded buildings, cannons, watchtowers and a ruined bell tower.

04 Having begun its life in 1873 as a 57-pupil school founded by French Jesuit missionary Francis Xavier Philip, the creeper-clad **St Michael's College** remains a prestigious academic institution.

05 Of Batti's many Hindu temples, **Anaipanthi Sri Siththi Vigneswarar** is the most striking; look out for the magnificent *gopuram* (gateway tower), decorated with a riotous procession of intertwined figures.

FROM TOP: AKANKSHA SINGH/LONELY PLANET, ALAN_LAGADU/GETTY IMAGES

49 Wildlife-Watching in GAL OYA

ELEPHANT-SPOTTING | LANDSCAPES | BIRDWATCHING

Around 20km west of Ampara and 80km southwest of Batticaloa, the little-visited 540-sq-km Gal Oya National Park is nothing short of spectacular. Centred on the island-dotted **Senanayake Samudra reservoir** – Sri Lanka's largest lake – it's a great swath of rainforested hills and craggy granite peaks. Here you have the unique opportunity to spot wild elephants during a boat safari.

FRANCESCO RICCARDO IACOMINO/GETTY IMAGES

How to

Getting here Take a bus from Batticaloa to Ampara, then get a tuk tuk to the village of Inginiyagala – the entrance to the park where you can hire a boat.

When to go From March to July you're most likely to see elephants swimming; November to April is best for birdwatching, coinciding with the migratory season.

Best lodgings **Gal Oya Lodge** (galoyalodge.com) organises boat and jeep safaris and other exciting experiences.

ROBERTHARDING/ALAMY

ISURU UDAYANGA PERERA/SHUTTERSTOCK

Boat Safaris

Gal Oya is Sri Lanka's only non-marine park that is best explored by boat. Arranged through your accommodation, boat safaris (US$65 for two people) let you spot wild elephants from the water and observe without disturbing them. Sailing past a jungle-clad shore and watching a solitary male bathing in the water, or seeing a small herd of females and baby elephants emerging on the grassy bank is nothing short of magical. The boatman cuts the motor and you float on the spot, motionless, while the elephants proceed to feed by knocking a patch of grass with their foot and shaking the dirt off with their trunk, or come to the water's edge to apply mud (elephant sun cream) to their backs.

Boat safaris depart at 6am and 3pm from the bottom of the dam in Inginiyagala village, 21km southwest of Ampara, and last around three hours.

Jeep Safaris

There are two bumpy forest tracks available for jeep safaris within the park, both around 10km long. They are more hit-and-miss when it comes to elephant-spotting, compared to boat safaris (with the exception of the December to February period, when you are likely to see elephants from the two tracks). However, these four-hour jeep safaris are ideal for birdwatchers, since you're likely to spot numerous endemic woodland species. November to April is best for birdwatching, coinciding with the migratory season.

Far left Boat safari
Bottom left Gal Oya Lodge
Left Gal Oya National Park

Walking with the Veddah

Veddahs are Sri Lanka's indigenous people. To learn about their traditional culture, join a jungle walk with a Veddha elder, organised by **Gal Oya Lodge** (galoyalodge.com; $US65 for 2 people).

Walking barefoot, the elder explains the medicinal use of numerous forest plants, demonstrates the use of a sling, shows how to trap animals, and how to use a specific tannin-rich plant to stun fish. Lighting a fire with a flint and tinder from his belt pouch, the elder might also share with you a unique way of preserving meat that involves honey.

50 Surfing ARUGAM BAY

SURFING | SURFING | SURFING

Arugam Bay (pictured below) is one of the world's top surf destinations, and it's easy to see why. The shoreline is a series of headlands that create consistent point breaks; whether you're a beginner or pro surfer, you'll find a wave to suit.

EPIC_SAM/SHUTTERSTOCK

Trip Notes

Getting around Tuk tuk drivers in Arugam Bay are used to transporting boards, with rates around Rs 100 per kilometre.

When to go Surf season is April to September, with the biggest swells in July and August. October means fewer surf days and smaller crowds.

Budget Surfing lessons cost Rs 5500 for 1¼ hours or Rs 9000 for 2½ hours. Board rentals are Rs 3000 for half a day.

Surf Camps & Tuition

Surf camps are a great option if you're a beginner or want everything taken care of. Top surf camps include **Surf & Yoga Arugam Bay** (surfnyogaarugambay.com), with seven-night packages from US$648; and **Banana Surf Camp** (bananasurfcamp.com), with six-night packages from US$600. **Arugam Bay Girls Surf Club** (abaygirlssurfclub.wixsite.com/website) offers women-only tuition.

01 An epic right-hander with a steep takeoff, **Main Point** put Arugam on the global surf map. With summer's peak swells, it fires off heavy, pitching walls with potential barrel sections.

02 If you're a beginner, opt for **Baby Point**, a slow swell with a gentle takeoff off Arugam Bay's southern headland. It's always packed with local surf schools.

03 Learners or intermediate surfers might also consider **Elephant Rock**, a fun right-hander south of Arugam Bay with a mellow takeoff, sandy bottom and consistent rides of up to 75m.

04 **Peanut Farm** consists of two peaks. If you're a beginner, go for the sand-bottomed right-hander close to the beach. Otherwise, hit the more powerful peak, which sometimes barrels.

05 A super-fun wave for shortboarders, **Okanda** awakens with the summer's biggest southeast swells and peels up to 300m along a wall of water you can rip from top to bottom.

FROM LEFT: EPIC_SAM/SHUTTERSTOCK, SHANTI HESSE/SHUTTERSTOCK

51 KUDUMBIGALA Monastic Complex

TEMPLE | CAVE | VIEWPOINT

Some 25km south of Arugam Bay, the site of Kudumbigala Monastery comprises Sigiriya-style outcrops protruding from dense tropical canopy, with over 200 shrines and hermits' caves. The site dates back to the 2nd century BCE and the reign of King Devanampiya Tissa – Sri Lanka's first Buddhist monarch – making it the country's oldest monastic retreat and place of pilgrimage.

ALEXPUNKER/GETTY IMAGES

How to

Getting here It's an hour's drive south of Arugam Bay; tuk tuks charge Rs 5000 return. If coming in a car, you need a high-clearance vehicle for the rough final stretch of road.

When to go It's best to visit during the May to September dry season, early in the morning, avoiding the hottest time of day.

Respectful attire Dress modestly by covering your shoulders and knees when visiting.

THOMAS WYNESS/SHUTTERSTOCK

RAMEES RA / SHUTTERSTOCK

Far left Kudumbigala Monastery
Bottom left Sudasharna Cave
Left Steps near Kudumbigala Monastery

Sudasharna Cave & Madhya Mandalaya

The site of **Kudumbigala Monastery** is 47 sq km big, but the main landmarks can be visited in an hour or so. Follow the footpath into the forest from the car park, passing between huge rocky outcrops. A 10-minute walk brings you to the **Sudasharna Cave** – an overhanging rock shading a small shrine; look for the faint traces of Brahmi script, dating back to the 5th century BCE, as well as a carving symbolising the Triple Gem.

Take the footpath to the left of the cave for another 10 minutes to reach the **Madhya Mandalaya** (Plain of Ruins) – a hilltop featuring a stupa and some other buildings. You may see monks making their way to the communal area; unlike the monks, casual visitors are not allowed inside the prayer hall.

Belum Gala

If you take the footpath to the right of the Sudasharna Cave, you may scale the vast Sigiriya-style rock summit of **Belum Gala**, crowned with a small dagoba. The ancient steps cut into the outcrop date back to the site's 2nd-century-BCE origins and it's a steep, vertigo-inducing slog of 10 to 15 minutes, with only a rough attempt at a handrail. The sacred summit presents you with magnificent views of the forest canopy punctuated by rock outcrops, Helawa Lagoon and the sand-bars that straddle Panama beach. You have to make the climb barefoot, without a hat, sunglasses or camera (store your belongings in a bag).

Triple Gem

The Triple Gem (also known as the Three Jewels) is a reference to the foundation of Buddhist practice – the three core 'refuges' in Theravada Buddhism:

- the Buddha – the Enlightened One
- the Dhamma – the Buddha's teachings; in particular, the Four Noble Truths and the Noble Eightfold Path that leads to liberation from the painful cycle of rebirth
- the sangha – the community of practitioners, with monastic life considered to be the best path for advancing towards enlightenment and the achievement of nirvana.

These are referred to as the 'refuges' because Buddhists 'take refuge' in and look to these three core tenets for guidance and spiritual support.

52 Safaris in KUMANA

ANIMAL-SPOTTING | LANDSCAPES | BIRDWATCHING

Some 30km south of Arugam Bay, the grasslands and riverine forest of the magnificent 357-sq-km Kumana National Park attract a fraction of the visitors of neighbouring Yala and are rich in wildlife such as elephants, buffaloes and crocodiles. Offroad jeep safaris from Arugam Bay also take in the Kumana Bird Sanctuary – important nesting and breeding grounds for over 250 bird species.

ALEXPUNKER/GETTY IMAGES

How to

Getting here Most guesthouses in Arugam Bay can arrange half-day or full-day trips to Kumana National Park; road conditions mean a two-hour drive each way.

When to go February to July is generally dry and good for animal-spotting, with wildlife congregating around water sources. Between May and July you'll see nesting migratory birds.

Budget Expect to pay around US$60/110 for a half-/full-day jeep safari.

PRAMIL THARANGA/SHUTTERSTOCK

YOSHAN KARUNARATNE/SHUTTERSTOCK

Far left Buffaloes
Bottom left Painted storks
Left Spotted deer

Spot Wildlife on a Jeep Safari

Neighbouring the popular Yala National Park, and 37km south of Arugam Bay, **Kumana National Park** (formerly Yala East National Park) is home to wild elephants, buffaloes, spotted deer, crocodiles and wild boar – all of which you may see during a jeep safari. Kumana's forest, grasslands and scrubland, dotted with numerous lagoons, are also inhabited by leopards and sloth bears, though you'd be lucky to catch sight of either. Since Kumana is little visited, you won't feel like you're crowding the wildlife. The birding here is also second to none year-round, though November to April is particularly good for spotting numerous migratory species.

Jeep safaris are easily arranged through your accommodation in Arugam Bay. Choose between a full-day or half-day trip, with the former involving a longer loop around the park. Half-day safaris leave Arugam Bay before dawn to catch the dawn chorus or at 2pm to make the most of the dusk, when the landscape is at its most photogenic and nocturnal animals begin to emerge.

You enter the park via the gate near the fishing settlement of Okanda, 22km south of Arugam Bay, after which the jeep initially follows the main 20km-long coastal track, which takes you past eight lagoons to the mouth of the Kumbukkan River. Much of the wildlife congregates around the lagoons. The southernmost lagoons, Yakala and Kumana, are best for birding.

Kumana National Park Birdlife

Over 255 bird species have been recorded in Kumana National Park, spread across the park's varied terrain of lagoons, ponds, *villu* grassland and riverine forest.

These include the Malabar pied hornbill, often seen hopping along the ground in unison (they mate for life), lesser whistling duck, crested serpent eagle, darter, chestnut-headed bee-eater, coppersmith barbet and the orange-breasted green pigeon.

Endemics include the gorgeous Sri Lanka junglefowl, and there are also large numbers of other crowd-pleasers, such as peacocks, painted storks and pelicans.

Binoculars and a copy of *Birds of Sri Lanka*, by Gehan de Silva Wijeyeratne, greatly enhance the experience.

Listings

BEST OF THE REST

Museums

Heritage Museum

Batticaloa's excellent museum explores the history of Arab traders and their impact on the local and national culture, including the spread of Islam in Sri Lanka. Dioramas and period objects abound.

Maritime & Naval History Museum

Trincomalee's fine museum inside a 17th-century Dutch residence focuses on Sri Lankan naval history since Marco Polo's time; underwater finds include Chinese ceramics, coins and an 8m-long artillery cannon.

Hindu Temples

Kali Kovil

This superbly painted Hindu temple in Trinco stands out for its remarkable *gopuram* (gateway towers) featuring coloured plasterwork with delightful details: a smiling lion, a medal-sporting peacock, bunches of bananas...

Buddhist Temples

Maligawila Monastic Complex

Shaded by magnificent banyan trees near Maligawila, these extensive remains of a 7th-century Buddhist monastery feature two well-preserved giant statues: the 10m-high Maitreya Bodhisattva and an 11m-tall Buddha.

Buddangala Raja Maha Viharaya

Rising above the forest north of Ampara, this 150m-high hill features an 1800-year-old Buddhist temple, with one of Buddha's teeth housed inside the dagoba and a museum within an ancient cave overhang.

Mosques

Al-Aqsa Mosque

Step inside Batticaloa's replica of Jerusalem's Dome of the Rock and admire the stained-glass windows, giant chandelier and the magnificent cupola, with its intertwined green, crimson and gold geometric shapes.

Ancient Wedding Sites

Magul Maha Vihara

At this 5th-century BCE wedding site, some 14km northwest of Arugam Bay, admire the *poruwa* (wedding platform), the *vatadage* (circular relic house) and the unique moonstone, depicting an elephant ridden by a mahout.

Beaches

Kalkudah Beach

Set against a backdrop of coconut trees and cashew plantations, the idyllic, long golden sweep of Kalkudah Beach is largely shadeless and good for swimming during dry season.

Passekudah Beach

Windsurfing and snorkelling are some of the water sports on offer at the white-sand, palm-fringed Passekudah Beach. Experienced scuba divers may want to check out several wrecks in Passekudah Bay.

Uppuveli Beach

Laze beneath the coconut trees on this wide, honey-coloured swath of sand. Rub shoulders with local fishers and go for a swim (unless red flags are flying, warning of strong currents).

Nilaveli Beach

Nilaveli's 4km-long, largely unpeopled sandy beach is one of Sri Lanka's finest; go beach-combing, sunbathe, or hire a boat to take you to Pigeon Island for excellent snorkelling.

Kallady Beach

Batticaloa's wave-battered, casuarina-edged Kallady Beach is lined with traditional fishing boats and sports reminders of the deadly tsunami of 2004: a ruined church belltower and prominent memorials to victims.

Seafood Restaurants

Crab $$$

Romance your seafood-lovin' sweetie at this romantic spot at Trincomalee's Trinco Blu. The superb crab curry is worth every penny.

Dhuwana Restaurant $$

Devilled cuttlefish, seafood *kotthu* and fresh catch of the day with fiery *sambols* titillate your palate at this cheerful, family-run restaurant on the waterfront near Trincomalee's Fort Frederick.

Nilaveli Moon Restaurant $$

A friendly little spot near Nilaveli Beach; order the whole barbecued fish, crab curry or giant grilled prawns.

Nature Huts $$

Curried crabs, succulent giant prawns fresh off the grill and other creatures of the sea star at this unassuming place 300m from Kalkudah Beach.

Sketch $$

After a day in the ocean in Arugam Bay, fortify yourself with fish *rotti* or splurge on crab curry with its attendant constellation of veggie curries.

Gecko $$

Local fish and seafood are given the Aussie spin at this laidback Arugam Bay joint; you'll find yourself returning for the amazing fish tacos.

Cooking Classes

Cooking with Mona

Craft spice concoctions from scratch with Arugam Bay's surfer Mona at her home kitchen. Learn which curries need added water and which don't and grate coconut for a fiery *sambol*.

Wildlife Experiences

Urani Lagoon

Join Eco Tourism Center Urani for a birdwatching excursion on a lagoon near Pottuvil, float on a catamaran along a mangrove-lined channel, and spot woolly-necked storks, herons, swamp hens and egrets.

Lahugala Kitulana National Park

Take a short walk from the A4 road to the viewpoint overlooking Lahugala Tank at the Lahugala Kitulana National Park, and watch wild elephants feeding on its shores.

Wilderness Lodges

Gal Oya Lake Club $$$

Luxury safari camp comprising individually styled thatch-roofed rooms near a bird-filled lake, perfect for twitchers with binoculars. Occasional visitors include fishing cats and giant squirrels.

Gal Oya Lodge $$$

The wood-and-thatch bungalows on a jungle plot within Gal Oya Valley National Park are visited by local wildlife. Scale nearby Monkey Mountain for amazing views of the park.

THE NORTH

TEMPLES | TAMIL FOOD | ISLANDS

RESEARCHED BY ZINARA RATHNAYAKE

THE NORTH
Trip Builder

Little visited, the Tamil-populated North is a region with heart, soul and abundant hospitality. Relish delicious, seafood-heavy feasts, cycle the culturally rich towns and retreat to offshore islands. Scattered around are sacred Hindu temples, fisheries, fresh-produce markets and birdlife-rich lagoons.

Practicalities

ARRIVING

Regular buses run between Jaffna and Colombo, including nighttime air-con coaches. A few buses to Trincomalee. Five trains daily operate to/from Colombo, and daily flights to/from South India's Chennai.

CONNECT

Wi-fi can be slow, so load up your local SIM (Dialog is preferred) with data to use navigation apps.

MONEY

Draw out cash before heading to small villages and offshore islands. Save money by taking local buses.

WHERE TO STAY

Town	Pros/Cons
Jaffna	Central to sights and transport; mix of luxe hotels and family-run homestays. Can get noisy.
Neduntivu (Delft)	Tented camps and guesthouses on a rustic offshore island. Limited ferries.
Mannar	Ideal for birdwatchers. Short on accommodation and restaurants.

GETTING AROUND

Tuk tuk or car Best way to explore; book through PickMe and Uber, or negotiate the fare with a driver.

Bus Connects Jaffna bus stand with small towns, Mannar, and Kurikadduwan ferry terminal.

Ferry Every 30 minutes (7.30am to 6pm) to/from Nainativu; four times daily to/from Neduntivu.

TOP: SANTHOSH VARGHESE/SHUTTERSTOCK
BOTTOM: NS NATURAL QUEEN/SHUTTERSTOCK

EATING

The North's cuisine varies remarkably from the rest of the island, with a mix of roasted, powdered spices flavouring specialties like crab, paired with *puttu* (steamed cylinders of rice flour and grated coconut; pictured top left). Snacks made from the palmyra palm are particularly loved. Look for *odiyal koozh* (seafood stew) and sweet *karthakolomban* mangoes (pictured bottom left).

Best breakfast
Lavin's (p229)

Must-try lunch
Amudham (p240)

JAN–MAR
Excellent time to visit. Migratory birds; kite and harvest festivals.

APR–JUN
Humid days, but with April New Year festivities.

JUL–SEP
Busiest time around the 25-day Nallur Festival.

OCT–DEC
Rainy season eases in December with slightly cooler, sunny days.

53 Tamil Tastes of JAFFNA

MARKETS | COOKING CLASS | TODDY

The strong cultural epicentre of Sri Lankan Tamils, Jaffna opens a window into the North's distinctive flavours, textures and feasts. It's here that uncles and aunties dig into plates of dosa and sip cups of sweet, frothy coffee; families gather in the backyard to prepare seafood stews; and fishing boats sail off at night to bring the bounties of the ocean.

S KUMAR KARAMANA/SHUTTERSTOCK

How to

Getting around Jaffna is easily accessible. You can walk, cycle, rent a motorbike, or hop on a tuk tuk through Uber or PickMe.

When to go Breakfast and dinner.

Reserve A local chef sets up a live kitchen in his backyard at **Tiki Jaffna**, preparing seafood and meat dishes to pair with classics like *idiyappam* (thin, steamed rice-flour mats).

Don't leave without Sipping palmyra toddy.

IAN FLEMING/ALAMY

Rooted in Earth's Abundance

Palmyra These palms are woven into local life and every part is put to use. Grounded sprouts thicken spicy seafood stews, and the flower's sap is boiled down to prepare sweet jaggery. At **Jaffna Market**, look for *kotta kilangu* (palmyra sprouts) and *nungu* (young palmyra fruit); drink the water, and eat the jelly-like flesh.

Toddy The fresh, mildly alcoholic sap extracted from the palmyra flower is a traditional – although disappearing – part of Jaffna's life, particularly among men. See tappers climb tall trees to collect the sap in **Manipay** by joining a tour with **Explore Yarl** (exploreyarl.com).

Seafood Every morning before 9am, locals flock to the **Kakkaitivu** and **Passaiyoor** fish markets, filled with loud calls of fishers auctioning the day's catch. Seafood is fried or made into stews and curry; sample them at **JAC Dining** or **Amudham**, and make them from scratch with **Jaffna Culinary Journey**.

Breakfast traditions South India influences are evident, with *idli* (steamed rice cakes) served with chutney and sambar (lentil-vegetable stew) and washed down with a cup of sugary coffee – get breakfast served on banana leaves at **Lavin's** (next to Thirunelveli Market). The women-run live kitchen **Ammachi Traditional Food Center** (Palali Rd) serves specialties like *kundu* dosa (fermented rice and lentil balls) and *paal appam* (bowl-shaped pancakes). These are also a dinner meal – grab them at **Thevshi Kutty Hoppers**, after 4.15pm.

Top left Palmyra sprouts
Bottom left Traditional Jaffna meal with crab curry

Jaffna's Very Own Cuisine

Our cuisine is rooted in our culture and celebrated for its rich aroma. You need to try *nandu kulambu*, crab curry with fresh drumstick leaves, and the mutton curry, prepared with organic meat that delivers exceptional flavour. We love roasted red rice string hoppers and *puttu* for their fragrance.

Vegetarian dishes are equally celebrated, from *kaththarikai piraddal* (fried eggplant curry) to *karunai kilangu piraddal* (elephant yam curry), *murukankai kari* (drumstick curry) and *rasavalli kanchi*, a purple-yam dessert. A cup of *chukku* coffee, a caffeine-free herbal drink, completes the experience.

Karthiga Athiththan, *a Jaffna local, hosts cooking classes at Jaffna Culinary Journey (+94 77 160 6322)*

Northern **ICONS**

03

01

02

06

05

04

01 Gopuram
This imposing, sculpture-covered tower at the entrance of the North's Hindu shrines is a unique feature of Dravidian temple architecture.

02 Palmyra Tree
A palm (the 'tree of life') used for roofing, timber, food and craft material.

03 Toddy
A favourite pastime drink, toddy is the mildly alcoholic sap of the palmyra flower, typically served in small toddy shops.

04 Jaffna Library
Set on fire by Sinhalese mobs in 1981, erasing rare Tamil history literature, the rebuilt library is a strong symbol of Tamil identity.

05 Greater Flamingo
These migrants – the largest and most widespread among flamingos – arrive in their thousands to the North's wetlands, escaping harsh winters.

06 Crab Curry
Fragrant spice blends heavy on fennel, cardamom and nutmeg flavour the North's most iconic coconut-based crab, garnished with drumstick leaves.

07 Nallur Festival
This 25-day celebration with colourful chariot

processions honours the residing Hindu god Murugan of Nallur Kandaswamy Temple.

08 Karthakolomban
Jaffna is known for these sweet, velvety mangoes, particularly from May to August. Also spelled *karutha kolamban.*

09 Puttu
Steamed tubes of rice flour layered with freshly grated coconut, this evergreen breakfast and dinner staple is best paired with crab curry.

10 Vadali
Across villages, you'll see these traditional fences guard local homes. They are made of dried palmyra palm fronds, creating natural patterns.

11 Jaffna Fort
In 1792 the Dutch expanded the Portuguese-built 17th-century fort with shielding triangles to create the star-shaped structure, surrounded by a moat.

12 Jaffna Curry Powder
This deep, smoky spice mix is prepared by grinding dry roasted whole spices like coriander, fennel, curry leaves and black peppercorns.

01 THOMAS WYNESS/SHUTTERSTOCK, **02** DEVAKA SENEVIRATNE/SHUTTERSTOCK, **03** SANTHOSH VARGHESE/SHUTTERSTOCK, **04** SEANKELLYPIX/SHUTTERSTOCK, **05** ASIRI62/SHUTTERSTOCK, **06** JONATHAN STOKES FOR LONELY PLANET, **07** THE ROAD PROVIDES/SHUTTERSTOCK, **08** SLCRAZYARTIST/SHUTTERSTOCK, **09** AALA IMAGES/SHUTTERSTOCK, **10** AMILA RANASINGHE/SHUTTERSTOCK, **11** ALEXPUNKER/GETTY IMAGES, **12** 3RD AXIS/SHUTTERSTOCK

54 Faith, History & HERITAGE

TEMPLES | HOLY SPRINGS | FORTS

Despite enduring a near 30-year civil war, contemporary Jaffna feels full of life. Delve into the region's history and traditions by exploring the colourful temples, sacred pools and colonial-era forts in and around Jaffna. Before the arrival of European powers, ancient Tamil dynasties ruled the region, with suburban Nallur being the capital of medieval kingdoms.

DAILY TRAVEL PHOTOS/SHUTTERSTOCK

How to

Getting around Most sights are connected by bus. Otherwise, consider booking a tuk tuk or renting a motorbike to explore at your own pace.

When to go Visit sights in the morning before the scorching sun. Go to Jaffna Fort for sunset views. The grand Nallur Festival falls in July/August.

Cycling A great way to explore the leafy lanes of Nallur, but look out for motorcycles and cars.

LEAGUTRAVELS/SHUTTERSTOCK

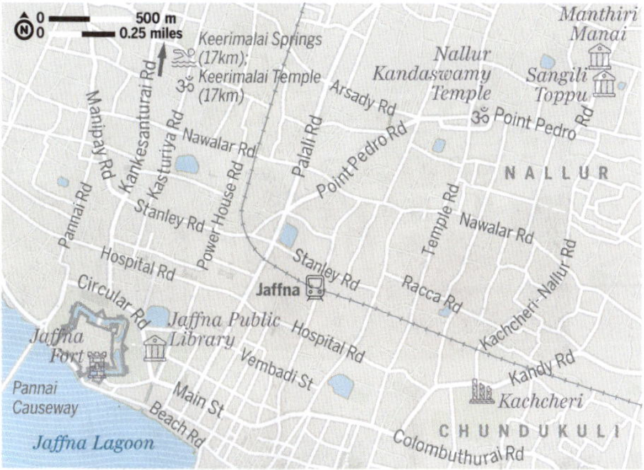

The Pilgrims' Trail

Temple visit Jaffna is peppered with Hindu temples, but if you visit just one, go to **Nallur Kandaswamy Temple** (nalluran.com). Visit during prayers (10am, noon, 4pm, 5pm, 6pm), when devotees bring flowers, fruits and coconuts as offerings, entering through a five-storey gilded, ornate tower with Dravidian architectural influences.

Sacred baths About 30km north of Jaffna are two striking azure pools by the ocean at **Keerimalai Springs**, filled with natural fresh water. For locals, it's holy and curative. Nearby is one of the region's oldest shrines, **Keerimalai Temple** (pictured pp224–5).

History Lessons

Rampart walk Locals gather at the walls of **Jaffna Fort** for sunset overlooking the lagoons and the Indian Ocean. Built by the Portuguese in 1618, and later expanded by the Dutch using a mix of stone, brick, mortar and coral, this pentagonal fort surrounds a moat once filled with crocodiles; walk along the ramparts and look for coral patterns. It was the scene of several battles during the civil war, reducing the interiors to crumbling masonry. Nearby, stop at the **Jaffna Public Library** housed in a three-domed building, a mark of Tamil history and resilience.

Royal footprints Strewn across Jaffna are crumbling ruins of the medieval Tamil kingdoms and colonial-era buildings. Examples include the **Kachcheri** near Old Park; the former minister's house **Manthiri Manai**, which dates back to 15th or 16th century; and the restored entrance of the royal palace, **Sangili Toppu**.

Top left Keerimalai Springs
Bottom left Kachcheri

Nallur Kandaswamy Temple Festival

Although the Portuguese destroyed the original Kandaswamy temples, the Dutch period saw the construction of the present temple in 1734. It is Sri Lanka's most prominent Hindu shrine.

The temple's annual 25-day festival – Sri Lanka's longest – takes place in July, August or September, with devotees from across the world coming to Jaffna. This vibrant celebration honours Hindu god Murugan, with devotional music, drumming and chariot processions around town, where images of deities are paraded in decorated vehicles.

Worshippers engage in acts of penance and self-mortification to express their deep reverence, including rolling on earth and piercing their flesh with metal hooks.

01 On **Karaitivu**, **Casuarina Beach**, named after the casuarina trees that line the soft sand, is a local favourite. Drive west to the British-era **Kovilam Lighthouse**.

02 Take a five-minute boat ride to stroll the coral-built walls of the Dutch-era **Fort Hammenhiel**, now turned into a navy-managed accommodation. It was once used to imprison communist leaders.

03 Jump on the ferry to **Nainativu** to visit **Nagapooshani Amman Temple** with four *gopuram* (gateway towers), the tallest at 33m. Walk 10 minutes south to **Nagadeepa Buddhist Temple**, believed to be a site Buddha visited.

05 Traverse the largely deserted **Mandaitivu** by tuk tuk, where wetlands conceal flocks of spoonbills, painted storks, lesser whistling ducks and even greater flamingos, best from November to April.

04 Cycle **Neduntivu**'s peaceful paths passing coral-fenced homes (pictured) and occasional traffic jams of cute goats. Visit Dutch-era ruins, walk inside a baobab tree, laze on empty beaches and sleep in a tented camp.

FROM TOP: TRABANTOS/SHUTTERSTOCK, THOMAS WYNESS/SHUTTERSTOCK
PREVIOUS PAGE: DARKYDOORS/SHUTTERSTOCK

56 Birds of MANNAR

FLAMINGOS | LAGOONS | BIRDWATCHING

Scattered around Sri Lanka's North are islets, sandbanks, lagoons, grassbeds and salt marshes, drawing native and migratory birds for feeding and breeding. Birdwatchers have plenty of company: pairs of spot-billed ducks; rare yellow-and-black songbirds found nowhere else; and huge flocks of greater flamingos forming in Mannar's wetlands, stopping by here along the Central Asian Flyway.

PRAMIL THARANGA/SHUTTERSTOCK

How to

Getting here and around Buses connect Mannar Island with Jaffna and Colombo; hire a tuk tuk to go around.

When to go The migratory bird season runs from November to April, reaching a peak around February.

Landmines Some of the North's landmine-laid waterbodies, like the Thondamanaru Lagoon on Jaffna peninsula, kept humans away from the wetlands during and after the nearly three-decade war, turning these places into crucial bird habitats.

ISURUMAAN WEERAWARDANA/SHUTTERSTOCK

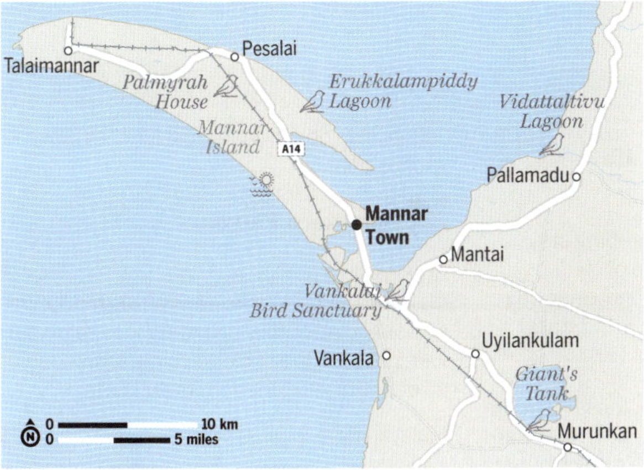

Top left Flamingos, Mannar
Bottom left Giant's Tank

Bird sanctuary Mannar's unique ecosystems are teeming with birds, particularly the sanctuary at **Vankalai Lagoon** in mainland Mannar, connected to Mannar Island via a causeway. During the birdwatching season, the mudflats, waterholes and seagrass beds at Vankalai conceal over 20,000 waterbirds. Among them are wading Eurasian spoonbills with their spatula-like bills, painted storks, sandpipers and, of course, flamingos. Marked as an important wetland by Ramsar, it's also home to marine turtles, saltwater crocodiles and rare dugongs.

Go around in a tuk tuk. Along the causeway, you'll find a birdwatching tower offering excellent views of the surrounding marshes. Other noteworthy spots include the **Erukkalampiddy Lagoon**, **Vidattaltivu Lagoon** and **Giant's Tank**.

Greater flamingos These gorgeous birds with their brushstrokes of reddish pinks and long, curved beaks lure visitors to an otherwise quiet, arid, wind-swept region, cut off from the world for decades during the war. Flamingos arrive in their thousands to Mannar's salt pans, beginning from November and reaching a peak in February, fleeing the harsh winters of the Indian state of Gujarat and beyond.

Birdwatching tours The region's birdlife is best explored by joining a tour. We highly recommend the Mannar-based naturalist Marynathan Edison at **HE4US Flamingo Guides** (+94 77 525 9550), who hosts flamingo-watching experiences. Mannar's only high-end hotel **Palmyrah House**, too, has guided tours with resident naturalists, and a 500m walkway through the surrounding wetland is ideal for birdwatchers.

Flamingo-Watching with an Expert

The flamingo season usually starts in November and ends in April. These months can change from time to time, but the flamingos always stay for six months.

Greater flamingos arrive in their thousands to our wetlands. They get their beautiful pink from the pigments in their diet, from things like algae and brine shrimp.

If flamingos arrive in Mannar's wetlands in November, February would be the best time to visit – by then they are well-fed and their pink colours are more visible. And when they just arrive in Sri Lanka, they are generally a little shy. It takes a month or so for them to get settled.

Marynathan Edison, *a Mannar-based coastal and marine environmentalist*

Listings

BEST OF THE REST

Camping & Island Life

Delft Village Stay

Everyone loves this no-frills camping stay on the remote coral-reef island of Neduntivu for its home-cooked food, groundwater well baths, sunset boat rides and cycling trails.

Borassus Nature Huts

Close to the sea in Mandaitivu, these wooden huts with thatched roofing in a palm grove are the best place to escape Jaffna's buzz, but are still only a 30-minute drive from the centre.

Learn Something New

Explore Yarl Cooking Class

Join a Jaffna aunty to prepare everything from crab curry to condiments like *pol sambol* (red-hot side dish of grated coconut, chilli and spice) at her home set in a leafy garden, and relish delicious lunches served on banana leaves.

Jaffna Culinary Journey

Learn to handscrape coconut and hand-press red rice flour into thin, noodle mats to prepare *idiyappam* with lawyer and home chef Karthiga Athiththan for dinner. Hosted at her restored heritage home.

Dilakshiya Pottery

Get behind the potter's wheel to learn the craft with artisanal potters at this fourth-generation pottery factory. You can buy souvenirs to take home from the adjacent shop.

Catumaran

Watch local women prepare *odiyal koozh* (seafood stew) at this woman-owned heritage boutique stay in Vaddukoddai, 13km from Jaffna. Also does banana leaf lunches. Reservations only.

Northern Flavours

Rio $

It's almost forbidden to say you visited Jaffna without going to this legendary ice-cream parlour; get the Rio Special, a colourful sundae loaded with jelly, dried fruits and nuts.

Malayan Café $

An old-school local favourite with a hand-written chalkboard menu. Gets busy during breakfast with ghee-loaded dosa and soft, spongy *idli* (steamed rice cakes).

Amudham $$$

This 3rd-floor restaurant at the luxury hotel Thinnai offers a crash course on Jaffna's bold, flavourful cuisine; sample classics like *thirukkai meen kulambu* (stingray slow-cooked in a tangy tamarind base) and country chicken dry curry.

Fox Jaffna $$$

Housed in a home once used as the intelligence headquarters by the LTTE, the boutique

ALANMORRIS/SHUTTERSTOCK

Rio

hotel's restaurant serves crab and mutton curry paired with *puttu* (cylinders of steamed rice flour and grated coconut) for dinner.

Spice of Jaffna $$

This small stall at the Cargills supermarket building's food court serves perhaps Sri Lanka's best *kotthu* (chopped *rotti* mixed with veggies, spices and meat).

Thevshi Kutty Hoppers $

Expect long queues at this unpretentious, roadside stand serving hoppers (bowl-shaped pancakes, aka *appam*) by the A9 Hwy. Sample the variety of hoppers, topped with chicken, prawns, cheese and coconut milk.

Tiki Jaffna $$$

Set out for an evening of interesting tales about northern life at chef-host Daniel's live kitchen in the backyard of his Jaffna home. The seafood and mutton dinners are fabulous.

Cakes & Brews

Zoco $$

Friends, couples, families and solo diners all gather at this popular waffle house. Sweet waffles aside, it also does delicious brownies, shakes, burgers and savoury waffle pizzas.

Kasun's Karma $$

Set in a tranquil garden with coconut palms and vines, this charming cafe serves Jaffna's best coffee. It's brewed from island-grown beans – also for sale on the racks!

Engada SPOT $

This local favourite in Manipay, 8km from Jaffna, is open until midnight. The menu is full of delicious cakes, crepes and ginger-infused tea.

Vijitha Cakes $

Choose from just-baked butter cakes, soft chocolate pastries and Jaffna's version of

KAVINDU R DE SILVA/SHUTTERSTOCK

Hoppers (bowl-shaped pancakes)

South Indian milk-based sweets at this local bakery-cafe.

Go on a Tour

Ellalan Tourism

The community from Jaffna's small fishing hamlet Guru Nagar runs educational tours of the vast lagoon, taking you to sea-cucumber farms. It also sets up beach picnics with barbecue on deserted strips of the peninsula.

Explore Yarl

Jaffna-born tour guide Arun Raj brings deep knowledge to his tours, which take you to the Nallur Kandaswamy Temple, Neduntivu, Nainativu, curative baths, caves and blue water wells scattered around town.

Adampan Organic Farm

In 2010 Nagesh Uruthiramoorthy returned home from Europe after 30 years (right after the end of the war) to run a self-sufficient farm two hours south of Jaffna, growing 42 rare, indigenous rice varieties. He's always happy for you to tag along on a farm tour. It's also possible to stay at the farm.

Practicalities

Right Nine Arches Bridge (p128)

GUARD
LUGGAGE

EASY STEPS FROM THE AIRPORT TO THE CITY CENTRE

For most visitors to Sri Lanka, Bandaranaike International Airport (BIA; pictured), a 40-minute ride north of Colombo, is the primary point of entry. Both departure and arrival terminals are in the same building. The airport serves over 50 international destinations directly across Asia, Oceania and Europe, and connects to other destinations in Europe, North America and Africa largely via transit hubs in the Middle East.

AT THE AIRPORT

SLSK PHOTOGRAPHY/SHUTTERSTOCK

SIM CARDS

SIMs and eSIMs are available at the arrival hall at BIA. Dialog and Mobitel have the fastest, widest coverage (from $4). International eSIMs purchased online, although pricier, can be more convenient, since you can activate them the moment you land.

CURRENCY EXCHANGE

There are 24-hour, 365-day Bank of Ceylon currency-exchange counters at the departures lobby, arrival hall and international transit area before the departure gates. Find better rates at banks and official exchange outlets in the city.

WI-FI

There's 30-minute free wi-fi available at BIA arrival and departure halls. Select #FreeWiFi@BIA. Can be spotty and slow.

ATMS

These are available at arrivals and departures.

CHARGING STATIONS

Very limited at both arrivals and departures. You'll also find a few scattered charging sockets here and there.

CUSTOMS REGULATIONS

Duty-free goods From outside Sri Lanka, limits include 1.5L of spirits, 2L of wine and 0.25L of perfumed spirits. Bringing any type of tobacco, including cigarettes and cigars, is prohibited.

Currency Money in any form amounting to US$15,000 or more, as well as gemstones carried in passenger baggage, has to be declared at customs.

GETTING TO THE CITY CENTRE

Rideshare Use Uber or PickMe, Sri Lanka's homegrown ride-hailing app that works similarly. Typically more cost-effective than taking taxis. Fares range from US$12 to US$16 and take 30 to 50 minutes (excludes highway tolls). Kangaroo has better cars and service, but pricier.

Bus Air-con buses (Bus no 187) run to/from Colombo Fort Stand 24 hours a day via Colombo–Katunayake Expressway. Buses stop at the outer porch of the departure terminal, which is easily walkable from the arrivals. A one-way journey costs Rs 290 and typically takes 50 minutes.

HOW MUCH FOR A...

Rideshare
US$12–16
30–50min

Bus 187
Rs 290
50min

Airport taxi
Rs 6570
30–50min

SLTB bus Air-con expressway coaches run five times a day to/from Makumbura (19km from Colombo), from where expressway buses run to Galle, Matara and elsewhere.

Taxi Airport taxis have a fixed rate. Prepay and book your ride at the taxi kiosk at the arrival hall. Typically costs more than ride-hailing services.

Cash For bus tickets, pay the conductor. Sri Lanka is rolling out card and Google Pay for public transport, but it's currently limited to a few buses departing from Makumbura.

Ride-hailing Pick-up and drop-off areas are directly outside airport arrivals and departures.

Highway toll Pay with card or cash at the toll gates.

OTHER POINTS OF ENTRY

Jaffna International Airport (JAF) A more convenient entry point for travelling to both Sri Lanka and India. Indian low-cost airline IndiGo operates daily flights from Chennai (in India) to the airport in Palali, 18km from Jaffna in Sri Lanka's north. Flights also run to/from the South Indian city Tiruchirappalli (Trichy) on Tuesdays, Thursdays and Saturdays. To get to/from JAF, book a taxi via your accommodation.

Mattala Rajapaksa International Airport (MRIA) Mostly only open to chartered flights or a few seasonal commercial flights from Russia and East European countries during peak tourist season.

Ferry to/from Kankesanturai (KKS) This runs from South India's Nagapattinam six days a week, but is highly dependent on weather conditions. The one-way journey takes about four hours and fares typically start from US$60 for economy class (with 40kg luggage allowance). Kankesanturai, 18km from Jaffna, is easily accessible via bus, taxi or rideshare.

Cruise-ship passengers Cruise ships typically enter at major ports, particularly in Colombo and Hambantota, 239km from Colombo. The latter is ideal for safaris in Yala National Park and beaches in the South.

TRANSPORT TIPS TO HELP YOU GET AROUND

Sri Lanka is easy to navigate using public transport. Train services can be limited, but regular buses link most cities and towns, and tuk tuks provide access when public services thin out. A car or motorbike allows travellers to go at their own pace. Be aware, however, driving is only for the experienced, as local drivers are notoriously reckless.

TRAIN

Railways are a fabulous way to experience the island, particularly along scenic routes like Colombo–Ella and Colombo–Galle. Book your tickets up to 30 days in advance (seatreservation.railway.gov.lk), and pick up the paper copy of your ticket at the station.

TUK TUK

Locally called three-wheelers; you can order them through Uber or PickMe in many cities and towns. Elsewhere, it's usually easy to flag down a tuk tuk, but settle on the price before you hop in. They only run on meters in Colombo.

HOW MUCH FOR...

Car rental per day Rs 5000–7000

Motorbike rental per day Rs 2500

Tuk tuk ride per km Rs 100

DRIVING IN SRI LANKA There's a saying: 'To drive in Sri Lanka, you need to drive like a Sri Lankan.' The island is infamous for hasty driving, and accidents are common. People rarely stick to lanes and traffic rules aren't strictly enforced. Only consider self-driving if you are a skilful, experienced driver with third-party insurance. Be on the alert for racing local buses. Rains can make driving dangerous in the mountains due to landslides.

DRIVING PERMIT To drive, you need your passport, a valid driving license from your country and a temporary Sri Lankan driving license from the Department of Motor Traffic office at BIA airport arrivals, next to SPAR supermarket. A one-month permit costs Rs 2000.

BOAT Operated by the Sri Lankan Navy, ferries similar to large motorboats connect the offshore islands of Jaffna Peninsula. Ferries run from Kurikadduwan Jetty (one-hour bus journey from Jaffna) to Neduntivu (Delft) and Nainativu, and from Karaitivu to Analaitivu and Eluvaitivu. A cable ferry connects Karaitivu with Kayts.

DRIVING ESSENTIALS

Drive on the left; the steering wheel is on the right.

You need a temporary Sri Lankan driving license/permit; get it at the airport.

50

The speed limit is 50km/h in urban areas, 70km/h to 100km/h on highways.

Helmets are mandatory for drivers and passengers on motorbikes.

Watch for elephant and peacock crossing signs. Slow down to 25km/h.

BUS An extensive bus network links cities, towns and villages. Most buses have no air-con. Rash driving, loud music and bright lights are also the norm on long distance rides, but they are a cost-effective way to get around. Comfortable air-con coaches run from Colombo to major hubs like Kandy, Anuradhapura and Jaffna, and along the Southern Expressway to Galle, Matara and elsewhere.

MOTORBIKE To hire a motorbike, you need a driving license with motorcycle endorsement, but rental firms rarely check this. If caught without a proper license, you'll be fined. And your insurance probably won't provide cover.

WILDLIFE ENCOUNTERS You'll come across peacocks, monkeys, buffalos, monitor lizards and wild elephants, especially on rural roads. Don't touch, pet or feed wildlife, and always maintain your distance, as animal behaviour can be unpredictable.

KNOW YOUR CARBON FOOTPRINT

A local bus from Colombo to Galle would emit 11.77kg of carbon dioxide per passenger. A luxury petrol-driven car would emit 59.6kg for the same distance.

There are a number of carbon calculators online. We use Resurgence at resurgence.org/resources/carbon-calculator.html.

ROAD DISTANCE CHART (KMS)

	Jaffna	Colombo	Galle	Matara	Tangalle	Ella	Nuwara Eliya	Kandy	Dambulla
Colombo	404								
Galle	502	130							
Matara	533	161	47						
Tangalle	560	188	75	589					
Ella	408	312	199	167	140				
Nuwara Eliya	427	168	256	223	195	60			
Kandy	317	121	221	250	295	135	76		
Dambulla	245	161	257	286	314	165	165	75	
Trincomalee	234	266	363	400	420	270	290	180	106

DANGERS, ANNOYANCES & SAFETY

Sri Lanka is generally safe for travellers. As with most destinations, use common sense to avoid scams, especially with random tuk tuks. Women travellers, especially solo, need to research before booking taxis and accommodations, and avoid walking alone at night.

TUK TUK SCAMS It's common for Colombo tuk tuks to approach solo travellers and offer rides to 'special' festivals, spas or gem boutiques. The driver will charge an exorbitant amount, or pressure you into buying overpriced products for a commission. Don't get onto these, and always use rideshare, metered tuk tuks or taxis booked through your accommodation.

RESISTANCE TO RIDESHARE Increasingly frequent in tourist hubs is the resistance shown to Uber and PickMe by drivers who aren't on rideshare apps. Avoid ordering Uber or PickMe where there's a tuk tuk or taxi parking. Walk a couple hundred metres away to book your ride, or order it to a known hotel, cafe or restaurant.

CATCALLING AND GROPING Women travelling alone can face sexual harassment on the streets or in public transport. Sit next to other women or families on buses and trains, and do not flag down a tuk tuk on the road. Stick to rideshare, or research for recommended drivers. Avoid walking alone after dark.

Floods and landslides Monsoons and storms can cause deadly landslides and floods, especially in mountain areas. News aggregator Newswire offers alerts and updates in English, based on warnings from the Disaster Management Centre.

NURPHOTO/GETTY IMAGES

DIMARIS/SHUTTERSTOCK

Drink spiking There have been several incidents of drinks/food being spiked with crystal meth, leading to robbery and theft, especially in the south-coast resort towns. Do not leave your drinks and food unattended.

MOSQUITOS

Mosquito-borne viral diseases like dengue and chikungunya can spread fast in Sri Lanka. Use bug repellent, especially when you are outside at sunset and at nighttime.

MEDICAL CARE

International health insurance is generally accepted, especially at major private hospitals and clinics. Sri Lanka has free universal public healthcare, but large state hospitals are often crowded. Medicines are widely available in pharmacies.

QUICK TIPS TO HELP YOU MANAGE YOUR MONEY

ATMS Commercial Bank, Bank of Ceylon and People's Bank are the most common banks and ATMs across Sri Lanka, with international banks like HSBC only in Colombo and Kandy. Almost all ATMs offer English options, and you'll find an ATM even in small towns. However, they are scarce in rural areas, and machines may run out of money. So carry extra cash with you.

TIPPING

Tipping is optional. Guides, servers and hotel staff, however, would appreciate it, so tip them (10% of the bill) if you liked their service.

BARGAINING

Fixed prices at stores. Locals sometimes bargain with market and street vendors. But remember that a few hundred rupees makes a big difference to small sellers.

CURRENCY

Sri Lankan rupee

HOW MUCH FOR A...

Cup of coffee
US$2

Can of Lion beer
US$1.50

Rice and curry for two
US$4–12

CASH Always carry cash with you. You'll need cash for tickets, transport and street food even in central Colombo. Take only what you need for daily expenses.

CREDIT CARDS

Credit cards are widely accepted in shopping malls, hotels and restaurants (midrange and up) in Colombo and tourist towns. Most fuel stations accept Visa and Mastercard. Major supermarkets, hotels and restaurants accept American Express.

MONEY CHANGING

Easy to do at banks, typically open from 9am to 3pm weekdays (except public and bank holidays). There are also a few official money exchangers in Colombo and bigger cities with better rates.

SERVICE CHARGE If a service charge is factored into your restaurant bill, there's no need for an additional tip.

ON CALL It's common for PickMe or Uber drivers to call to confirm location and method of payment. Drivers may cancel rides with card payments.

DOLLARS Although Sri Lankan rupee is the official currency, high-end hotels and restaurants may quote prices in US$. You can still pay in rupees. Note: If you pay in dollars, you'll still get the change in rupees.

BUDGET HACKS

To save money, stick to public transport; long-distance trips on non-air-con buses and trains cost less than US$5. Stay in family-run homestays with breakfast included in the rate. Join group safaris to split costs and eat local food (US$1 for takeaway vegetarian rice and curry from a hole-in-the-wall).

POSITIVE-IMPACT TRAVEL

Tips to leave a lighter footprint, support local and have a positive impact on local communities.

ON THE ROAD

Walk or cycle. Most tourist attractions are walkable. Hotels, hostels and homestays often have bicycles to use for free or for a small fee.

Bus it everywhere. Buses are better for reducing emissions and fuel use than tuk tuks and private cars. Local buses connect pretty much every town.

Ride the train. Trains, although slow, can be fun and are a more ecofriendly way to travel, especially if you've got time (commuter tickets: pravesha.lk, which is geo-restricted; reservations: seatreservation.railway.gov.lk).

Do-good travel. For wildlife and nature-based experiences, book with certified ethical tour companies and guides who prioritise environmental conservation. Look out for companies like Eco Love Tours (@ecolovetours), and learn about mangrove and wetland conservation (wetlandwatch.lk).

Eco stays. Seek out sustainable accommodations and farm stays that support the community and care for the environment. Be aware, however, of greenwashing businesses.

NURPHOTO SRL/GETTY IMAGES

GIVE BACK

Visit wildlife parks and conservation projects. The Elephant Transit Home in Uda Walawe looks after injured and orphaned calves until they can release them back into the wild. Support small cat research initiatives (scar.lk).

Support non-profits that actively involve tea-estate communities. The Malaiyaha Tamils working in Hill Country estates are underpaid, with little to no access to proper housing, nutrition and sanitation. Organisations like the Tea Leaf Trust (tealeaftrust.com) create social and educational pathways, empowering the community to take ownership of their stories.

Surf with local women. Local surf culture is largely male-dominated. Support women's surf clubs and schools changing the narrative. Visit Arugam Bay Girls Surf Club (@abay_girls_surf_club) and SeaSisters (seasisterslk.com).

DOS & DON'TS

Don't photograph impoverished communities. Always ask before you take photos. Respect their livelihoods and homes.

Do stay at local-owned accommodation. Locals are increasingly priced out, while foreigners own many southern hotels.

Don't stay at hotels run by armed forces in the North. Support local Tamils, who are working hard to rebuild after the war.

LEAVE A SMALL FOOTPRINT

Pack reef-safe sunscreen. It's difficult to find sunscreen without oxybenzone and parabens in Sri Lanka, so bring plenty of it.

Learn about sustainable, native farming practices on a tour with Naveen Lakshan (@kumbuk.group), and join his mother's cooking class.

Go wild. Hike, trek and walk national parks, rainforests and botanical gardens. Along the Pekoe Trail, be mindful of the communities you pass through.

Stick to the trail. And avoid feeding or petting wildlife, which leads to long-term human-animal conflict. Maintain distance.

IAN PETER MORTON/SHUTTERSTOCK

SUPPORT LOCAL

Buy souvenirs directly from artisans. Go to Colombo's Saturday Good Market (@goodmarket.lanka), women-run Sooriya Weaving Mills (pictured; sooriyaweaving.com) for handlooms, and Jez-Look Batiks (@jezlookbatik) for batik fabrics.

Eat locally. There's no shortage of family-run restaurants for delicious, homemade food. The Ministry of Agriculture's Hela Bojun and Ammachi (in the North) support female entrepreneurs.

Book your workshops with Sarana (@saranalanka), who works with skilled artisans.

CLIMATE CHANGE & TRAVEL

Lonely Planet urges all travellers to engage with their travel carbon footprint, which will mainly come from air travel. While there often isn't an alternative, travellers can look to minimise the number of flights they take, opt for newer aircrafts and use cleaner ground transport, such as trains.

One proposed solution – purchasing carbon offsets – unfortunately does not cancel out the impact of individual flights. While most destinations will depend on air travel for the foreseeable future, for now, pursuing ground-based travel where possible is the best course of action.

The UN Carbon Offset Calculator shows how flying impacts a household's emissions:

The ICAO's carbon emissions calculator allows visitors to analyse the CO2 generated by point-to-point journeys:

RESOURCES

www.dwc.gov.lk

rainforestprotectors.org

tealeaftrust.com

wnpssl.org

UNIQUE & LOCAL WAYS TO STAY

Sri Lanka is home to a mix of accommodations to suit all styles and budgets, from luxury safari lodges to private villas, ecofriendly treehouses, wellness retreats and family-run homestays. Generally, though, you'll want to stay close to Sri Lanka's stunning tropical landscapes, beaches and ancient cities. Expect to pay high prices for anything beachfront, but you can still find good deals outside peak season.

HOW MUCH FOR A...

Homestay
Rs 5000

Beach villa
Rs 60,000

Resort room
Rs 25,000

JON CHICA/SHUTTERSTOCK

HOMESTAYS

Living with a Sri Lankan family is a meaningful way to experience everyday life. Think of traditional breakfast spreads, cycle trails through paddy-lined villages, swimming in lotus-filled lakes and claypot cooking classes. Increasingly popular now, you'll find homestays almost everywhere, even in Colombo, but especially when you travel to rural areas.

Most homestays are simple, no-frills stays, but are clean, comfortable and good value. They're particularly great for solo travellers, especially women. Always read reviews before you book.

SURF CAMPS

Great for beginners to learn surfing or experts to sharpen their skills, surf camps are set up every season in Arugam Bay (pictured left) and along the South – Ahangama, Weligama and Hiriketiya are popular. Camps run for a week or longer, and include accommodation, surf lessons, yoga, tuk tuk shuttles to surf spots, breakfasts and internet.

LUXURY SAFARI CAMPS

Some of Sri Lanka's most remarkable stays include luxury safari camps and glamping lodges within the fringes of the island's wildlife-heavy national parks, particularly in Yala and Wilpattu (pictured). All-inclusive tented camps, with private plunge pools and sundecks, feature daily game drives, gourmet meals, evening tea, lantern-lit sundowners and after-dinner nightcaps.

TORSTEN PURSCHE/SHUTTERSTOCK

IVAN BATINIC/ALAMY

AYURVEDA RETREATS

A wellness system focusing on balancing mind, body and spirit, Ayurveda has a history going back 5000 years to ancient India. It's a key part of Sri Lankan life, along with the island's own indigenous healing practices. If you are looking for a relaxing holiday while staying close to nature, wellness retreats are a great way to experience a slice of Sri Lanka. They range from plush all-inclusives to thatched cabana-like accommodations, from spa massages and yoga sessions to rigorous programs with medical assessments.

RETREAT LIFE

Life at a wellness retreat is largely defined by where it is, and the kind of program you sign up for. Design-led Santani sits in Kandy's forested hills, and is known for its excellent packages: days begin with yoga and breathing sessions, followed by breakfast and 90-minute treatments, pool time, and evening yoga before dinner.

Staying at a retreat doesn't always mean you are cut off from the world. There's plenty of opportunity to climb waterfalls, go on a wildlife safari and add a city tour. By the beach, Mango Tree Spa is fabulous; it's only steps away from Hiriketiya's buzz. Less than 30 minutes from Galle Fort, you'll find the low-key Niyagama House (pictured) with personalised yoga sessions. Bonus: monkeys, peacocks and squirrels are your jungle companions.

BOOKING

The best way to find accommodation is through online travel search engines. To book small family-run accommodations in rural areas, you might need to text through WhatsApp or call them – this is also a great way to get perks like discounts and upgrades, particularly during the low season. You'll find good deals for resorts, safari lodges and villas on these websites.

Book in advance, particularly around Christmas and New Year during the peak season (December through March). The April New Year is a busy time for the Hill Country as domestic tourists flock to cooler towns. Rooms fill up in the East from May to September.

Airbnb (airbnb.com) Good for homestays, boutique hotels, beach villas and apartments. Great deals for longer stays.

The Pekoe Trail (thepekoetrail.org/accommodation) Lists accommodations along the 300km tea-country hiking route and directs you to third-party booking sites.

Booking.com Has a range of options, from hotels to homestays and hostels.

HERITAGE STAYS

You'll find beautifully restored colonial-era mansions woven with history and character across the island, but more specifically in Galle Fort. Design enthusiasts can stay at Geoffery Bawa's Colombo home No 11 and country estate Lunuganga (geoffreybawa.com).

ESSENTIAL NUTS & BOLTS

DRESS CODE

Cover knees and shoulders at religious places, except in a few Hindu shrines like Nallur Kandaswamy Temple where men need to remove shirts. Carry a shawl or sarong.

SHOES & HATS

Always take off your shoes and hats when you visit Buddhist temples, kovils (Hindu temples) and mosques. Shoes are generally off inside private homes, too.

SILENT, PLEASE

Treat places of worship with respect and maintain silence inside shrines, mosques and temples.

FAST FACTS

Time Zone
GMT+5:30

Country Code
+94

Electricity
230V/
50Hz

GOOD TO KNOW

Most visitors need to apply for an Electronic Travel Authorization (ETA; eta.gov.lk).

For emergencies, dial 119. To order a free ambulance anywhere anytime, dial 1990 (1990.lk).

Contact 24-hour tourist police (dial 1912) in cases of scams, theft and harassment.

The legal minimum age to buy alcohol in Sri Lanka is 18; it's illegal to drink on the streets.

Sri Lanka has three national languages: Sinhala, Tamil and English.

ACCESSIBLE TRAVEL

The airport (BIA) in Colombo provides wheelchair assistance for passengers with reduced mobility.

Public transport is not wheelchair friendly and best avoided. Hire an experienced driver instead.

Larger hotels and resorts have wheelchair-friendly vans, buses and buggies, as well as other accessible features, spacious rooms and helpful staff.

Big supermarket chains (Keells and SPAR) have entrances with ramps and wheelchair parking spots.

Footpaths are uneven and challenging to navigate in a wheelchair. In some areas there are no footpaths.

Accessible dining is limited, except for food courts in shopping malls. You're more likely to find wheelchair ramps and other accessibility features in restaurants within upmarket resorts.

Attractions National parks can be visited with accessible safari vehicles. The Temple of the Tooth relic, Botanical Gardens in Kandy, and sacred cities of Anuradhapura and Polonnaruwa can be navigated in a wheelchair with assistance.

Specialised tour companies offer accessible tours, including Ceylon Expeditions (ceylonexpeditions.com) and Access the Globe (@accesstheglobe).

SELFIES

It's disrespectful to take selfies with your back to statues of Buddha, Hindu deities, altars and sacred temple trees.

ETHICAL TRAVEL

Research on socio-environmental impact before visiting elephant orphanages and turtle hatcheries – some may exploit wildlife.

NO PDA

Sri Lanka is a conservative island; public displays of affection are considered disrespectful, especially around children.

TRAIN TRAVEL Don't jump on unreserved and crowded train cars that are a lifeline for locals and connect some of Sri Lanka's remotest parts. Book your seat, or pick a tourist train like Ella Odyssey or Calypso. It's also dangerous to hang off train doors.

FAMILY TRAVEL

Buses and trains have half-off tickets for kids aged five to 12. Free for kids under five. It's common for Sri Lankans to give their seat to parents with toddlers. Breastfeeding on public transport is completely accepted.

Facilities can be found in big restaurants, which often have high chairs. Changing tables are rare outside malls and larger resorts. Supermarkets have nappies and formula.

Visitors under 12 can often visit archaeological sites, temples and museums for free or at a discount.

EAT THE LOCAL WAY Sri Lankans eat with their right hand. While tourists are not expected to do this, it's a great way to dive into local culture, and make friends along the way. Restaurants, cafes and hole-in-the-walls will have wash basins to clean afterwards.

NURPHOTO/GETTY IMAGES

LGBTIQ+ TRAVELLERS

Attitude Although homosexuality is deemed illegal under Sri Lanka's British colonial-era law (which hasn't been repealed since), public perception is slowly shifting. However, homophobia and discrimination against the LGBTIQ+ community persist.

Checking in Tourists are unlikely to face outright discrimination, and same-sex couples typically won't have problems getting a hotel room.

Local knowledge Follow activist Aritha Wickramasinghe (@aritha.w) and communities like Bridge to Equality (bridge2equality.org) and Equal Ground (equal-ground.org) to familiarise yourself with issues, campaigns and events.

LANGUAGE

Sinhala and Tamil are official languages in Sri Lanka. While English may be widely spoken in the main centres, off the beaten track it's spread thin. Have a go at speaking Sinhala or Tamil – you'll soon strike up a conversation with an always-smiling Sri Lankan aunty and find yourself sitting in a local home, digging into plates of rice and curry.

If you read our pronunciation guides as if they were English, you shouldn't have problems being understood. To enhance your trip with a phrasebook, visit shop.lonelyplanet.com.

SINHALA BASICS

Hello.	*aayu-bowan*
Yes.	*oww*
No.	*nee*
Thank you.	*istuh-tee*
Sorry.	*samah venna*
What's your name?	*oyaaghe nama mokka'da?*
My name is ...	*maaghe nama ...*
Do you speak English?	*oyaa in-ghirisih kata karenawa da?*
I don't understand.	*matta therenne ne*
Help!	*kau-ruth nadh-dhah?* (lit: anyone isn't here?)
Call a doctor!	*dostara gen-nanna!*
Call the police!	*polisiyata kiyanna!*
Go away!	*methanin yanna!*
I'm lost.	*maa-meh nativelaa*
What time is it?	*veh-laah-vah kee-yah-dhah?*
It's (one) o'clock.	*dhan veh-laah-vah (e-kai)*
morning	*u-dheh*
afternoon	*dhah-vahl*
evening	*han-dhaa-wah*
yesterday	*ee-yeh*
today	*ah-dhah*
tomorrow	*he-tah*

1	*e-kah*	**6**	*hah-yah*
2	*dhe-kah*	**7**	*hah-thah*
3	*thu-nah*	**8**	*ah-tah*
4	*hah-thah-rah*	**9**	*nah-vah-yah*
5	*pah-hah*	**10**	*dhah-hah-yah*

TAMIL BASICS

Hello.	*vanakkam*
Yes.	*aam*
No.	*il-lay*
Thank you.	*nandri*
Sorry.	*mannikavum*
What's your name?	*ungal peyr en-na?*
My name is ...	*en peyr ...*
Do you speak English?	*nin-gal aangilam paysu-virhalaa?*
I don't understand.	*enakku puriyavillai*
Help!	*udavi!*
Call a doctor!	*daktarai kuppidunga!*
Call the police!	*polisai kuppidunga!*
Go away!	*pohn-goh!/poi-vidu!*
I'm lost.	*naan vali tavari-vittehn*
What time is it?	*ma-ni en-na*
It's (one) o'clock.	*ma-ni (on-dru)*
morning	*kaa-lai*
evening	*maa-lai*
yesterday	*neyt-tru*
today	*in-dru*
tomorrow	*naa-lai*

1	*on-dru*	**6**	*aa-ru*
2	*i-ran-tu*	**7**	*ey-zu*
3	*moon-dru*	**8**	*et-tu*
4	*naan-ku*	**9**	*on-pa-tu*
5	*ain-tu*	**10**	*pat-tu*

Index

000 Map pages

000 Map pages

C

D

E

000 Map pages

T

U

V

000 Map pages

W

Y

'When I first visited the Knuckles Conservation Forest, it rained non-stop. When the sun finally came out and I saw the pristine nature and abundant fauna, Knuckles easily became one of my favourite places on the island.'

MARISA MEGAN PASKA

'When I arrived at a woman-owned heritage homestay in Jaffna at 4am, she welcomed me with tea and local sweets.'

ZINARA RATHNAYAKE

'Master architect Geoffrey Bawa's beautifully designed home preserves icons of mid-century modernism, from Eero Saarinen 'Tulip' chairs to Eames sculptures and '60s Quasar-France inflatable furniture.'

MONIQUE CHOY

'The first time I visited the Temple of the Tooth in 2011, I was able to see the Buddha's sacred tooth itself (my best friend's family had long been Temple Custodians).'

ANNA KAMINSKI

'The time I drove my rental scooter down an innocuous sandy road, only to end up at the most perfect and totally empty stretch of golden beach; fantastic.'

BRADLEY MAYHEW

FROM TOP: NICOLASDECORTE/SHUTTERSTOCK, CREATIVE FAMILY/SHUTTERSTOCK

THIS BOOK

This 1st edition of Lonely Planet's *Experience Sri Lanka* guidebook was researched and written by Zinara Rathnayake, Monique Choy, Anna Kaminski, Bradley Mayhew and Marisa Megan Paska.

This guidebook was produced by the following:

Destination Editor
Akanksha Singh

Coordinating Editor
Simon Williamson

Production Editor
Barbara Delissen

Cartographer
Anthony Phelan

Image Editor
Jo-Anne Riddell

Assisting Editor
Laura Crawford

Cover researcher
Matthew Dekneef

Thanks Katie Connolly, Melanie Dankel, Jenna Myers